TRILLIONS

TRILLIONS

How a Band of
Wall Street Renegades
Invented the Index Fund
and Changed Finance
Forever

Robin Wigglesworth

PORTFOLIO / PENGUIN

PORTFOLIO / PENGUIN
An imprint of Penguin Random House LLC
penguinrandomhouse.com

Most Portfolio books are available at a discount when purchased in quantity for
sales promotions or corporate use. Special editions, which include personalized covers,
excerpts, and corporate imprints, can be created when purchased in large quantities.
For more information, please call (212) 572-2232 or e-mail
specialmarkets@penguinrandomhouse.com. Your local bookstore can
also assist with discounted bulk purchases using the Penguin Random House
corporate Business-to-Business program. For assistance in locating a
participating retailer, e-mail B2B@penguinrandomhouse.com.

Image credits: photo page 1 © Tim Seides; page 2 top courtesy of Markowitz's office;
page 2 bottom courtesy of Stanford News Service; page 3 middle, page 5 top,
page 5 bottom © Dimensional Fund Advisors LP; page 3 top courtesy of John A. McQuown;
page 3 bottom courtesy of Batterymarch Financial Management; page 4 top courtesy of Institutional
Investor; page 4 bottom courtesy of Jan Twardowski; page 6 top copyright © 2021 by Eric T. Clothier,
all rights reserved; page 6 bottom courtesy of BlackRock; page 7 courtesy of the Leuthold Group

Library of Congress Cataloging-in-Publication Data
Names: Wigglesworth, Robin, author.
Title: Trillions : how a band of Wall Street renegades invented the index
fund and changed finance forever / Robin Wigglesworth.
Description: New York : Portfolio, 2021. |
Includes bibliographical references and index. |
Identifiers: LCCN 2021027549 (print) | LCCN 2021027550 (ebook) |
ISBN 9780593087688 (hardcover) | ISBN 9780593087695 (ebook)
Subjects: LCSH: Index mutual funds—History. | Investments. | Finance.
Classification: LCC HG4530 .W524 2021 (print) | LCC HG4530 (ebook) |
DDC 332.63/27—dc23
LC record available at https://lccn.loc.gov/2021027549
LC ebook record available at https://lccn.loc.gov/2021027550

ISBN 9780593421314 (international edition)

Printed in the United States of America
1st Printing

BOOK DESIGN BY TANYA MAIBORODA

To
Matilde and Finn
Pappa loves you more than
infinity supermassive black holes are big

CONTENTS

CAST OF CHARACTERS

WARREN BUFFETT. Chairman of Berkshire Hathaway, and the world's most famous investor. Won the investment industry's bet of the century by pitting an index fund against a panoply of hedge funds.

TED SEIDES. The cofounder of Protégé Partners, a hedge fund investment firm, who took Buffett up on his bet that an index fund could beat the finest money managers in the world over a decade.

JACK BOGLE. The founder of Vanguard, one of the biggest index fund managers in the world, and often dubbed "Saint Jack" due to his exhortation for the investment industry to give more people a "fair shake" through cheap passive investment vehicles.

LOUIS BACHELIER. An early-twentieth-century French mathematician who died in obscurity, but whose work on the "random walk" of stocks would make him the intellectual godfather of passive investing.

ALFRED COWLES III. The wealthy tuberculosis-plagued heir of a newspaper fortune who undertook one of the first rigorous studies of how well investment professionals actually performed versus the broader stock market.

JAMES LORIE. A gregarious University of Chicago professor tasked by Merrill Lynch to find out the long-term return of stocks. The result was the biggest and most comprehensive study of the equity market to date, providing the raw fuel for the development of index funds.

HARRY MARKOWITZ. The cerebral economist whose groundbreaking 1952 PhD thesis on financial markets became one of the most influential papers in finance, winning him the Nobel Prize in Economics, and laying the groundwork for the subsequent passive investment revolution.

WILLIAM SHARPE. A onetime medical student who became one of the first programmer-economists, building on his mentor Markowitz's work to demonstrate the power of a broad "market portfolio"—in other words, an index fund.

EUGENE FAMA. A onetime jock turned legendary economist at the University of Chicago, whose efficient-markets hypothesis helped explain why markets are so hard to beat, and inspired the birth of passive investing.

JOHN MCQUOWN. A ferociously determined, computer-obsessed banker who convinced Wells Fargo to establish a skunk works and assemble the biggest crew of economic superstars. They would go on to launch the first passive investment fund, which reshaped finance.

REX SINQUEFIELD. A former Fama student who became the self-styled "Ayatollah" of the efficient-markets hypothesis, establishing the first S&P 500 index fund at American National Bank of Chicago. He would later go on to found Dimensional Fund Advisors (DFA) with McQuown's protégé David Booth.

DEAN LEBARON. A resolutely unorthodox money manager who made his name in the go-go stock market boom of the 1960s, but established one of the first index funds at his firm Batterymarch—even if it initially found no takers.

JIM VERTIN. The head of research at Wells Fargo's trust department. He was initially a ferocious opponent of McQuown, but eventually became a convert to the cause and a zealous proselytizer for passive investing.

WILLIAM FOUSE. A mustachioed bon vivant who put himself through university by playing jazz. After being pushed out of Mellon Bank, he became an instrumental bridge between the cutting-edge research of McQuown's skunk works and the rest of Wells Fargo's investment department.

JIM RIEPE. Bogle's main lieutenant at Wellington, who followed him over in the "great bifurcation" and the founding of Vanguard and played a pivotal role in the launch of the First Index Investment Trust.

JAN TWARDOWSKI. Bogle's young "quant," who helped design Vanguard's inaugural index mutual fund using a now-defunct programming language. Despite the fund initially bombing with investors, he was able to make sure that it didn't deviate too far from its index.

BURTON MALKIEL. An economist whose book *A Random Walk Down Wall Street* popularized many of the theories developed by the likes of Fama. He would later become a board member at Vanguard, and the chair of the American Stock Exchange's (Amex) new products division, which invented the exchange-traded fund (ETF).

JACK BRENNAN. A patrician Bostonian who was Bogle's trusted lieutenant and successor, and who proved instrumental in building Vanguard into a huge investment group. But the two men fell out dramatically, leading to a bout of strife that threatened to blow Vanguard off course.

DAVID BOOTH. A basketball-loving Kansan who dropped out of Chicago's PhD program to work for John McQuown at Wells Fargo. He then founded DFA with fellow former Fama student Rex Sinquefield, and helped extend the index fund revolution to new frontiers.

LARRY KLOTZ. One of AG Becker's top salesmen who joined Booth and Sinquefield in founding DFA, winning many of its first big clients before he was summarily ejected by his two partners.

JEANNE SINQUEFIELD. Rex Sinquefield's brilliant and exacting wife, who went from a PhD in sociology to designing financial derivatives, and then became head of trading at DFA. Every new recruit had to pass her "Jeanne Test."

DAN WHEELER. A loquacious former Marine turned financial advisor, who helped build up DFA's retail operations and established its boot camps, which helped spread the gospel of efficient markets to new corners of the financial industry.

NATE MOST. A geeky, avuncular former physicist and submariner, who after a long, nomadic career in the backwaters of finance was instrumental in the invention of the ETF at the Amex.

STEVEN BLOOM. Most's youthful, brainy sidekick at the Amex, whose classical Harvard economics PhD complemented his mentor's eclectic creativity perfectly. He later worked at Nasdaq before teaching at West Point and the Eisenhower School for National Security and Resource Strategy.

IVERS RILEY. A former Navy pilot who joined the Amex after losing out on the top job at the New York Stock Exchange to Dick Grasso. He saw the potential for Most and Bloom's invention to be a "destiny-changing product" for the struggling exchange.

FRED GRAUER. A former academic unceremoniously sacked from Wells Fargo Investment Advisors (WFIA), before later returning to lead it. Grauer turned around the troubled unit and set it on a course toward becoming one of the biggest investment groups in the world.

PATTIE DUNN. The charismatic journalism student who first joined WFIA as a secretary, and rose quickly through the ranks. She eventually replaced her mentor Grauer as chief executive of Barclays Global Investors (BGI)—much to his consternation.

LEE KRANEFUSS. An entrepreneurial former consultant tasked by Dunn to build World Equity Benchmark Shares (WEBS) into a separate ETF business called iShares. He could ruffle feathers internally, but succeeded far beyond anyone's expectations.

LARRY FINK. Once a star bond trader at First Boston with the world at his feet, but pushed out after a humiliating loss. He then dusted himself off, founded BlackRock, and built it into the world's biggest investment empire.

ROB KAPITO. Fink's former right-hand man at First Boston and his key lieutenant at BlackRock. A wine lover known for his aggressiveness and abrasiveness, he was instrumental in BlackRock's growth.

RALPH SCHLOSSTEIN. A former Treasury official and Lehman banker who partnered with his friend Fink to found BlackRock. His statesmanlike and diplomatic approach meant that he was in charge of integrating the company's acquisitions of State Street Research and Merrill Lynch Investment Managers (MLIM).

MARK WIEDMAN. An outgoing former lawyer and Treasury official, who led the integration of BGI into BlackRock. His success means that he is one of the leading contenders to pick up the reins should Fink ever retire.

TRILLIONS

Chapter 1

BUFFETT'S BET

IT WAS A SLOW, LANGUID summer day in 2007 when Ted Seides settled in behind the oblong modern desk in his swish corner office on the fifteenth floor of New York's MoMA building. CNBC was blaring in the background, but with little else to do, he decided to work through his email inbox. There he spied something intriguing.

A friend had sent him a transcript of a recent meeting between Warren Buffett and a bunch of college students. Seides had long been a fan of the legendary "Oracle of Omaha" and was a devoted attendee of the annual meetings hosted by Buffett's vast investment conglomerate, Berkshire Hathaway. But something in the transcript made him sputter that morning.

One of the students had asked Buffett about a wager he had offered a year earlier, that a fund that simply tracked the US stock market would beat any group of high-flying hedge fund managers. Berkshire's chairman noted that no one had dared to take him up on the bet, "so I guess I'm right," he told the students. The scorn vexed

Seides, a normally unflappable thirty-six-year-old Wall Streeter with a passing resemblance to a clean-shaven Judd Apatow. After all, hedge funds were his bread and butter.

He had learned the skill of picking out the finest ones from the master himself, Yale University endowment's David Swensen. A few years earlier Seides had helped found Protégé Partners, an investment group that specialized in unearthing the industry's most skilled financial wizards for pension funds and private banks—a "fund-of-hedge-funds." By 2007, Protégé managed $3.5 billion of hedge fund investments on behalf of its clients, and had generated 95 percent returns, handily beating the returns of the US stock market.[1]

The hedge fund industry first emerged in the 1960s, but had enjoyed explosive growth over the last decade, and by 2007 managed nearly $2 trillion on behalf of investors around the world. Big hedge fund managers like George Soros and Ken Griffin had amassed vast fortunes, attracting envy even in other well-paid corners of the financial world. By the mid-2000s, most young Wall Streeters dreamed of running a hedge fund, not toiling away in investment banking or—perish the thought—doing unglamorous work such as lending money to companies.

The boom frustrated Buffett, who had long felt that the investment industry overflowed with mediocrities who in practice did little more than line their own pockets with the ample fees they charged clients. At Berkshire Hathaway's annual meeting in 2006, when he first proposed the wager, he gave the industry both barrels.

"If your wife is going to have a baby, you're going to be better off if you call an obstetrician than if you do it yourself. And if your plumbing pipes are clogged, you're probably better off calling a plumber. Most professions have value added to them above what the laymen can accomplish themselves. In aggregate, the investment profession does not do that," Buffett had told attendees. "So you have a huge group of people making—I put the estimate as $140 billion a year—that, in aggregate, are and can only accomplish what some-body can do in ten minutes a year by themselves."

Seides was somewhat sympathetic to Buffett's point that many professional money managers in practice do a poor job, but the pro-posed bet just looked dumb to him. As CNBC was trumpeting in his office that summer morning, the subprime mortgage crisis had just begun to rumble, and Seides thought that things would get worse before they got better. The hedge fund industry's free-wheeling buccaneers looked like they would be far more adept at navigating the coming storm. After all, hedge funds can profit from markets moving both up and down, and invest in far more than just the S&P 500 index of US stocks that Buffett had offered up to fight in his corner. They may charge plenty, but Seides was confident that they could leap over that hurdle and comfortably beat the S&P 500, which was at the time still trading at exceptionally high valuations, oblivious to the brewing financial crisis.

Seides had missed the 2006 Berkshire Hathaway meeting when Buffett first offered the wager, but since no one had seemed to re-spond in the interim, and it was a slow day, he started writing an old-fashioned letter to Buffett, proposing to accept his wager. "Dear Warren," it started:[2]

> Last week, I heard about a challenge you issued at your recent Annual Meeting, and I am eager to take you up on the bet. I wholeheartedly agree with your contention that the aggregate re-turns to investors in hedge funds will get eaten alive by the high fees earned by managers. In fact, were Fred Schwed penning sto-ries today, he likely would title his work "Where Are the Custom-ers' G5s?"
>
> However, my wager is that you are both generally correct and specifically incorrect. In fact, I am sufficiently comfortable that unusually well managed hedge fund portfolios are superior to

*market indexes over time that I will spot you a lead by selecting 5
fund of funds rather than 10 hedge funds. You must really be licking your chops!*

To Seides's delight, Buffett promptly replied, scrawling a terse message on Seides's letter and sending it back to his New York office,
starting an extended back-and-forth about how to arrange the bet.
Eventually, they settled on a million-dollar wager that pitted two
diametrically opposed investment philosophies against each other:
imperious, expensive investment managers who scour the planet
for the most lucrative opportunities, against cheap, "passive" funds
that blindly buy the entire market. It represented reigning wisdom
against scrappy underdog.

▲

DESPITE HIS RENOWN as an investor, Buffett has long had a jaun-
diced view of his own profession—something revealed in a remarkable 1975 letter to Katharine Graham, the former *Washington Post*
owner and grandee of DC society. "If above-average performance is
to be their yardstick, the vast majority of investment managers must
fail," Buffett glumly noted.[3]

The main subject of the letter was pensions. With his signature
wit, Buffett explained to his friend the dry actuarial arithmetic of
retirement plans that promise to provide members a certain, regular
retirement payment. But his most brutal points were on the usefulness of professional fund managers whom pension plans hire to manage their money.

As Buffett laid out with devastating clarity, expectations of
above-average performance by all pension funds were "doomed to
disappointment." After all, they in practice *were* the market. Buffett
compared it to someone sitting down at a poker table and declaring,
"Well, fellows, if we all play carefully tonight, we all should be able

to win a little." Add in the trading costs and the cost of paying their managers' salaries, and investment funds would on average inevitably do worse than the broader market.

Of course, many investment groups—and the pension fund executives who entrust them with their money—will counter that the trick is to invest only in above-average managers. Sure, many will be poor, lazy, or wrong, but rigorous research can unearth the stock-picking stars who can consistently beat their market.

This elite would, in the era of laxer regulations, also wine and dine company executives to get discreet but vital market-moving information ahead of the unwashed masses of ordinary investors, and enjoy privileged access to the research of Wall Street firms desperate for their business. Moreover, a lot of trading was still done by individual investors, dentists and lawyers who acted on the recommendation of an army of stockbrokers of often dubious expertise and ethics. In such an environment, the premise that professional fund managers could consistently beat the market surely didn't seem so unreasonable?

This was certainly the common wisdom at the time. The 1960s saw the emergence of the first superstar mutual fund managers, cerebral stock-pickers who became celebrities for their investment acumen. Up until then, the industry had been dominated by "prudent men in hallowed institutions, quietly tending casks of slowly maturing capital," as *Institutional Investor*, an industry magazine, said at the time. But the 1960s bull market—dubbed the "go-go" era—changed everything. "Now the thirst for gains is so great in the fund business that managers are stars, and they get a piece of the profits. Just like Paul Newman and Elizabeth Taylor," *Institutional Investor* noted.[4]

These stars aimed to thrash the market by investing in racy, fast-growing companies like Xerox and Eastman Kodak, many of which were dubbed the "Nifty Fifty" for the power of their stock market performance. But their luster dimmed quickly when the boom ended in the late 1960s and the Nifty Fifty fell to earth.

In his letter to Graham, Buffett used an apt metaphor to explain why relying even on fund managers with exemplary track records was often a fallacy, comparing it to a coin-flipping contest. If a thousand people predict the outcome of a series of coin flips, mathematically thirty-one should manage to guess five flips in a row correctly. Highly educated, hardworking fund managers would naturally bristle at the insinuation that they are mere coin flippers, but the laws of probability are clear.

As Buffett later highlighted in a celebrated 1984 speech, one could even imagine a national coin-flipping contest of 225 million Americans, all of whom would wager a dollar on guessing the outcome. Each day the losers drop out, and the stakes would then build up for the following morning. After ten days there would be about 220,000 Americans who had correctly predicted ten flips in a row, making them over $1,000. "Now this group will probably start getting a little puffed up about this, human nature being what it is," Buffett noted.[5] "They may try to be modest, but at cocktail parties they will occasionally admit to attractive members of the opposite sex what their technique is, and what marvelous insights they bring to the field of flipping."

If the national coin-flipping championship continued, after another ten days 215 people would statistically have guessed twenty flips in a row, and turned $1 into more than $1 million. And still the net result would remain that $225 million would have been lost and $225 million would have been won. However, at this stage the successful coin flippers would really begin to buy into their own hype, Buffett predicted. "They will probably write books on 'How I Turned a Dollar into a Million in Twenty Days Working Thirty Seconds a Morning,'" he joked.

Buffett conceded that it was possible to unearth some fund

managers with a real edge. Naturally, as a protégé of Benjamin
Graham—a famous investor and academic who established an approach dubbed "value investing"—Buffett has often highlighted
how many successful money managers shared Graham as their
"common intellectual patriarch." But investors who can consistently
outperform the market are few and far between, he argued.

In the conclusion to his letter to the *Post*'s owner, Buffett therefore laid out his recommendations: Either stay the course with a
bunch of big, mainstream professional fund managers and accept
that the newspaper's pension fund would likely do slightly worse
than the market; find smaller, specialized investment managers who
were more likely to be able to beat the market; or simply build a
broad, diversified portfolio of stocks that mirrored the entire market.
Buffett obliquely noted that "several funds have been established
fairly recently to duplicate the averages, quite explicitly embodying
the principle that no management is cheaper, and slightly better than
average paid management after transaction costs."

At the time there was no real term for such a seemingly lazy
investment strategy—at the time championed only by some odd-
balls working at third-tier, parochial banks in San Francisco, Chicago, and Boston—but today they are called index funds, and the
approach is dubbed "passive investing."

Index funds are investment vehicles that simply try to mimic an
index of financial securities. These indices can be big and well
known—like the United States' Dow Jones Industrial Average, the
UK's FTSE 100, or Japan's Nikkei—or more niche or exotic, such
as benchmarks that track the debt of developing countries. While
traditional "active" funds managed by professionals try to pick winners and shun losers, index funds do nothing but buy everything in
their benchmark according to predetermined rules of construction.
Take the S&P 500, an index generally accepted as the best and
broadest measure of the US stock market. An S&P 500 index fund

buys every single one of the five hundred stocks in the index, exactly according to their relative stock market value—so it buys more of Apple than it does Alaska Air Group.

This may seem like a bizarre approach, yet as Buffett had realized, even savvy Wall Street pros can be pretty bad at picking financial securities. Moreover, given the costs of paying a fund manager and their staff, they have to comfortably beat their benchmarks for investors to break even. In sporting terms, by selecting an expensive, actively managed fund, they are starting every game a goal down. Worse, there seems to be no way of consistently identifying those with the skill needed to score two goals to overcome the deficit.

Data is a hard taskmaster, but has consistently shown that while someone might get lucky for a few years, very few do so in the long run. The exact statistics vary between countries and types of market that they invest in, but roughly speaking, only 10 to 20 percent of active funds beat their benchmarks over any rolling ten-year period. In other words, investing is a rare walk in life where it generally pays to be lazy and choose a cheap passive fund.

Nonetheless, back in the 1970s, this data just wasn't well known, and "index investing" was still in its infancy. Many in the industry simply scoffed at the ludicrous idea that someone should or would lazily settle for whatever the entire stock market did. For the *Post*, dumping its pension money into such an oddball idea proved far too much of a leap. Instead, it entrusted its pension to a handful of fund managers personally recommended by Buffett.

To be fair, his prudence helped ensure the newspaper a well-endowed pension at a time when many corporate plans are struggling. However, Buffett's discreet nod to a bunch of innovative funds that merely tried to cheaply mimic the stock market would prove prescient, and decades later it would help him win the investment industry's bet of the century.

▲

SEIDES INITIALLY PROPOSED to make the bet $100,000—Buffett's annual salary—but Buffett wanted to make the stakes more interesting. Given his age and the complications that a decade-long bet might cause for the settlement of his estate in case he passed away, he said he would be interested in a bet only of at least $500,000. Even so, "my estate attorney is going to think I'm out of my mind for complicating things," he wrote Seides.[6]

That was a bit rich for Seides, so Protégé Partners itself became the counterparty to Buffett's bet. Each party put up about $320,000, which would be used to buy a Treasury bond that would be worth $1 million at the bet's conclusion in 2018. If Protégé won, the proceeds would go to Absolute Return for Kids, a charity backed by prominent members of the hedge fund community. If Buffett triumphed, the money would go to Girls Inc., a venerable charity that the Buffett family had long supported.

Rather than the ten hedge funds that Buffett had first proposed back in 2006, Protégé selected five funds-of-funds like Protégé Partners itself—investment funds that in turn invest in an array of hedge funds. In total, these five funds-of-funds were invested in over a hundred hedge funds. That way, the overall performance would not be distorted by the results of a single awful or awesome money manager. Ever the showman, Buffett insisted that he would announce a tally of how things were going at Berkshire Hathaway's annual meeting every year.

Due to legal restrictions on gambling in some US states, the bet was arranged through something called Long Bets, a forum for big wagers on the future backed by Amazon's Jeff Bezos. Although seemingly frivolous, friendly gambles can have a lot of power. In 1600, Johannes Kepler entered into a bet with a Danish astronomer that he could calculate a formula for the solar orbit of Mars in eight days.

In the end, it took him five years, but the work help revolutionize astronomy.[7] This was precisely what the Long Bets Project wanted to encourage, and the Buffett-Protégé wager was perfect. It was eventually formally announced in a June 2008 *Fortune* article by Carol Loomis, a well-known journalist and friend of Buffett.

Buffett thought that Protégé's choosing a fund-of-funds was a mistake, even if it meant that one bad apple was less likely to spoil the barrel. Hedge funds are expensive, often charging 2 percent annually of the assets they manage, and taking another 20 percent cut of any profits they generate. Funds-of-funds put an extra layer of fees on top. In contrast, the passive US stock-market-mimicking investment vehicle that Buffett chose—one of the index funds whose invention he had mentioned to Kay Graham years earlier—charged just 0.04 percent a year.

"A number of smart people are involved in running hedge funds. But to a great extent their efforts are self-neutralizing, and their IQ will not overcome the costs they impose on investors," Buffett argued.[8] Seides acknowledged that traditional mutual fund managers who focus just on stocks will on average underperform a "narrow" benchmark like the S&P 500. But he maintained that it was an apples-to-oranges comparison, given that hedge funds can also profit from falling securities, and invest in a far broader array of markets.

"For hedge funds, success can mean outperforming the market in lean times, while underperforming in the best of times. Through a cycle, nevertheless, top hedge fund managers have surpassed market returns net of all fees, while assuming less risk as well," Seides argued. While the extra cost was an issue, he was confident that funds-of-funds should be able to surmount this by selecting the best hedge funds.

Indeed, Buffett initially estimated his chances of winning at a modest 60 percent, given that his opponent was an "elite crew, loaded with brains, adrenaline and confidence."[9] Seides, on the other hand, put his chances of besting Berkshire's chairman at a more confident 85 percent.[10] "Fortunately for us, we're betting against the S&P's performance, not Buffett's," he said.

And initially it did look like the Oracle of Omaha would have to eat some humble pie. Buffett declined to discuss the bet at Berkshire's annual meeting in 2009, when he was trailing well behind. While the hedge funds were down by over 20 percent in 2008, the index fund chosen by Buffett had lost 37 percent of its value as the financial crisis rattled markets. It looked like Seides's argument that hedge funds would do a better job of preserving value in a bear market was bearing fruit.

Things didn't look much brighter in 2010, when Buffett for the first time discussed the bet at Berkshire's annual meeting—albeit perfunctorily. The next year he was somewhat more fulsome, but mostly to land a jab at an old target. "The only people that are ahead so far are the investment managers," he noted, before the shareholder meeting broke for lunch. By year four, the S&P 500 had begun to narrow the difference, but Buffett was still behind. Given the mounting crisis in Europe at the time, the outcome looked like it rested on a knife's edge.

▲

IN DECEMBER 2016, John Clifton Bogle received an enigmatic note from an old friend, a former Morgan Stanley strategist named Steven Galbraith, asking him to block off the first weekend of next May, when Bogle would be turning eighty-eight. Galbraith wanted to do something special to celebrate his friend, but refused to tell Bogle what he had cooked up.

Jack Bogle had four decades earlier founded Vanguard, the investment group that brought index-tracking funds to the masses.

After an inauspicious start in 1974, Vanguard had, thanks to the messianism of its headstrong founder, become one of the world's biggest money managers, with an array of dirt-cheap funds that do nothing but attempt to mimic markets rather than beat them. Indeed, it was a Vanguard fund that Buffett had chosen as his champion in his bet with Seides—a bet whose victor would coincidentally be declared around Bogle's birthday.

As his eighty-eighth birthday approached, Bogle had lost his earlier imposing physical presence. His angular features had softened, the severe crew cut he had sported for most of his life had become thin and sparse, and his posture had been eroded by scoliosis, age, and other afflictions. Bogle suffered his first of many heart attacks at thirty-one, at age thirty-eight he was diagnosed with a rare heart disease called arrhythmogenic right ventricular dysplasia, and at sixty-seven he finally had a heart transplant. But his voice still boomed like a foghorn, his mind was as sharp as ever, and he had lost none of his appreciation for adventure. So he gamely agreed to whatever mysterious plan Galbraith had hatched.

On the morning of May 5, 2017, Bogle and his family drove from their house in Bryn Mawr to Atlantic Aviation, Philadelphia's private plane airport. There, a Citation jet with Galbraith aboard picked them up and flew straight to Omaha, for Bogle to attend his first-ever Berkshire Hathaway annual shareholder meeting.

The event is often called the Woodstock of capitalism, a forum for anyone who owns a share in Berkshire Hathaway to ask Buffett and his partner Charlie Munger about everything from business to geopolitics and personal values. The duo revel in the attention, Buffett responding with his well-honed folksy wit and Munger with terse acidity.

Checking in at the Omaha Hilton, Bogle received his first awkward but pleasant surprise: A horde of guests armed with iPhones gave Vanguard's founder the full paparazzi experience, snapping photos of the latest financial celebrity to make a trek to Nebraska's carnival of capitalism. "It felt like escorting Bono around," Galbraith recalls. Bogle's wife, Eve, was a little concerned about the frenzy, given his frailty, but Bogle lapped it up. The shower of photography continued throughout the day, including over dinner at the hotel later that evening. "I quickly learned that saying 'yes' was infinitely more efficient than saying 'no' and then arguing about it," Bogle later wrote.[11]

It was when he woke up on Saturday morning and looked out the hotel room window that Bogle realized just how big a deal the Berkshire meeting is. A line four people wide snaked from the conference center to as far as the eye could see, thousands of people braving the chilly Nebraska morning for the chance to sit closer to Buffett and Munger. That year, forty thousand people attended, with over half forced to watch a video link from a nearby overflow site. Bogle, his family, and the Galbraiths were, however, given prime seating near the front of the cavernous arena, right behind Berkshire's longest-standing shareholders and next to its directors.

As usual, the duo opened with a limp joke. "You can tell us apart because he can hear and I can see. That's why we work so well together," Buffett wisecracked. He went on with the usual discussion of Berkshire's last annual results, and as interesting as it was, after a while Bogle began wondering why Galbraith had brought him all the way to Omaha at his advanced age and poor health. But then Buffett made a sudden detour, and all became clear.

"There's one more person that I would like to introduce to you today and I'm quite sure he's here. I haven't seen him, but I understood he was coming," Buffett said, scanning the audience. "I believe that he made it today and that is Jack Bogle . . . Jack Bogle has probably done more for the American investor than any man in the country. Jack, could you stand up? There he is." To thunderous applause, the gaunt but beaming Bogle, dressed in a dark suit and checkered open-neck shirt, stood up, waved to the crowd, and took a small bow toward Buffett and Munger's podium.

To attendees who might not know who the old man was, Buffett explained how index funds like those pioneered by Vanguard had taken on and upended the money management industry. "I estimate that Jack, at a minimum, has saved and left . . . tens and tens and tens of billions into their pockets, and those numbers are going to be hundreds and hundreds of billions over time," Buffett said. "So, it's Jack's eighty-eighth birthday on Monday, so I just [want to] say, 'Happy birthday, Jack.' And thank you on behalf of American investors." Another round of hearty applause broke out in the arena.

For Bogle, being lauded by Buffett himself in front of thousands of people was an immensely emotional experience. "I don't get verklempt about a lot of stuff, but this was really really awesome," Galbraith said. "It meant a lot to him." The number of people who wanted a photo with him reached the point where Vanguard's founder had to start leaving sessions early to give himself enough time to get out. Bogle later wrote that he "began to understand why rock stars among our entertainers are so eager to avoid the paparazzi." Nonetheless, for someone who was near the end of a long and eventful life that had left him wealthy but hardly rich, the sense of an astonishing legacy being recognized and burnished was unmistakable.

"I confess that, on this one grand occasion, I found huge satisfaction in being recognized for my contribution to the world of investing, and to the wealth of the human beings who have entrusted their assets to Vanguard's index funds," Bogle later said.[12] "I'm only human!"

But Buffett is also only human, and Bogle's visit was akin to a victory lap for the Oracle of Omaha as well.

▲

JUST DAYS BEFORE BERKSHIRE'S shareholder meeting, Seides had officially conceded that he had lost the bet. He had left Protégé a couple of years earlier, but on its behalf he admitted that with only eight months of the bet remaining he was doomed to lose.

Commenters on the Long Bets forum were already gloating. "Warren is mopping the floor with Protege," one said. "No big nail-biter finish here . . . Index funds rule." In one of the last articles of her remarkable six-decade career at *Fortune,* Carol Loomis hailed how Buffett "scorches the hedge funds." Members of Bogleheads, an online forum for fans of Vanguard's founder, were understand-ably smug. "The Sage of Omaha proved what Jack and Bogleheads knew all along, passive investing is the way to go," chortled one of them.

It wasn't even close. The Vanguard 500 Index Fund—ironically viewed as a dismal failure when launched by Bogle four decades earlier—had returned 125.8 percent over the decade. The quintet of funds-of-hedge-funds had an average return of only 36.3 percent. In fact, not one of the five individual hedge fund investment vehi-cles had managed to beat the S&P 500 index that the Vanguard fund tracked.

In his annual report, Buffett was not above some gloating. "Bear in mind that every one of the 100-plus managers of the underlying hedge funds had a huge financial incentive to do his or her best," he wrote. "Moreover, the five funds-of-funds managers that Ted selected were similarly incentivized to select the best hedge-fund managers possible because the five were entitled to performance fees based on the results of the underlying funds. I'm certain that in almost all cases the managers at both levels were honest and intelligent people. But the results for their investors were dismal—really dismal."

Seides agrees with Buffett's assertion that costs matter greatly, but still thinks that Buffett overplays his message. He argues his mistake was to pit a US stock market fund against a broad array of hedge funds, many of which primarily focus on lower-returning corporate bonds or government debt. Moreover, the decade the bet spanned was an exceptionally good one for US stocks, despite the blow of the financial crisis.

In the end, the proceeds that actually went to Girls Inc. amounted to $2.2 million, thanks to a timely switch of the bet's collateral from US Treasury bonds into Berkshire stock—highlighting how human discretion can still play a valuable role. The money helped finance a Girls Inc. program for vulnerable young women at a converted convent on the outskirts of Omaha, now appropriately renamed Protégé House.

However, in retrospect Seides does make one damning concession: If he was a young man today, he would not choose a career in investing. The profession has become increasingly competitive and difficult, and judging whether someone's results are due to luck or skill is almost impossible. Moreover, it is a rare career path where experience does not necessarily make you more proficient, and being mediocre is of no value. "Your average doctor can still save lives. But your average investor detracts value from society," Seides admits.

Naturally, Buffett argues that being a professional investor is not an impossible task, but he is skeptical that many can succeed. Even those who do often see their results atrophy over time. A good track record means a fund manager typically attracts a lot of new investors. But the more money one manages the harder it is to find lucrative opportunities. Since most people in the industry are paid largely according to the amount of money they control, they have little incentive to keep their size manageable. "When trillions of dollars are managed by Wall Streeters charging high fees, it will usually be the managers who reap outsized profits, not the clients. Both large and small investors should stick with low-cost index funds," Buffett argues.[13]

▲

THE BET IS SYMBOLIC OF a broader shift in the investment industry. The *Washington Post* may have eschewed the embryonic index funds that had cropped up by the mid-1970s, but today those funds are gobbling up vast chunks of the investment industry. The public universe of index funds stood at almost $16 trilllion by the end of 2020, according to Morningstar, a prominent data provider on the investment industry. But many big pension plans and sovereign wealth funds also have huge internal index-tracking strategies, or pay an investment group to do it for them outside of a formal fund structure. BlackRock, the world's biggest money manager, estimated in 2017 that there was another $6.8 trillion in nonpublic passive equity strategies, managed internally or by the likes of BlackRock. Assuming a growth rate similar to the public index fund world, that means that over $26 trillion—and that is likely a conservative estimate—now does nothing more than slavishly track some financial index, whether the S&P 500 for American stocks, the Bloomberg Barclays Aggregate for the US bond market, or the JPMorgan EMBI index for developing country debt.

The biggest equity fund in the world is now an index fund. The biggest bond fund is as well. The leading gold index fund now holds more of the yellow metal than most central banks, an astonishing eleven hundred tons. That is equivalent to a quarter of all the bullion in Fort Knox. No wonder that Bloomberg's podcast on a form of index funds known as exchange-traded funds (ETFs) is called *Trillions*, a tongue-in-cheek reference to *Billions*, Showtime's series on the fictional hedge fund manager Bobby Axelrod.

The boons are being reaped by nearly everyone, directly or indirectly. Paul Volcker, the former chair of the Federal Reserve, famously said in 2009 that the only valuable innovation the finance industry has conjured up in the past twenty years was the ATM. Broaden that to the past fifty years, and I would argue that the index fund—first born in the early 1970s—is up there. The average cost of mutual funds in the United States has halved over the past two decades, largely thanks to the growth of index funds and the pressures they bring to all investment fees.

The net savings over that period amount to trillions of dollars, money that goes straight into the pockets of savers, rather than highly paid finance industry professionals. For example, the overall annual cost to investors of the entire $8 trillion universe of ETFs—a next-generation version of index funds that will be explored in later chapters—is, roughly speaking, $15 billion. That is way less than just Fidelity's revenues in 2020, and a tiny fraction of the hedge fund industry's total earnings.[14]

The finance industry has historically been adept at inventing new products that line its own pockets more than those of Main Street. The index fund is a rare exception to the rule. At a time when the gap between the haves and have-nots is widening everywhere, the positive impact that an initially much-maligned invention by a motley group of self-described finance industry renegades and heretics can have in the space of a few decades is inspirational.

Nonetheless, new technologies—and that is essentially what the index fund is—always have side effects, and not all of them are positive. As index investing has grown, the initially snide comments have been replaced by concern, even fear. Over the past decade, it has become a crescendo. Paul Singer, a famous hedge fund manager, even argues that passive investing has grown into a "blob" that is now "in danger of devouring capitalism."

"We are always amazed by decent ideas and insights which are stretched so far beyond their original version that they become caricatures of themselves and then sometimes contra-functional. So it may be with passive investing," the head of Elliott Management wrote in a letter to his investors in 2017.[15]

Singer is hardly a dispassionate observer. Index funds make his life harder, both by pressuring the eye-watering fees that the hedge fund industry has historically charged and by making the corporate crusades Elliott is famous for a lot more complicated. Nonetheless, his criticism, although shrill, has a kernel of truth to it.

For proponents of index investing, it is important to recognize the potentially negative implications and try to ameliorate them, rather than blindly deny that they exist. The growth of passive investing will prove one of the most consequential challenges that we face in the coming decades, not just to markets and investing but to the way capitalism functions. That may seem overblown, especially at a time of pandemics, resurgent nationalism, and widening inequality. But as we saw in 2008, whether we like it or not, finance touches every aspect of our society in ways that are often hard to fathom.

▲

BUFFETT'S PUBLIC SHOUT-OUT TO BOGLE, the creator of the S&P 500 index fund that he had chosen to be his champion in the bet with Seides, was well deserved. Bogle was a titan of the investment industry, a force of nature who arguably did more than anyone to popularize and proselytize for index funds. Much of their growth can be attributed to the messianic fervor that he brought to their cause, in the face of widespread scorn, derision, and mockery from the investment industry.

However, Bogle was far from the only zealot in a revolution that eventually grew to reshape finance. He may have championed the cause of index funds like none other, but he did not provide their intellectual foundation stones, invent their structure, or shape their later evolution into a modern-day phenomenon.

I have tried to avoid writing a "Dummy's Guide" to index funds, eschewing shunning jargon and exhaustive minutiae of mechanical processes in favor of personal stories and narrative verve. I wanted to write something that would help readers appreciate the remarkable rise of index funds, understand their context in the broader history of investing, and help them see where we are now heading.

The people behind the invention and growth of passive investing—though many of them hate the term, given its slothful connotations—are brilliant and fascinating, and many of them kindly shared extraordinarily liberally of their time. Memories fade and accounts differ, and it has at times been tricky to reconcile them into one clear, accurate narrative. But I hope I have written a book that does justice to the magnitude of the story I wanted to tell.

As we shall see over the following chapters, this is a revolution whose seeds were sown in Belle Époque Paris, first harvested in boho San Francisco, and transformed into a world-conquering invention by Wall Street's financial engineers. It features a colorful cast of former farmhands turned computer geeks, amateur jazz musicians, former seminarians, fallen academics, avuncular acoustic physicists, a charismatic secretary turned CEO, finance industry titans, and even a brief cameo from the Terminator. They faced enormous hurdles, public lack of interest, and often widespread scorn from the investment world's haughty mainstream. But what they achieved is nothing short of staggering.

Chapter 2

THE GODFATHER

LEONARD "JIMMIE" SAVAGE, a University of Chicago statistics professor with Coke-bottle glasses and an eclectic, brilliant mind, was rummaging through the university library in 1954 when he made a discovery: a book by a little-known turn-of-the-twentieth-century French mathematician named Louis Bachelier with ideas astonishingly far ahead of their time. Savage sent postcards lauding the work to some of his friends and asked if they had "ever heard of this guy?"[1]

One of the recipients was Paul Samuelson, a rock-star economist who would go on to become the first American to win a Nobel Prize in the field. Samuelson could not find a copy of the book in MIT's library, but he did locate Bachelier's French PhD thesis. That proved enough to whet his interest. He had it quickly translated and spread the word among his economist colleagues, remarking, "Bachelier seems to have had something of a one-track mind. But what a track!"[2] Indeed, that innocuous 1954 postcard from Savage would arguably change the arc of financial history.

Seldom in the history of finance has someone so inconsequential in their own time gone on to enjoy such an outsized influence as Louis Jean-Baptiste Alphonse Bachelier. The son of a prosperous but otherwise unremarkable French wine merchant would quietly lay the groundwork for ideas that continue to shape our world—thanks to the idle rummaging of a nearly blind US statistician with uncommon perception and unusual reach in the US economics community.

Bachelier was born in Le Havre in March 1870, at a time of immense political turmoil and intellectual ferment, a Belle Époque that birthed artists, writers, and scientists like Henri Matisse, Émile Zola, and Marie Curie. Yet little in Bachelier's background hints at the enormous legacy he would leave. Indeed, the relative lack of details on large swaths of his life indicate how little appreciated he was in his own time. Le Havre's famous seaport made it an international, thriving trading entrepôt, but it remained a largely unremarkable city, distant from the cafés, galleries, and *grandes écoles* of Paris.

Though the young Bachelier was initially groomed to take over the family wine business, his father was also an amateur scientist who inculcated a love of physics and mathematics in his eldest son. Bachelier was sent to study for his baccalaureate at a secondary school in nearby Caen, the capital of Lower Normandy, from which he graduated in 1888, intent on a career in mathematics. But then tragedy struck.

Bachelier's father died on January 11, 1889, and just four months afterward his mother also passed away, forcing the eighteen-year-old to abort plans for further study and return home to take over the family business and care for his older sister and three-year-old brother. When Bachelier turned twenty-one he was conscripted into the army.

After a year of military service he finally made it to the Sorbonne, where he studied under the tutelage of mathematical giants such as Henri Poincaré, who supervised his doctorate.[3] Bachelier's grades were unremarkable, but in 1900, shortly after his thirtieth birthday, he successfully defended a doctoral thesis in applied mathematics on "the application of the calculus of probabilities to stock market operations," likely inspired by a part-time job at the Paris stock exchange while studying at the Sorbonne.[4]

Embarrassingly, although Poincaré praised it as "very original," Bachelier's thesis received only an "honorable" mark, below the "very honorable" grade generally required to gain an academic position. Perhaps it was the subject itself—finance was then considered a grubby field not worthy of serious scientific study—that cost him, with Poincaré noting that "the subject is somewhat remote from those our candidates are in the habit of treating."

This was a huge blow, and it meant Bachelier had to largely give unpaid lectures on probability mathematics at the Sorbonne and survive on ad hoc scholarships until he was called up to serve in World War I. When he returned he was unable to obtain a full professorship, bouncing between jobs at the universities of Besançon, Dijon, and Rennes. In a confidential note to the rector at Besançon in May 1921, the French director of higher education wrote, "He is not a high flier, and his work is rather peculiar. But he has served well during the war, and we had not been sufficiently fair to him. In effect, he has been placed on trial in your faculty."[5]

Most humiliatingly, he was briefly blackballed by the University of Dijon, when the department's chair—who favored another candidate for an available tenured position—sought to discredit him by sending an out-of-context excerpt of one of Bachelier's papers to the École Polytechnique in Paris to highlight an apparent error.[6] It was only in 1927 that Bachelier finally gained a tenured professorship at the University of Besançon, where he taught until retiring to Brittany a decade later. In 1946, he passed away in relative obscurity.

His work on probability received some attention in mathematical circles, but remained largely unknown until Jimmie Savage—

himself a fabled polymath whom the economist Milton Friedman described as "one of the few people I have met whom I would unhesitatingly call a genius"—discovered his work. Savage zealously proselytized its importance to American economists, and ensured that it belatedly received its deserved prominence.

Bachelier's thesis *Theory of Speculation* is now widely considered one of the seminal works in the history of finance, the first-ever rigorous, mathematical examination of how financial securities appear to move in unpredictable and random ways. Paul Cootner, a leading scholar of finance in the 1960s, later remarked that "so outstanding is his work that we can say that the study of speculative prices has its moment of glory at its moment of conception."[7]

Inspired by his time at the Paris stock exchange, Bachelier attempted to construct a "probability law" for market fluctuations, using mathematics rather than the gut instinct of traders. The paper is inaccessible to lay people, riddled with mathematical formulae and written with the typically academic disregard for literary flair or even comprehensibility outside of a narrow group of industry readers. But the crucial nub was Bachelier's observation that "contradictory opinions in regard to [market] fluctuations are so divided that at the same instant buyers believe the market is rising and sellers that it is falling . . . It seems that the market, that is to say, the totality of speculators, must believe at a given instant neither in a price rise nor in a price fall, since, for each quoted price, there are as many buyers as sellers."

In other words, while a clever buyer might think he may be landing a bargain, a presumably similarly intelligent seller must be assuming he is getting a good price. Otherwise no deal would be struck. Therefore, at any given moment in time financial securities are priced at the level that investors as a whole and on average consider fair. This was a groundbreaking realization.

And that was not all. Bachelier showed that financial securities appeared to follow what scientists call a "stochastic," or random, movement. The most famous form of random movement was discovered by the Scottish botanist Robert Brown. While examining grains of pollen under a microscope in 1827, Brown saw tiny particles ejected by the pollen that moved around willy-nilly with no discernible pattern, a phenomenon that subsequently became known as Brownian motion.

To better understand the seeming randomness of markets, and to try to estimate the value of financial securities, Bachelier constructed for the first time ever a method to analyze these jittery stochastic movements. He did this a full five years before Albert Einstein independently performed the same in a physics-focused analysis. Today, it is more commonly referred to as a "random walk" similar to that of a drunkard stumbling down a dark road. Markets, by and large, seem to perform the same inebriated wandering that a student might after a particularly heavy day at the university bar.

Although little appreciated in his own time, Bachelier is today considered one of the great academics of the nineteenth century, the father of a field now known as mathematical finance. He might have died in obscurity, but in 2000 his admirers formed the Bachelier Finance Society and started a series of biannual conferences dedicated to mathematical finance.

Moreover, Bachelier's work laid the groundwork for a theory that helped explain one of the most puzzling aspects of the investment industry—why most professional money managers seemed to do such an abysmal job.

▲

THE ROARING TWENTIES ENDED WITH a bang. On the overcast and chilly fourth Thursday of October 1929, a jittery US stock market suffered a catastrophic collapse. Desperate attempts by leading banks and investment trusts to quell the panic through mass purchases of stocks—a playbook that had helped in previous crises—bought only a temporary respite. Between mid-September and mid-November 1929, the US stock market lost nearly half its value, a calamity that reverberated across the world and ushered in the Great Depression.

The Great Crash of 1929 was one of the first severe blows against the credibility of the nascent industry of professional money managers. During the boom, confidence in the judgment of "investment trust" managers—professional investors who managed big pools of money on behalf of thousands of individual savers—was so high that only annual disclosures of their holdings were required, as more frequent transparency could trigger a speculative frenzy in the stocks they bought. But the crash revealed that many of these emperors of money were naked. As John Kenneth Galbraith noted in his seminal history of the episode, "The mightiest of Americans were, for a brief time, revealed as human beings."[8]

In 1940, a former Wall Street stockbroker named Fred Schwed captured the soured view of his industry in a seminal book titled *Where Are the Customers' Yachts?*, a phrase that still endures as an acerbic take on how well many investors have done compared with their brokers and financial advisors. Yet the first empirical, rigorous study of just how well professional investors performed came from an unlikely source.

As his generational suffix hints, Alfred Cowles III was born in 1891 into wealth and privilege. His grandfather, the first Alfred, was one of the *Chicago Tribune*'s founders. His father, Alfred Jr., was a prominent lawyer who later helped run the newspaper. The third Alfred dutifully followed in his father's footsteps and attended Yale University, before joining the newspaper to be groomed for a senior position.

But then fate intervened and dramatically changed the path young Cowles's life would take. After he was struck down by tuberculosis at some point in the 1920s, his family sent him to Colorado Springs, where the fresh mountain air, low humidity, and plentiful sunshine were said to help victims recuperate. To keep busy, Cowles began helping his father with the management of the family's fortune. He subscribed to a mass of investment services and newsletters to help him navigate markets, but to his shock none of them managed to predict the calamity of the 1929 crash nor navigate the aftermath particularly well. Cowles therefore resolved to determine whether stocks really were predictable.[9]

Cowles analyzed the track records of sixteen financial subscription services; the "Dow Theory" first espoused by *Wall Street Journal* founder Charles Dow; the two dozen investment publications he had started with; and the public purchases and sales of twenty leading fire insurance companies.[10] It was quite the undertaking. He had to detail and measure the performance of 7,500 separate recommendations by the financial services, for a total of 75,000 entries, four years of transaction data by the insurance companies, 255 *Wall Street Journal* editorials, and 3,300 recommendations by the investment publications.

The result was a 1933 article in *Econometrica*—a new journal dedicated to mathematical economics funded by Cowles himself—titled "Can Stock Market Forecasters Forecast?" Cowles summed up the results of his study in a terse, brutal three-word abstract: "It is doubtful."[11]

Cowles's calculations indicated that only a minority of prognosticators actually managed to do better than the stock market as a whole, and blind luck might explain those. Even the fire insurance industry—which he noted had "long years of experience and large amounts of capital at its disposal"—did miserably, underperforming the market by an average of 1.2 percent a year over the 1928–31 period. Cowles's conclusion was damning: "The best of these records, since it is not very much more impressive than the record of the most successful of the sixteen financial services, fails to exhibit definitely the existence of any skill in investment."[12]

Compiling all the data and measuring the forecasters' success was a herculean task, performed on a primitive punch-card computer supplied by a then up-and-coming company called International Business Machines (IBM). A bigger follow-up study in 1944 reviewed 6,904 market forecasts over a period of more than fifteen years. Again, the researchers failed to find any evidence that the stock market could be successfully predicted.[13]

Understandably, the investment profession failed to appreciate the sunshine Cowles had shone on their prowess. "Of course, I got a lot of complaints," he later recalled. "Who appointed me to keep track? Also, I had belittled the profession of investment adviser. I used to tell them that it isn't a profession, and of course, that got them even madder."[14]

But that was not the newspaper scion's only contribution to finance. In 1932, he set up the Cowles Commission for Research in Economics, with the motto "Science is Measurement." Measurement was his lifelong passion, with his son later revealing that among his copious papers were facts and analyses on subjects as varied as admission rates to Yale, blindness in the United States, the most popular breeds of dogs, the weather in Palm Beach, and sharks.[15] The Cowles Commission would go on to host and support an all-star cast of great economists and financial academics over the years, such as James Tobin, Joseph Stiglitz, Abba Lerner, Kenneth Arrow, Jacob Marschak, Tjalling Koopmans, Franco Modigliani, and Harry Markowitz, several of whom would go on to win Nobel Prizes for work at the commission. In fact, one could argue that in its heyday it was the most influential economic think tank in history. Not bad for the tuberculosis-ridden son of a newspaperman based in scenic but remote Colorado.

▲

THE COWLES COMMISSION ALSO DID vital work in another growing area of importance: measuring the overall stock market. In 1938, Cowles published another major study, which painstakingly collected data on all the shares listed on the New York Stock Exchange since 1871 and created an overall index to "portray the average experience of those investing . . . in the United States."[16]

This effort highlights just how important stock market indices were starting to become at the time. The first ones were generally compiled by financial newspapers, but calculated haphazardly and intermittently. The first daily stock market index appeared in 1884, published by Charles Dow in his "Customer's Afternoon Letter." His initial effort calculated only an average of eleven transportation stocks, almost all of them railways. In 1889, the newsletter was renamed the *Wall Street Journal*, and in 1896 Dow calculated his first daily index of purely industrial stocks—the now-famous Dow Jones Industrial Average.

It wasn't until the stock market boom of the Roaring Twenties that financial indices really started proliferating. Yet despite their rising popularity they long remained primitive by modern standards. Without computers they had to be compiled and calculated manually, an arduous task for benchmarks with more than a handful of members. But Standard & Poor's launch of its own index of America's biggest companies in 1957 was a landmark, "a symbol of the beginning of the electronic era in finance," according to Robert Shiller, the Nobel laureate.[17]

The S&P 500, as it was called, despite initially tracking only 425 companies, was calculated by a Datatron computer linked directly to the stock market ticker machines now set up on Wall Street, and could continuously measure the new index. That was a tremendous improvement. By 1962, the S&P 500 was computed every five minutes (and every fifteen seconds by 1986).

But bizarrely, no one really knew exactly the long-term return of stocks. After all, the indices captured only the biggest, most heavily traded listed companies, and didn't account for dividend payments, mergers, spin-offs, or sometimes even share splits (when a stock becomes too expensive for ordinary investors, so the company slices it up into smaller increments to make it more affordable). Complicating matters further, there are many different types of stocks. So no one could really conclusively say what kind of long-term returns investors should be able to expect from the stock market.

This was a problem for Wall Street firms that were trying to drum up interest among prospective clients, many of which still vividly remembered the Great Depression, and overwhelmingly preferred the safety of bonds issued by solid companies and the US government.

In 1948, Louis Engel, the head of marketing at the brokerage house Merrill Lynch, Pierce, Fenner and Smith, ran a full-page advertisement in the *New York Times* promising to explain "what everyone ought to know . . . about this stock and bond business," using "plain talk about a simple business that often sounds complicated."[18] At over six thousand words, it is probably one of the most verbose ads ever run. But it proved a huge success. The ad ran for nearly two decades in some form, generated enormous traction for Merrill's famous "thundering herd" of stockbrokers, and ultimately resulted in a book by Engel titled *How to Buy Stocks* that sold four million copies.[19] But when Engel in 1960 wanted to run an ad arguing explicitly that stocks were a good investment for ordinary people, it was nixed by the Securities and Exchange Commission. Wall Street's financial watchdog argued that he needed evidence to make that claim.

So Engel called up his alma mater, the University of Chicago, to find out if anyone could conclusively and empirically answer the question of what stocks really returned in the long run. Merrill Lynch granted $50,000 to James Lorie, the associate dean of Chicago's business school, who in March 1960 set up the Center for Research in Security Prices (CRSP) in Chicago to collect the necessary data. Initially he hoped to have a definitive answer within a year. "We spent $250,000 and took four years," he later joked.[20]

Despite the setbacks, Lorie was the right person to lead the project, for both his professional and personal qualities. Although he never achieved the fame or Nobel Prizes of some of his Chicago contemporaries, his contributions to the intellectual ferment of the university's economics department—and, ultimately, the invention of the index fund—are undeniable.

▲

BORN IN 1922 IN KANSAS CITY, the horse-loving, backgammon enthusiast[21] Lorie combined a genial temperament and a love for jokes—Johnny Carson was one of his favorite comedians[22]—with a crackerjack, eclectic mind. This proved instrumental in luring a wide array of other famous economists to Chicago. He was much loved by his MBA students, who dubbed his finance course "Lorie's Stories" because of his affection for colorful anecdotes and asides.[23] But CRSP, usually just called Crisp, proved his crowning achievement.

The work he embarked upon for Merrill was no humdrum task, as he noted with his usual wit in a speech to the American Statistical Society on his findings: "Some people say that sex is not as important as Freud thought; and as I get older, I am increasingly inclined to agree with them. Others deny that money is as important as the Socialists say. They may be right. Nevertheless, sex and money are undoubtedly both popular and even important," Lorie said, noting that twenty million Americans owned about $600 billion worth of stocks at the time, both directly and via pension funds.[24]

He paid tribute to the pioneering work that Cowles had done, but noted that previous examinations had been conducted by people who might know a great deal about the stock market, but very little about statistics. "While this combination of knowledge and ignorance is not so likely to be sterile as the reverse—that is, statistical sophistication coupled with ignorance of the field of application—it nevertheless failed to produce much of value," he argued.[25] Enlisting his computer-savvy colleague Lawrence Fisher to do much of the actual number-crunching, Lorie thought he could do better.

They resolved to calculate the average rate of returns of common stocks listed on the New York Stock Exchange, collecting the closing monthly prices of seventeen hundred companies listed there, and any other data relevant to measuring their returns. This was easier said than done, given the multitude of ways that US corporations had over the years distributed their profits to shareholders, varying commission costs, tax treatments, and even the different types of securities that companies issued. Lorie and Fisher found over fifty different types of common stock—in other words, securities that carried some ownership rights and claim to the income of the issuing company—that weren't actually called so, and some common stocks that were in reality no such thing.

Of the almost four hundred thousand price quotations they collected, over thirty thousand required serious checking and cleaning up, as the fastidious Fisher wanted to make the data even cleaner and more accurate than the raw source material, "a possibly laudable and assuredly extravagant ambition," Lorie later remarked.[26] But the results finally unveiled in 1964 were fabulous. Their dataset—compiled on a magnetic tape that unreeled would stretch for over three miles[27]—showed the rates of stock market returns for twenty-two distinct periods between 1926 and 1960, with and without dividends, and with varying tax assumptions. Overall, someone investing money in all the stocks of the NYSE in 1926 and reinvesting all dividend payments would have made 9 percent annually by 1960—far higher than previously thought.

Thrillingly for the sponsors of the study at Merrill, even someone who had invested at the peak of the 1920s bull market, just before the Great Crash of 1929, would have made 7.7 percent a year. And since 1950 the average annual rate of return had been over 10 percent. This was music to the ears of Merrill's stockbrokers, who promptly reprinted the study in a full-page advertisement in the *Wall Street Journal*,[28] distributed it to over seven hundred thousand people across the United States, and hammered it home in a series of conferences held from London and Geneva to New York and San Francisco.[29] It was a bombshell—especially to many investors who had historically thought bonds were both safer and higher-returning in the long run. They were now forced to revisit their assumptions.

However, the equally momentous revelation of the data crunched by CRSP was that the long-term return of US stocks was actually slightly higher than the average returns of investment trusts and mutual funds. These were for the first time beginning to be collected more systematically by consultancy firms such as AG Becker. This was curious, Lorie gleefully noted in a 1965 speech.[30] "The managers of the funds controlled by these organizations are competent, responsible professionals whose careers depend in large part on success in selecting securities and in timing their purchase and sale," he said. "Yet throwing darts at lists of stocks and dates is on the average as satisfactory a method of making investments as is reliance on competent professional judgment."

This uncomfortable truth was further underscored by a pioneering 1967 paper by Michael Jensen, another prominent University of Chicago graduate. The intellectual heir to Cowles's first effort to examine the performance of professional investors pored through the results of 115 mutual funds between 1945 and 1964, and found that they were on average unable to outperform the broader market even before their expenses. Moreover, the damning research indicated that there was "very little evidence that any individual fund was able to do significantly better than that which we expected from mere random chance."[31]

This hardly trickled into the offices of the rapidly growing mutual fund industry. After all, the tribe of swaggering star money managers that had emerged in the 1960s bull market had little time for the idle pontification of academics in their ivory towers—if they were even aware of it. In the pre-internet era, information traveled slowly, and unwelcome information was easier to ignore. Fund managers like Fidelity's Gerald Tsai could point to eye-watering returns from investing in hot "Nifty Fifty" stocks, but as mad as it might sound today, most investors didn't ask for and fund managers didn't provide relative performance data.[32] And the idea that someone could do well by just buying the entire market was considered preposterous.

A good example is the backlash suffered by a radical, ahead-of-its-time 1960 paper by Edward Renshaw, a Chicago economics graduate who taught economics at the University of California, and one of his students, Paul Feldstein. He made the case for the establishment of "an unmanaged investment company" that would merely track a stock market index, like the Dow Jones Industrial Average.[33] Although it avoided attacking the skill of money managers and was primarily couched in terms of convenience for inexperienced investors attempting to sift through the cornucopia of mutual fund managers popping up around the time, the paper was roundly dismissed. One senior industry veteran, writing under the pen name John B. Armstrong, was even handed an award for his rebuttal[34] in the *Financial Analysts Journal*, and the idea sank without a trace. Thus investment groups could continue to counter the attacks from academia by saying that one couldn't buy the entire market anyway. For the mainstream financial press, the debate was too recondite to care about—especially when copy about rock-star fund managers sold far better.

But the magazine *BusinessWeek*—coincidentally where Merrill's Engel had been managing editor before he joined the brokerage house—noted the implications of CRSP's results: "For a sizable area of Wall Street—mutual funds, security analysts, investment advisers and the like—the study should prove unsettling. Everyone in this area makes his money, to one degree or another, by selling his skill to [the] less expert."[35]

Some finance industry insiders were slowly beginning to wrestle with the implications. In 1975, Charles Ellis, a Donaldson, Lufkin & Jenrette banker who later founded an influential consultancy called Greenwich Associates, wrote an article titled "The Loser's Game" in the *Financial Analysts Journal*, which argued, "The investment management business (it should be a profession but is not) is built upon a simple and basic belief: Professional money managers can beat the market. That premise appears to be false."[36]

The CRSP data was the wellspring from which a lot of this dawning realization sprung. Rex Sinquefield, then a student at Chicago's business school, noted, somewhat tongue-in-cheek, that "if I had to rank events, I would say CRSP is probably slightly more significant than the creation of the universe."[37]

Lorie himself stressed that professional investors "can be and almost certainly are useful." They performed a valuable service in simply convincing people to invest in stocks—which, as he had shown, offered superior returns to bonds and money deposited in a bank account—and provided a relatively efficient way of gaining a diversified portfolio of them. After all, the cost of bookkeeping and custodial work could be significant, and the service that professionals offered smaller investors in reducing the "agony of choice and responsibility" was valuable, Lorie argued.[38]

Nonetheless, he took a stab at explaining why the average returns of professional money managers didn't seem to be able to beat the market. Some were fairly obvious, he noted, for example the fact that mutual funds typically charged investors an 8 percent fee up front—the "load," in the industry's jargon—and then an annual management fee. Mutual funds and investment trusts were also only rarely fully invested in the stock market, as they usually try to keep some cash in reserve in case some investors want to pull out, or an enticing buying opportunity suddenly presents itself. But holding cash is a drag on performance when markets are rising. Moreover, professional investors were becoming increasingly important players in the stock market, and thus in many respects *were* the market—as Buffett later pointed out in his letter to Katharine Graham.

Finally, Lorie discussed a controversial but increasingly popular theory that was spreading out of the confines of academia, that stocks took a "random walk" and thus cannot actually be accurately and consistently predicted—the idea that Bachelier had first proposed in 1900 but had only recently been rediscovered thanks to the efforts of the likes of Savage and Samuelson.

In 1964, Paul Cootner, a colleague of Samuelson at MIT, published a five-hundred-page tome titled *The Random Character of Stock Prices*, which contained much of the academic work done by himself, Cowles, and others in the field. One of the more colorful descriptions of the apparent path of stock prices came from Maurice Kendall, a famous British statistician who in 1953 had published a study of fluctuations in UK stocks, Chicago wheat prices, and New York cotton. He noted that the price series all seemed haphazard, "almost as if once a week the Demon of Chance drew a random number."[39]

Cootner's book also included the first fully translated reprinting of Bachelier's original 1900 thesis, helping bring it to a broader audience. "His work was seminal but the gestation period was long," Lorie noted. "Only within the last 10 years has his work been redis-covered by persons interested in testing it and extending it with other data."[40]

Bachelier is arguably the index fund's intellectual godfather. But economics and finance are fields where everyone stands on the shoulders of giants. The expansion of the random-walk theory into a vibrant, multifaceted model for how markets function and how investors should approach them—laying the academic groundwork for the passive investing earthquake to come—came primarily from three unusually brilliant members of the profession: Harry Mar-kowitz, William Sharpe, and Eugene Fama, each of whom would go on to win a Nobel Prize for their work.

Chapter 3

TAMING THE DEMON OF CHANCE

HARRY MARKOWITZ WAS WAITING PATIENTLY in the anteroom of his University of Chicago supervisor's office when the cerebral, gangly young economics student decided to strike up a conversation with a visiting stockbroker.

It was 1950; the first *Peanuts* comic had just been printed, James Dean got his big break by appearing in a Pepsi-Cola ad, and Cold War tensions were on the rise, with North Korea invading its southern neighbor that summer. Yet the cross-currents of popular culture and geopolitics felt remote at the University of Chicago, so they instead talked idly about how Markowitz was struggling to think of a subject for his PhD thesis. "Why don't you do a dissertation on the stock market?" the broker suggested.[1]

It proved a serendipitous meeting, one that would set Markowitz on a path toward a peculiar form of fame—the kind where one can walk undisturbed in public, but the cognoscenti whisper your name with reverence. Samuelson, arguably the preeminent US economist of the twentieth century, is said to have argued that "Wall Street stands on the shoulders of Harry Markowitz."[2] His groundbreaking work continues to inform the money management principles of billionaire hedge fund managers, sprawling investment banks, and vast pension plans to this day.

It was an odd fate for Markowitz, who initially had little knowledge of or even interest in the world of finance. Born in 1927 and growing up as the son of two comfortable Jewish grocers in Chicago, he enjoyed a quiet, sheltered life. Even the Great Depression—which had naturally stirred interest in economics—left no lasting impression on him. Markowitz grew up playing baseball, football, and the violin, but his growing passion was philosophy, particularly David Hume and René Descartes. After doing a two-year bachelor's degree at the University of Chicago, he chose to specialize in economics on a whim, largely because he liked mathematics.

But his natural aptitude was obvious enough that Markowitz was invited to become one of the student members of the Cowles Commission set up by Alfred Cowles III two decades earlier. Its former director Jacob Marschak became Markowitz's supervisor, and it was outside Marschak's office that the young economist ended up chatting with the visiting stockbroker. When Markowitz eventually knocked and entered, he told his supervisor about the conversation and broached the idea of some kind of dissertation on the stock market.[3]

At the time, this was an unconventional idea. Although Chicago had a thriving business school, the stock market itself was still considered a little grubby for serious, intellectual academic research. But Marschak agreed that it could prove a fertile field, explaining that Cowles himself had been fascinated by it. Marschak confessed to knowing little about the subject personally, so he directed his student to Marshall Ketchum at Chicago's business school, who supplied a reading list to get Markowitz started.

So he duly headed to the library, and within the afternoon had the kernel of an idea that would eventually have a seismic impact. Indeed, many in the industry argue that modern finance was in practice born that day.

Markowitz quickly read one of the first recommendations on Ketchum's list, John Burr Williams's *The Theory of Investment Value.* Williams had worked on Wall Street, but after the crash of 1929 and the Great Depression he had gone to Harvard to get a PhD in economics, to better understand the calamity that had just happened and bring some more rigor to his profession. In the book, Williams proposed that the price of a stock should be equal to the present value of the expected dividends it would in the future pay to shareholders. That sent Markowitz pondering in Chicago's voluminous university library.

At least in theory, that should mean that people should invest only in the single security that offered the greatest expected return. But Markowitz knew this would be insanity in practice. Future dividends are inherently uncertain, and investors care about both the risk of their investments and their return. So he thought diversification—spreading the eggs across several baskets—would reduce the risk. Using the volatility of a stock as a proxy for risk, he empirically proved that diversification across a large number of independently moving securities—a "portfolio," as the finance industry calls a collection of securities—did indeed reduce the risks for investors.

In fact, Markowitz suggested that all investors should really care about was how the entire portfolio acted, rather than obsess about each individual security it contained. As long as a stock moved somewhat independently of the others, whatever its other virtues, the overall risk of the portfolio—or at least its volatility—would be reduced. Diversification, such as can be achieved through a broad, passive portfolio of the entire stock market, is the only "free lunch" available to investors, Markowitz argued.

Of course, most investors already intuitively knew that putting all their eggs in one basket could be dangerous. But at the time, how to best construct a portfolio of stocks largely amounted to "rules of thumb and folklore," according to the financial historian Peter Bernstein.[4] Markowitz's thesis—first published in the prestigious *Journal of Finance* in 1952—showed for the first time quantitatively how they could try to optimize the balance between risk and return. The article, titled "Portfolio Selection," became the foundation stone for what eventually became known as "modern portfolio theory," which to this day informs how most investors manage their holdings, and won Markowitz a Nobel Prize in 1990. "It happened in the twinkle of an eye," he later recalled. "People ask me if I knew I'd get a Nobel prize. I always say no, but I knew I'd get a PhD."[5]

However, despite Markowitz's confidence—and the huge legacy it would leave—whether it would actually qualify for a PhD in economics was oddly uncertain. Markowitz had in 1952 left Chicago for the RAND Corporation, a prestigious think tank in sunny California, and had to return to defend his thesis to the faculty. He was unconcerned, thinking as he landed in Chicago, "I know this subject cold. Not even Dr. Milton Friedman [the University of Chicago's legendary economics professor] can give me a hard time."[6]

Unfortunately, Friedman was unconvinced. Five minutes into Markowitz's defense, the university's towering intellect interjected: "Harry, I've read your dissertation. I don't find any mistakes in the math, but this isn't a dissertation in economics. We can't give you a PhD in economics for a dissertation that's not economics." That resulted in a heated debate, with Marschak defending his protégé. In the end, they sent Markowitz out into the hall to await their decision. Roughly five minutes later, Marschak emerged and said, "Congratulations, Dr. Markowitz."

The economist's move to RAND proved fortuitous. It was there that Markowitz first met William Sharpe, a brilliant young economist who would become his own protégé and dramatically expand upon his work—something that Markowitz later appreciated enormously. "Bill always says that he received a Nobel Prize because he followed me using portfolio theory, and I said that I got a Nobel Prize because he transformed the field from business administration to economics," Markowitz later observed. "Otherwise, I would not have gotten a prize in economics."[7]

▲

SHARPE GREW UP IN RIVERSIDE in Southern California, and initially planned on becoming a doctor. But once he started at Berkeley in 1951, he quickly realized that his queasiness at the sight of blood might be an impediment. So he transferred to UCLA to pursue a degree in business administration. The accounting courses mostly consisted of bookkeeping, which Sharpe found turgid. But an introductory course to a mysterious subject called "economics" promptly had him hooked, so he switched lanes again. "I just thought it was beautiful, so I changed to an economics major. I had no notion how I would earn a living, but I just had to do it," he later recalled.[8]

However, this was a different time, and the good grades Sharpe attained didn't help him get into Wall Street. Quite the contrary. When he interviewed for a job at a bank, the interviewer took one look at his grades and suggested he'd be better off going to graduate school than working in finance. "I got the impression they didn't really want people [with good grades] in banking," he recalls. Sharpe pointed out that he was also the commodore of the local sailing club, was in the Reserve Officers' Training Corps, had—at least briefly—been in a fraternity, and insisted that he was "actually a rounded human being." Nonetheless, in the end he decided to pursue a master's degree in economics. After that, he had to serve two years in the Army, stationed at Fort Lee in Virginia.

Sharpe luckily avoided combat duty in the Korean War, and

although he enjoyed service, he discovered that he could shorten the two years of active duty to just six months if he went to work for a government contractor. One of his UCLA professors had recommended that he join the RAND Corporation after he was finished in the Army anyway, and since RAND was an Air Force–backed research institute, Sharpe was able to join it as an economist in 1956 while pursuing a doctorate at UCLA.

RAND proved formative. Some of its employees joked that it stood for "Research And No Development," and its intellectualism was inspiring to the young economist. The think tank's ethos was to work on problems so hard that they might actually be unsolvable.[9] Four days of the week were dedicated to RAND projects, but the fifth was free for freewheeling personal research. Ken Arrow, a famous economist, and John Nash, the game theorist immortalized in the film *A Beautiful Mind*, both consulted for RAND around the time Sharpe was there. The eclecticism of RAND's research community is reflected in his first published works, which were a proposal for a smog tax and a review of aircraft compartment design criteria for Army deployments.

The nascent field of computing also rubbed off on Sharpe. He learned to program on a hulking RAND computer designed by John von Neumann—one of the greatest American mathematicians of the twentieth century—which staff had nicknamed "Johnniac," as well as a state-of-the-art IBM machine. This then-novel skill, honed through countless brutal nighttime keypunch sessions, would prove invaluable for the young economist. Aside from helping Sharpe counter his weakness at pure mathematics, becoming one of the first-ever economist-programmers ultimately helped him secure a doctorate.

Perhaps most important, he got to work with Markowitz. Sharpe's first stab at a doctoral thesis had bombed, but he had become familiar with the Chicagoan's work as a student, and when

Markowitz arrived at RAND, Sharpe sought him out for advice. It proved a fertile collaboration.

Sharpe wrote a computer program that simplified Markowitz's models so that they were more usable in practice. In 1952, the only computers that could actually run the analysis that Markowitz had described were controlled by the US government and used to design nuclear weapons.[10] Using Fortran, a programming language Sharpe learned at RAND, he developed an algorithm that could crunch the analysis on a hundred different securities in thirty seconds, rather than the thirty-three minutes it would normally take an IBM 7090 computer to run the full Markowitz process. At the time, computing time was costly, and this was a major leap forward.

That was not all. To simplify Markowitz's model, Sharpe stipulated one fundamental underlying factor—the return of the overall stock market—and instead calculated the variation of individual securities relative to this, rather than each security relative to each other. In his formula, it was given the Greek letter beta. So if Coca-Cola's shares rise by 0.8 percentage points for every 1 percent the broader stock market climbs, it has a beta of 0.8. If a racier stock gains 2 percent, it has a beta of 2. Higher-beta stocks are more volatile, and should therefore offer greater returns than steadier, lower-beta securities. And thus beta became the lingua franca for the returns of the stock market as a whole, while "alpha" later emerged as the term for the extra returns generated by a skilled investor.

Not only did this gain Sharpe his PhD, but it eventually evolved into a seminal paper on what he called the "capital asset pricing model" (CAPM), a formula that investors could use to calculate the value of financial securities. The broader, groundbreaking implication of CAPM was introducing the concept of risk-adjusted returns—one had to measure the performance of a stock or a fund manager versus the volatility of its returns—and indicated that the best overall investment for most investors is the entire market, as it reflects the optimal tradeoff between risks and returns.

This laid the intellectual groundwork for the coming invention of the index fund. Sharpe never made explicit mention of any index funds—after all, none had been invented yet, and he was unaware of the radical Renshaw paper proposing an "unmanaged investment company." Sharpe called it simply "the market portfolio." But the implications were clear. Independently, similar models were developed by the likes of Jack Treynor, John Lintner, and Jan Mossin around the same time as Sharpe's CAPM paper. But it was his work that in time became one of the most influential publications in economic history.

Ironically, the CAPM paper initially met with a limp reception. Sharpe was confident that it was the best paper he would ever write when he submitted it for publication in early 1962, and he waited for the phone to ring with plaudits. Instead, it was rejected by the *Journal of Finance* on the grounds that its many assumptions were too unrealistic. Stubbornly, he resubmitted it, and it was eventually published in 1964. Yet the early reaction was tepid. "Man, I had just written the best paper I'm ever going to write, and nobody cares,"[11] the normally cheery Sharpe thought to himself. But over time, its importance shone through, and it ultimately helped him—and Markowitz—win the Nobel Prize in Economics in 1990.

Nonetheless, it took another Chicago economist to construct a fully fledged argument for precisely *why* the "market portfolio" is optimal and to help supercharge the financial-academic ferment into a full-blown revolution.

▲

IT WAS THE QUINTESSENTIAL STORY of American immigration. Sometime in the early 1900s,[12] Gaetano and Santa Fama joined the Italian exodus to America, uprooting their lives in Sicily and moving to chilly New England. Gaetano became Guy, found work as a barber, and settled down with Santa in north Boston's Little Italy, where they raised seven children. There, their son Francis met the daughter of another couple of Italian immigrants. When they married, Francis Fama and Angelina Sarraceno moved to the solidly working-class town of Malden, just north of Boston. On Valentine's Day 1939, they welcomed a little baby boy they christened Eugene Francis Fama, the third of what ultimately became four children.[13]

Gene's formative memory from those early years was World War II, and anxiety that his father would be drafted. Francis Fama was a truck driver, but during the war he worked in Boston's shipyard building battleships. Although he escaped the draft, the ships were lined with asbestos, which ultimately led Francis to die at seventy of asbestosis, a form of lung cancer, despite his never having smoked or drunk alcohol in his life. Soon afterward Angelina would also pass from cancer, caused by high doses of hormones that were at the time prescribed for women going through "the change of life."[14]

Still, Gene Fama enjoyed a happy childhood. Francis and Angelina had banded together with an aunt and uncle to buy a two-flat building across Boston's Mystic River in the town of Medford, which abuts Malden. Despite a rather small frame that measured a shade under five foot eight and 160 pounds even at his prime, Gene became quite the jock, excelling at basketball, baseball, track, and football—in which he claims to have invented the "split end" position, as a result of the beatings he received when trying to block much bigger opponents. Regardless of the veracity of this claim, Gene's sporting prowess earned him a permanent slot in his high school's athletic hall of fame.

Around this time he also met a pretty, diminutive girl named Sallyann Dimeco who attended the neighboring Catholic girls' school. They married soon after high school. Nonetheless, despite the distractions, Fama excelled academically as well, and his mother encouraged him to pursue further education. Hoping to become a high school teacher himself—and perhaps a sports coach on the side—he went to Tufts University to study Romance languages, becoming the first of his family to go to college. The track of his life looked firmly set toward happy middle-class obscurity.

However, the subject bored him to tears. "I just got stuck," he recalls. After two years of seemingly endless Voltaire, he took a class in economics on a whim, and fell in love—with both the subject and the prospect of "escaping lifetime starvation on the wages of a high school teacher."[15] The last two years at Tufts he took all the economics courses he could, and applied for graduate school at a host of top universities. He received an offer from nearby Harvard, but heard nothing from the University of Chicago. In another fork of history, Chicago might never have admitted the person who would go on to be one of its preeminent economics professors. But curious about the silence, Fama called the school's dean of students office, and by chance the phone was picked up by the dean himself—Jeff Metcalf.

"Gee, we have no record of your application," Metcalf told Fama.[16]

"Well, I did send it," Fama insisted.

"What kind of grades do you have?" Metcalf asked.

"All A's!" Fama said.

Metcalf continued chatting to the young student, and something about him tickled the dean. So he told Fama about a scholarship at Chicago specifically for students from Tufts. And that's how the precocious former jock ended up at the University of Chicago. Aside from a two-year stint as a visiting professor at the University of Leuven in Belgium in the mid-1970s, Fama has stayed true to Chicago ever since the fateful call, and is still teaching in his eighties.

It was at Chicago that Fama first met Benoit Mandelbrot, a brilliant Polish-French American mathematician. The peripatetic polymath would occasionally visit the university and give presentations to its graduate students, and ended up taking many long walks around the university's quadrangles with the young Fama. Crucially, it was Mandelbrot who told the young Italian American about the apparent randomness of financial markets, and Bachelier's groundbreaking work over half a century earlier. Mandelbrot was intimately familiar with *Theory of Speculation* from his time in France, and together with Samuelson and Savage he played a pivotal role in making Bachelier's work more widely known, especially in Chicago.

When Fama had to decide on his PhD thesis he presented five ideas to his supervisor, Merton Miller, a superstar economist in his own right. "He gently stomped on four of my topics, but was excited by the fifth," Fama later recalled.[17] During his last year at Tufts, the young economist had worked for a professor who ran a stock market forecasting service on the side. Fama was tasked with finding ways to do so. The problem was that methods based on the historical data never seemed to work on "out of sample" tests—in other words, fresh market data not used in the model.

For example, perhaps the data indicated that one could make money from always buying carmaker stocks on a Monday, but when one actually did so the returns evaporated. Out-of-sample tests are a tool that statisticians use to check that a pattern might actually be predictive, rather than just a spurious random correlation—such as per capita cheese consumption seemingly being closely linked to how many people die annually from getting tangled in their bedsheets.[18]

Although Fama never found a successful way of forecasting the stock market, through his work he had painstakingly collected a database of daily information on the thirty stocks that made up the Dow

Jones Industrial Average. At the time, the CRSP data was still being collected by Lorie and Fisher in a nearby building on campus, so this was a treasure trove of information. Fama proposed to Miller that he would produce detailed evidence of Mandelbrot's hypothesis that stock returns conform to "non-normal" distributions—in other words, they are nearly random and exhibit far more wild swings than one might expect—and a detailed examination of returns over time. Although there was already some academic work on this, Fama promised a "unifying perspective" thanks to the data he had collected.

He delivered. His PhD thesis showed—in "nauseating detail," as he later admitted—that the stock market did indeed suffer from extreme movements outside the normal. Most natural phenomena normally distribute along what statisticians call a "bell curve." For example, there are more people who are six feet tall than seven, or four. When mapped out on a graph, the distribution takes the shape of a bell, with most observations clustered evenly around the most common datapoint. This normal shape is also called a "Gaussian distribution," after the eighteenth-century German mathematician Carl Friedrich Gauss.

The stock market conforms to this, but only to a degree. Stocks do fall or rise 1 percent more often than 2 percent—but they also tend to fall by a statistically improbable amount far more often than a normal distribution would imply, Fama's 1964 thesis showed. In the jargon of statisticians, stock market returns show a nasty tendency of having "fat tails" on an otherwise normal bell curve. Moreover, Fama's thesis—titled "The Behavior of Stock-Market Prices"—corroborated earlier work by the likes of Mandelbrot and Samuelson which argued that markets are close to random, and therefore impossible to predict. As the young economist wrote in the introduction, "The series of price changes has no memory, that is, the past cannot be used to predict the future in any meaningful way."[19]

But why? Fama's big contribution was to present an overarching hypothesis explaining this conclusion. Although his doctoral thesis makes no explicit mention of it, the term "efficient markets" made its first appearance in "Random Walks in Stock Market Prices," a paper he published in the *Financial Analysts Journal* in 1965, which was reprinted in a simpler form by *Institutional Investor*, the money management industry's leading magazine, later that year.

Fama proposed that in an efficient market, the competition among so many smart traders, analysts, and investors meant that at any given time, all known, relevant information was already reflected in stock prices. And new information would continually be baked into the price virtually instantaneously.

This was eventually dubbed the "efficient-markets hypothesis." It wasn't an entirely novel observation. In 1889, George Rutledge Gibson had written in *The Stock Exchanges of London, Paris, and New York* that when "shares become publicly known in an open market, the value which they acquire may be regarded as the judgment of the best intelligence concerning them."[20] But Fama was the first to combine theory and data into one overarching framework. In 1970, he brought it all together in "Efficient Capital Markets: A Review of Theory and Empirical Work," which became the seminal piece of the efficient-markets hypothesis.

The hypothesis quickly became de rigueur among the academic cognoscenti at business schools across the United States. In Chicago, it practically became religion. Professor Ketchum, who had first inspired Markowitz decades earlier, still taught a class on analyzing financial securities, but it fell out of favor as Fama's work became dogma. "If you were cool, you wouldn't take Ketchum's class," recalls David Booth, a student at Chicago at the time.

Yet the efficient-markets hypothesis was, and remains to this day, controversial. After all, if markets are so efficient, why are they prone to booms and busts? Why do at least some people seem to manage making money relatively consistently? How on earth can the hypothesis be true when stocks can very clearly be enveloped by obvious, wild manias, such the "meme stonk" craze of early 2021? Even at the time, it was laughed at outside the confines of academia. Stockbrokers may have embraced the returns shown by Lorie's CRSP, but shunned less convenient studies. One 1968 advertisement placed by Oppenheimer & Co. captured the finance industry's attitude to the theory:[21]

> *Random walks in the park with pleasant company are most enjoyable; in the stock market, however, they might lead down a perilous path. Despite the observations of some learned theoreticians, there is no substitute for qualitative research in the management of money and we doubt there ever will be.*

The financial crisis of 2008 was a particularly hard blow to efficient-markets proponents, even though Fama himself had shown that markets are prone to improbable "fat tail" meltdowns, and later did seminal work on factors that have in the long run made investors above-market returns (research we will return to later). Fama notes that markets are rarely perfectly efficient, and acerbically argues that the theory "is only controversial among people that don't want to believe in it." His view is that events like the dotcom bubble, the financial crisis of 2008, or the wild post-coronavirus market rally of 2020–21 might show that prices may not always be "right," but it is in practice impossible to know when they aren't before the fact.

Yet the best argument for the enduring value of the efficient-markets hypothesis comes from the eminent twentieth-century British statistician George Box, who is said to have quipped that "all models are wrong, but some are useful." The efficient-markets hypothesis may not be entirely correct. After all, markets are shaped by humans, and humans are prone to all sorts of behavioral biases and irrationality. But the hypothesis is at the very least a decent approximation for how markets work—and helps explain just why they have in practice proven so hard to beat. Even Benjamin Graham, the doyen of many investors, later in his career became a de facto believer in the efficient-markets hypothesis.

Fama later presented an apt, if lewd, metaphor to tweak the noses of investors who disagreed with his ideas, likening traditional money management to pornography: "Some people like it but they're not really getting better than real sex. If you're willing to pay for it, that's fine. But don't pay too much."[22]

▲

ALTHOUGH THERE WERE SEVERAL OUTPOSTS in the academic rebellion against the investment industry, Chicago was clearly its stronghold. In the two hundred acres of leafy quadrangles and Gothic houses wedged between Washington Park and Lake Michigan, the biggest and brainiest congregation of economic thinkers the world had ever seen quietly revolutionized the financial universe.

However, the intellectual ferment was slow to permeate the real world of finance. Most people on Wall Street had little time, inclination, or sometimes even capability to understand the transformative work that was taking place in academia. But there was one significant breach in its immune system, which slowly helped spread these radical ideas like a virus through the finance industry.

CRSP's contribution went beyond providing much of the raw material of financial data the industry used. After their findings were published, Lorie and Fisher began organizing a series of twice-yearly seminars at the University of Chicago's center for continuing education, next to the Midway Plaisance park that cleaves through the school's neighborhood. Lorie and Fisher brought their data, many of the world's leading economists presented their papers and ideas, and a motley bunch of unusually open-minded investment professionals and bankers came to learn what the academics were cooking up.

They included John Clifton Bogle, a hotshot executive at Wellington Management Company, one of the country's biggest mutual fund groups; Rex Sinquefield, a student at Chicago's business school who went to work in the American National Bank's trust department; Burton Malkiel, an investment banker at the prominent Wall Street brokerage Smith Barney; William Fouse, a stock analyst at Mellon National Bank and Trust; John McQuown, a strong-willed executive at Wells Fargo; and Dean LeBaron, a gregarious, eclectic money manager at the mutual fund group Keystone. Many of them were dubbed "Quantifiers" for their use of computers—which were finally starting to become less rare in the investment world—to more rigorously quantify what had for centuries been a human, qualitative endeavor. As *Institutional Investor* wrote in April 1968:

> *Not all revolutions are bloody takeovers on a day in May. Some creep up slowly. At first the guerillas roam ineffectually on the hills. Then there are a few leaders disturbingly different from those of the past. At the end their friends begin to appear everywhere in government, and you know you have to change your tune to stay alive. Investment departments are in the midst of such a silent struggle, and it is clear that the revolutionaries are going to win. Their name: the Quantifiers. Their weapon: the computer.*

The semiannual seminars run by Lorie and Fisher thus became the way that new, heretical ideas were transmitted from the stilted language of academic papers and into the bloodstream of finance.

Take Malkiel. After drinking deeply from the CRSP well and seeing firsthand the woes of the investment industry, he left Wall Street to get a PhD in economics at Princeton and entered academia. In 1973, he wrote *A Random Walk Down Wall Street*, a book that brought a lot of these academic theories into the mainstream, and included the memorable barb that "a blindfolded monkey throwing darts at a newspaper's financial pages could select a portfolio that would do just as well as one carefully selected by experts."

In the book, Malkiel called for someone to set up a fund that "simply buys the hundreds of stocks making up the market averages and does no trading . . . Fund spokesmen are quick to point out 'you can't buy the averages.' It's about time the public could."[23]

Indeed, while Malkiel was researching and writing his bestselling tome, the race was already on to create the first-ever investment fund that encapsulated the waves of innovative research coming out of financial academia, with a motley group of iconoclastic industry executives in Boston, Chicago, and San Francisco all jostling to become the first to launch a product that would eventually humble the investment industry and reshape finance forever.

Chapter 4

THE QUANTIFIERS

APPROPRIATELY DRESSED FOR THE OCCASION in one of his few suits, John McQuown strode confidently up to the lectern at the nondescript conference center in San Jose, California. It was January 1964 and he was in town to present some of the zany research he was doing on whether stock market prices could be predicted using computers. Unbeknownst to him, it was a talk that would alter the course of his life.

McQuown was a fresh-faced investment banker at Smith Barney, the New York brokerage house. This was a calmer era of Wall Street, when most firms remained sleepy partnerships and before the ascendance of swaggering traders who placed freewheeling bets with the bank's own money. Most of the time McQuown worked in corporate finance, helping US companies raise money—worthy, if in practice often unglamorous, work.

But on the side McQuown—a forceful man with thick dark eyebrows, a mop of bushy hair, and the physique of a former farmhand turned Navy engineer—had taken a job at a fledgling start-up that was attempting to divine whether past stock market patterns could be mined to predict future prices.

To do so, McQuown and his partner were renting the massive IBM 7090 mainframe computer in the bowels of the Time-Life Building on Manhattan's 51st Street and Sixth Avenue, for $500 a shift. Given his day job and the cost, the work had to be done at night and over weekends. The slowness of computing at the time meant that McQuown was often forced to crawl into a sleeping bag to catch some shuteye while the machine creaked its way through the calculations.[1]

The work ultimately proved fruitless. No matter what patterns they detected in the financial data, none actually yielded any clues on what stocks would do from one day to the next. Everything seemed, well, random. But the long nights spent punching in the numbers, and the reams of exotic data the computer would as a result spit out, aroused the curiosity of the local IBM manager. Intrigued, and keen to show off more potential uses of its computers, IBM invited McQuown to present his preliminary work to a gathering of current and prospective clients in San Jose.

When he landed in San Francisco, the city could make a decent claim to be one of the most interesting places in the world. The Summer of Love was still three years away, but the combination of cheap housing and relaxed social mores had nurtured a vibrant countercultural movement, the Warriors' Wilt Chamberlain was setting the NBA alight, and the rise of a nascent technology industry in what became known as Silicon Valley was starting to make a mark. Writers like Hunter S. Thompson and Tom Wolfe chronicled 1960s San Francisco and helped bring its cultural cross-currents to light for a broad audience.

This hubbub felt remote at IBM's anodyne San Jose business center, but the conference it hosted in early 1964 arguably proved just as serendipitous. In the audience was Ransom Cook, the chairman and chief executive of Wells Fargo. At the time Wells Fargo was a venerable, respectable bank, tracing its lineage all the way back to California's 1850s gold rush, but of little consequence outside of its West Coast heartland. It wanted to be something more, however, and Cook was impressed by the young midwesterner and his command of technology.

After the conference he wandered over to chat with McQuown, telling him that computers were the fastest-growing expense at Wells Fargo, but so far the results were disappointing. "As far as I can tell, what we're doing today is the same thing we did in the 1930s, with green eye shades and armbands and handwritten letters," Cook groused. "Aren't computers capable of doing more?" McQuown insisted that they were.

After a brief chat, Wells Fargo's chairman asked McQuown if he was planning to stick around for a few days. As it happens, he was, so the next day McQuown popped into the bank's headquarters for a longer conversation with its chairman. Cook wasted little time getting down to business. "I'm very concerned about the investment performance of portfolios, even though I don't know what it really is. And I don't think anyone else does either," Cook admitted. "Can you really run money with stuff?" he asked McQuown,[2] in reference to all the reams of computer-generated data he had seen presented at the IBM conference.

McQuown argued that a more scientific approach to investing was the future. In his telling, the traditional approach followed a version of the "Great Man" theory first espoused by the nineteenth-century philosopher Thomas Carlyle. Some preternaturally gifted hero would pick stocks that he thought would rise. When his touch inevitably deserted him at some point—and in the 1960s it was invariably a "him"—the investor would simply transfer their hopes onto another Great Man. "The whole thing is a chance-driven process. It's not systematic and there is lots we still don't know about it and that needs study," McQuown argued.[3]

Clearly, his arguments persuaded Cook, who made McQuown a job offer on the spot, to establish and lead an internal think tank to explore ways to improve various aspects of Wells Fargo's business, including investment management. McQuown, flattered but wrong-footed by the suddenness of the offer, said he would have to return to New York to mull it over with his wife, Judith Turner, who was currently enrolled at Columbia. She was skeptical, but Cook hounded McQuown by phone over the next few weeks. Eventually McQuown relented. In March 1964, he moved to San Francisco to set up a new unit called "Wells Fargo Management Sciences"— answering directly to the chairman himself—while his wife enrolled at Berkeley to finish her MBA.

It was a compelling offer, after all. McQuown was on $6,000 a year at Smith Barney, but Cook offered him $18,000, helping assuage some of his wife's qualms about moving west. Cook asked his new protégé what kind of a budget he envisioned for the new division. Uncertain, but wary of asking for too little and receiving less, McQuown answered "about a million a year to start."[4] To his delight, Cook thought that entirely reasonable, starting a pattern of extraordinary largesse in the pursuit of breakthroughs.

One of the first things McQuown did at the newly established Wells Fargo Management Sciences was to seek approval from Cook to sign up for CRSP's seminars and stock market information, becoming the first commercial user of the database. Backing Jim Lorie's project was expensive, and McQuown was uncertain of just how truly committed Cook was to the new skunk works. But the chairman didn't flinch.

"Go spend whatever you need to spend," Cook reassured him. "Let me know when you need money, and I'll figure it out." From that day on, McQuown had essentially carte blanche to spend whatever he wanted, on whatever he wanted, all in the pursuit of exploring new frontiers of finance. "He basically just opened up the coffers," McQuown recalls, still marveling at his good fortune. This patronage was continued under Richard Cooley, who replaced Cook as chairman and chief executive of Wells Fargo at the end of 1966. "There was something about the water that they were drinking that gave them the courage to do these kinds of things," McQuown notes.

▲

MCQUOWN GREW UP ON HIS family's farm in rural Illinois, where Wall Street might as well have been an alien dimension. When the townsmen were called up to fight in World War II, the eight-year-old "Mac" had to start helping out as a farmhand. While that nurtured an abiding appreciation for nature, it was the farm machinery that fascinated him, eventually leading to a degree in mechanical engineering from Northwestern, as he became the first in his family to gain higher education.

There, he did an internship at a company that produced steel office furniture, hoping to learn how an engineering background might be useful in the world of business. It was there that he for the first time encountered a computer—an IBM 305 RAMAC that ran on a stack of 24-inch magnetic disks and punch cards—which the company used for the inventory control of products and component parts. "It sounded like a freight train when it was whirling, but I loved it,"[5] he later recalled. But a new passion soon emerged. During his degree he stumbled into a corporate finance class, and the complexity appealed immediately, leading to an immersion into the world of bonds and stocks.

McQuown had joined the Reserve Officers' Training Corps while at Northwestern, so after graduating in 1957 he was commissioned as an ensign in the Navy and sent to serve two years on the

World War II–era destroyer USS *Wiltsie*, based out of San Diego. In his second year—at just twenty-four years of age—he was made chief engineer ahead of a seven-month deployment in the western Pacific. It was an abrupt crash course in both practical engineering and leadership for the young McQuown. "To say it was character building would not give it close to sufficient due," he later said.[6]

The experience left a deep mark, solidifying an already steely determination in the young midwesterner. Friends and former colleagues describe his drive as extraordinary. At worst it could tip into bullheaded impatience and bellicosity, but it got things done. Even age did little to temper his stubbornness, with one friend describing how McQuown, in his sixties and his leg in a full cast after smashing it in a skiing accident, once took him on a wild Army jeep ride to his vineyard in Sonoma despite the apparent pain from the break. "This guy was tough," his friend reminisces.

After the two-year Navy stint, McQuown decided to pursue an MBA at Harvard Business School, where his earlier interest in computers blossomed into a love affair. HBS itself had no computers available to students, so he would have to trek over the Charles River to MIT to get his regular fix. There, he met an MIT professor who was attempting to see if he could predict future stock market prices from past trading volumes and patterns. McQuown became his "data dog," collecting the raw numbers of stock market prices from the magazine *Barron's*, converting them into a machine-readable form, and testing the professor's hypotheses through MIT's IBM mainframe.

McQuown graduated in 1961, but his background and interests raised eyebrows among some of the investment banks he interviewed with. "What the hell would an engineer want to do on Wall Street?" one interviewer inquired.[7] These days, degrees in engineering, physics, and mathematics are de rigueur in finance. But at the time McQuown himself struggled to answer the question, so he ended up at

Smith Barney, a storied Wall Street firm, mostly because it had a more comprehensive training program on the practicalities of finance. On the side, he kept working with the MIT professor's project—which ultimately led to the serendipitous meeting with Wells Fargo's chairman in early 1964 and the establishment of the Management Sciences unit.

The skunk works was not formally housed inside Wells Fargo's trust department, where the actual investment management business resided. Moreover, it was tasked with a wide variety of other projects, such as quantifying the economics of individual branches, or estimating the profitability of lending to large companies versus the statistical risks of their defaulting.

An effort to create a computer-generated metric for consumer creditworthiness later became part of the analytical framework behind Fair, Isaac and Company's credit scores, now known just as FICO.* Wells Fargo's Management Sciences unit also played a role in the Interbank Card Association (ICA), a group of West Coast banks that had banded together to launch a credit card to compete with Bank of America's successful BankAmericard. The ICA was the genesis of what ultimately became Mastercard.

A project on analyzing the performance of the trust department and ways it could be improved started on McQuown's first day, which also yielded some attention. "Wells Fargo is a veritable laboratory for the application of the computer to investment work," *Institutional Investor* gushed in a profile of the emerging "quantifiers" in 1968. "The reason for it all is John A. McQuown."[8] His zeal came at a cost, however. McQuown's wife, Judith, never took to the West Coast lifestyle; the marriage dissolved in 1966, and she moved back east.

It wasn't without professional challenges either. The biggest

---

*Cooley was a friend of Bill Fair, who founded Fair Isaac.

hurdle was that the executives of Wells Fargo's investment department were profoundly antagonistic to McQuown's efforts. James Vertin, the head of its financial analysis department—which serviced the trust business with research and portfolio management—was particularly hostile. He dubbed his opponent "Mac the Knife," described the Management Sciences unit as "guys in white smocks with computers whirring," and saw its encroachment into his territory as "the fin of the shark cutting through the water."[9] Inevitably, this caused a lot of internal friction. "It felt like shovelling shit against the tide," McQuown later recalled.[10]

Meanwhile, there were several other players lurking in the background, looking to be the first to launch a groundbreaking passively managed index-tracking investment fund informed by the cutting-edge academic work of Markowitz, Sharpe, Fama, and their colleagues.

▲

REX SINQUEFIELD WAS AN UNUSUAL member of the financial fraternity, growing up in grinding poverty and briefly flirting with a career in the clergy. But the mark he would leave was as large and indelible as any of the East Coast liberal elite that he often liked to mock.

He grew up in St. Louis, and for a period had to live in a Catholic orphanage overseen by strict German nuns after his father passed away and his mother was unable to provide for him and his four-year-old little brother. Sinquefield's older sister was by then in high school, so she stayed with her mother. The pain of the family separation was intense, but Sinquefield eventually thrived under the discipline imposed by the St. Vincent Orphan Home, and after six years there was able to return home, once his mother had found work as a secretary.

After high school he went to seminary, initially planning on becoming a priest, but left after three years. Departing seminarians were never asked why, given how intensely personal the decision can be, and Sinquefield has stayed schtum on his reasons. "It wasn't right for me," he says. "The church is better off." Every seminarian is a philosophy major, but he thirsted for something radically different, so he remained a philosophy major at Saint Louis University, but bolted on business studies, and eventually took an extra year to get a bachelor's in finance.

His grades were so good that his teachers urged Sinquefield to apply to the University of Chicago's Graduate School of Business, where he went after a brief but fortunately safe, unremarkable clerical stint in the Army, having been drafted during the Vietnam War that was then raging. Already an avid chess player, he learned judo to pass the time at Fort Riley, and entered tournaments around Kansas.

Chicago proved to be another type of epiphany. Sinquefield was entranced by brilliant professors like Merton Miller and his protégé Gene Fama, and became a fervent believer in the theory of efficient markets. "It has got to be true," Sinquefield thought to himself at the time. "This is the only thing that creates order in the universe, in the markets."[11] He would later describe himself as the "Ayatollah" of efficient markets, such was the strength of his belief in Fama's theory as an absolute truth.[12] As an added bonus, at the local judo club he also met a brilliant PhD student in sociology (focused on demography) named Jeanne Cairns, a third-degree brown belt he would soon marry.

After graduating, Sinquefield knew he wanted to work in investing, thirsting to implement everything he had learned. But despite a Chicago MBA, he got turned down by all of the big banks in Chicago, New York, and Los Angeles that he interviewed with, his zealous desire to shake up the investment management business going down poorly. His only offer came from American National

Bank of Chicago, a respected if modestly sized local commercial bank, with an even smaller trust department.[13]

He was initially hired to work in stock market research in the trust department, housed in the bowels of the bank's beautiful, iconic art deco tower in the heart of the city's vibrant financial district. It was quite the adjustment for an ardent apostle of efficient markets. Researching stocks with the aim of picking the best ones was not what he wanted to do. The first report he had to write was on Anheuser-Busch, the brewer, and it felt painful for Sinquefield. "Cindy, it's all bullshit," he told his secretary one day. "Everything we do, it's all bullshit."

On the side of his day job, he worked with University of Chicago professor Roger Ibbotson to update and expand on CRSP's research into the long-term returns of bonds and bills (a kind of short-term government debt) as well as inflation rates. *Stocks, Bonds, Bills, and Inflation* was first published in 1977, and became a long-running series of books akin to the investment industry's annual sports almanac.

Sinquefield's educational background and all the chatter about the groundbreaking academic research coming out at the time piqued the interest of Gordon Campbell, the dignified former Air Force captain who ran the trust department. He asked the young efficient-markets enthusiast to explain the subject to some of the unit's staffers. The talks went so well that Campbell then asked Sinquefield to give the same presentation to the bank's board of trustees, which also proved receptive.

Eventually he managed to parlay his Chicago degree into a move to the portfolio management group, where he landed in January 1972. The very next month, Sinquefield made a radical proposal that he had been stewing on for some time. He sent a one-page memo to his bosses urging the bank to start a "passive" portfolio of stocks that mimicked the S&P 500, a vehicle that he at first dubbed

"The Market Fund." His memo tersely laid out the financial theory underpinning the idea, and the empirical evidence that most active fund managers did a dismal job.

Getting little response, Sinquefield cornered Campbell about his memo. The trust department head admitted he thought it was a good idea, and it might be a project they could explore in a couple of years. Sinquefield walked away thinking, "Two years? Bullshit. We're going to get this done now."

To his pleasant surprise, the board soon gave him the go-ahead to research his zany idea and prove that he really could accurately and cheaply replicate the stock market index. "I really admired them," Sinquefield later recalled. "Here are people that really don't know this stuff the way I do, and yet they're putting the reputation of the entire bank on the line."

Over the summer of 1973, Sinquefield went into high gear, carefully constructing a paper portfolio and pricing it every night to show that the deviations between what they could produce and the S&P 500 were tiny. He was ably helped by many of the trust department's administrative staff, whom he had converted through his earlier efficient-markets presentations. Yet whether he would get the final go-ahead from American National Bank's top brass to set up a live index-tracking fund was far from certain.

▲

LIKE MCQUOWN AND SINQUEFIELD, Dean LeBaron was another iconoclastic outlier in the financial world. Where many are aloof and controlled, he is gregarious and impulsive. And in an industry where almost everyone professes a desire to be the best, LeBaron has always insisted that he would rather be first. "It's easy to be the best. Just do something someone else is doing and do it better and with more pizzazz," he jokes. "But being first is hard."

LeBaron entered the investment industry in 1960, after an MBA from Harvard,[14] mostly because he dreaded simply becoming another man in a "gray flannel suit who aspired to be an assistant plant manager for General Motors someplace."[15] Although he made his name as a skilled portfolio manager for Keystone Investment Management in the growth-oriented 1960s stock market boom, LeBaron—a contrarian at heart—became entranced by the cutting-edge financial research being pumped out by the University of Chicago, Stanford, and nearby MIT, and started attending some of the semiannual CRSP seminars in the Windy City.

On the side, he started learning Fortran, a popular programming language at the time. Underscoring his maverick credentials, LeBaron—an avid pilot—bought a twin-engine Cessna Skymaster and a bright red "Amphicar," a German-made amphibious vehicle that he'd drive around Boston Harbor, flashing his headlights at diners by the pier.[16]

But in 1969, he fell out with Keystone's management over his refusal to adhere to the company's policy that all senior employees must set aside some money for political donations[17] and spend some of their time writing position papers—something LeBaron interpreted as de facto industry lobbying. Internally, his intransigence was met with consternation. "At that point I began hearing them hammering away in the other room, building a box of approximately my size," he says, laughing.

Jumping before he was pushed into the metaphorical coffin being constructed, he left to set up Batterymarch Financial Management in 1969, envisioning it as a kind of engineering firm for financial services, a company that would combine human judgment with computers to crunch the numbers and construct better portfolios from a collection of smaller, undervalued stocks. Joining him was Jeremy Grantham, a brilliant young British money manager LeBaron had hired at Keystone.

Cheekily, the company took its name from the street and building where it would be based, to give prospective clients the impression that they were named after the new firm, rather than vice versa. Initially it was tough sledding for Batterymarch, with the early 1970s bear market hitting them hard. Only an old World War II flight simulator[18] LeBaron had bought and dragged in provided some office levity. But his hunger for innovation over success would soon be slaked by a bit of both.

In 1971, Grantham attended a dinner at Harvard Business School, where the attendees discussed the best ways to evaluate and select fund managers. Tongue-in-cheek, Grantham suggested that the best choice might be for many investors to hand their money to "the gentlemen of S&P," given how its index committee that selects which companies go into the S&P 500 benchmark appeared to beat most money managers in the long run. Unsurprisingly, the suggestion was met with a limp reception. "It went down like a lead balloon," Grantham recalls with relish.

Yet LeBaron was intrigued by the idea, having separately had a conversation with a visiting Columbia Business School professor about the subject. LeBaron was familiar with the relevant financial theory, and loved the idea of engineering a brand-new product that would tweak the noses of the industry. Most of all, he realized that what a lot of prospective clients were asking for was basically an index-based product: a large, diversified, simple, low-turnover portfolio of stocks issued by well-known blue-chip US companies. LeBaron was no efficient-markets zealot: He still thought that skilled managers might still be able to perform well in less covered, less efficient corners of the stock market—such as the small companies, or in the developing world. But in the mainstream reaches of the financial markets, such a product made sense, he thought.

By 1973, Batterymarch thought they had figured out the best way to do it. The Batterymarch Market Portfolio was offered through "separately managed accounts"—individual investment accounts rather than a traditional mingled investment fund—to pension funds. The strategy would be housed in Batterymarch's Program Selected Portfolio division, buy the 250 biggest stocks of the S&P 500, which LeBaron reckoned would be enough to most cost-efficiently mimic the performance of the full index, and charge investors a flat $100,000 annual fee.

Nonetheless, it initially failed to attract any investors, even after Batterymarch subsequently lowered its fee to $25,000. "While we get many queries regarding PSP, I've yet to see an armored car drive up to our door with money in it to invest," LeBaron observed in November 1973.[19] That led a columnist for *Pensions & Investments*, an industry magazine, to give Batterymarch a "Dubious Achievement Award," for its endurance in touting its index fund for an entire year without winning a single client.[20] Like a good sport, LeBaron went to *P&I's* offices to pick up his award, framed the certificate, and hung it in his office.[21]

The San Francisco–based investment management arm American Express was also at the time in the process of setting up an index fund—advised by William Sharpe at nearby Stanford—but progress was slow and success uncertain. For a while, it seemed like the *Field of Dreams* model—build it and they will come—might not actually work for the handful of companies willing to explore a new frontier of finance. "We were renegades," Sinquefield recalls. But the renegades would eventually prove successful, and their invention would ultimately humiliate many of the industry luminaries who had long heaped scorn upon them.

Chapter 5

BASTIONS OF UNORTHODOXY

IN SAN FRANCISCO, WAR HAD broken out. The battles between McQuown's Management Sciences and Vertin's financial analysis department were epic, across multiple fronts and spanning several years. Mac may have been headstrong, but Vertin was no shrinking violet himself.

A World War II–era Navy lieutenant, avid outdoorsman, and keen duck hunter with the eyesight of an eagle, Vertin drove a bright red car, occasionally donned a red sports jacket that clashed with the generally staid couture of banking, and "strode the earth like an invincible warrior," according to the financial historian Peter Bernstein. A magazine journalist interviewing Vertin noted his "bushy grey eyebrows," which seemed to belie his youthful energy.[1] He was no intellectual slouch either, with a keen, inquiring mind and—like McQuown—a somewhat skeptical view of his own industry.

Vertin compared many professional money managers to witch doctors who would jump up and down to cure a patient. Eventually the sickness would fade by itself, but the medicine man would naturally claim credit for the miraculous recovery.[2] In his office, he had hung a poster that stated, "None of us is as smart as all of us."[3]

Still, Vertin wasn't going to bow down to McQuown and his attempts to bulldoze the trust department into submission. Vertin passed away in 2018, but confirmed shortly before his death that he often found McQuown "a pain in the ass."[4] He wasn't the only one. Many subordinates at Wells Fargo thought McQuown "dominating and patronizing."[5] But given his direct line to the bank's chairman, there was little they could do. "It was really stormy, people argued a lot," recalls one former trust department employee. Even intellectual allies like professor Sharpe said McQuown could be "wild and crazy" at times.

Nonetheless, Vertin eventually relented, convinced by the reams of data that Management Sciences' brainiacs produced to make their case. To aid their crusade—and financed by the executive office's largesse—McQuown had assembled an all-star cast of academics to consult for Wells Fargo, which at various points included William Sharpe, Jim Lorie, Lawrence Fisher, Michael Jensen, Harry Markowitz, Merton Miller, and Jack Treynor, as well as Fischer Black and Myron Scholes—two emerging superstar economists. Mac had met many of them at the twice-yearly CRSP seminars in Chicago, which he would religiously attend, and Dick Cooley willingly opened Wells Fargo's purse strings to fund any research they wanted to do.

Gene Fama never worked formally for Wells Fargo, but did contribute research, and served as an intellectual godfather for the group. It was Fama who sent one of his brightest students, David Booth, to work for McQuown, and introduced Scholes and Black to the Management Sciences unit. His rising fame helped give the small, nascent but fervent cabal of indexing proselytizers the intellectual cover they needed. Altogether, Management Sciences arguably amounted to the Manhattan Project of financial economics.

Working with the assembled academic rock stars was humbling even to McQuown, whom no one would describe as particularly shy. "It was an education and a half, holy mackerel," he reminisces.

Scholes and Black proved pivotal. Scholes had already started consulting for Wells Fargo, and in the summer of 1968 he recommended that the bank set up some kind of passive investment vehicle that would buy and hold a slice of the entire stock market. McQuown was interested, but wanted more in-depth research into the potential tradeoffs and pitfalls. Although Scholes was just twenty-seven at the time, he was already an assistant professor at MIT, and could devote only a few days a week to the project. So he asked Black—whom he had recently met for the first time after being introduced by fellow Chicago grad Michael Jensen—if he could help.[6]

It proved the beginning of an exceptionally fertile collaboration. The two economists in 1973 published a groundbreaking mathematical model to price derivatives, which reshaped the finance industry and continues to be a foundation stone of modern-day Wall Street. It won Scholes and Robert Merton, another MIT professor who built further on the model, the Nobel Prize in Economics in 1997, with Black denied only by his untimely passing in 1995.

Less noticed at the time, Scholes and Black also laid the analytical groundwork for Wells Fargo's efforts to set up a "passive" fund, by which they meant a portfolio of equities constructed "without using subjective measures of the future performance of selected stocks, or the market as a whole."[7] McQuown's Management Sciences people—primarily Larry Cuneo and Wayne Wagner—did the grunt work, but the two academics would fly out regularly to pore over the data while drinking copious amounts of heavily sweetened iced tea.[8]

Against this array of intellectual brainpower, and the number of groundbreaking academic papers now being published on what seemed to be a daily basis, Vertin's resistance eventually crumbled. Indeed, he ultimately embraced the new way of thinking with the zeal that only a late convert can muster.

Yet they still needed someone to be, as Vertin put it, a "bridge between the theoretical new and the operating old." Wells Fargo found an unlikely one in a former jazz saxophonist and bon vivant from West Virginia, with a mind to match McQuown's and Vertin's.

▲

WILLIAM FOUSE'S CHUBBY FRAME, big square glasses, small mustache, and ready smile masked what was a brilliant, eclectic brain. In the history of index funds, he may not have enjoyed the widespread fame of some of his contemporaries, but everyone who worked with him says that he deserves plenty of the credit, for both their invention and their subsequent growth.

He was born on September 20, 1928, in Parkersburg, West Virginia,[9] where his father was a banker and his mother a teacher. Fouse played clarinet in his high school marching band,[10] and his musical talent later helped pay for degrees in industrial administration and business administration from the University of Kentucky, where he played in various jazz bands to make ends meet. Jazz— and good food—remained a passion until he passed away in 2019. "He believed it was about quality not quantity when it came to living," according to one longtime friend and colleague.[11]

In 1952, Fouse joined the trust department of Mellon Bank in Pittsburgh as a junior analyst, initially to research railroad stocks, and eventually became assistant director of investment research. Yet despite Mellon being a "bastion of orthodoxy in its purest form,"[12] Fouse was no orthodox thinker.

He fell in love with computers, voraciously consumed new research being produced by the new generation of financial academics, and became a regular attendee at CRSP's seminars, where he got acquainted with kindred spirits. His superiors at Mellon were less entranced by all this newfangled talk of beta, efficient frontiers, and modern portfolio theory being spread by the likes of Markowitz, Sharpe, and Fama. Fouse's efforts to keep track of the performance of Mellon's fund managers—finding "nothing, nothing, nothing, or worse than nothing," as he put it[13]—went down like a bucket of cold vomit.

Inspired by Sharpe's work, Fouse in 1969 recommended that Mellon launch a passive fund that would try to replicate only one of the big stock market indices, like the S&P 500 of America's biggest companies. It got nixed by Mellon's management. In the spring of 1970, he then proposed a fund that would systematically invest according to a dividend-based model devised by John Burr Williams—who had nearly two decades earlier inspired Markowitz's work—but that too was summarily squashed. "Goddammit Fouse, you're trying to turn my business into a science," his boss told him.[14] For the normally gregarious Fouse, it felt like a sword going through his midriff.[15]

It proved the final straw. Fouse resolved to work for someone who valued innovation, and picked up the phone to call McQuown, whom he had met through the CRSP conventions for heretical investment thinkers. He even sent McQuown a long memo explaining why Wells Fargo should hire him, describing himself as "keenly analytical, innovative, independent of thought, dedicated to the scientific method, outspoken, and somewhat impatient with ignorance." McQuown snapped him up, and Fouse was promptly made head of stock market research in Wells Fargo's financial analysis department, working under Vertin, who finally had his bridge between the new and the old.

At this stage, Vertin's shift was far along, but there were still plenty of office politics skirmishes. Fouse felt that he had been sent by McQuown into the trust department like a missionary bishop into a land of heathens led by Vertin. "He got religion, but I don't know whether he would have if we hadn't forcibly converted him," Fouse later recalled.

Even so, McQuown at one point himself tried to have Fouse sacked, after a heated clash over the dividend-based model of investing that Fouse tried to introduce at Wells Fargo after being unceremoniously shot down by his former bosses at Mellon. "I was like a ping-pong ball being bounced around," Fouse said. "It was an interesting time. But I persevered." Occasional martini-fueled lunches at San Francisco's North Beach Restaurant—a Tuscan restaurant that opened up in 1970 a stone's throw away from Washington Square—helped keep a fragile peace.

▲

BY THE TIME FOUSE ARRIVED at Wells Fargo, they had already started work on some kind of passive investment fund. At first, the effort was not quite a "pure" index fund, however. The research done by Scholes and Black had indicated some market inefficiencies that could potentially be mined, such as the tendency for less volatile stocks (those with a lower "beta," to use Sharpe's original jargon) to actually produce greater returns, contradicting CAPM and Fama's work.

In a December 1969 report to Wells Fargo, Scholes and Black therefore proposed three options: (1) a passive fund that would buy the entire stock market and juice its returns by also borrowing money, or "leverage," in financial jargon; (2) a passive fund that would buy only low-beta stocks but again use borrowed money to lift its overall volatility to the market average; and (3) a fund that would buy low-beta stocks and actually bet against—to "short" in market parlance—higher-beta stocks.[16]

The third option is more akin to a hedge fund, but Wells Fargo enthusiastically started work on the second option, and dubbed the nascent initiative the Stagecoach Fund, in an homage to the bank's famous gold rush–era logo. The hope was to launch a fund that used modern research to consistently beat the stock market, which would appeal to Wells Fargo's retail clients and pension funds alike.

But the newly arrived Fouse stomped on it. He argued that just buying lower-beta stocks would come at too great a cost to diversification, as these stocks tended to be found in only a few stable industries. Instead, he wanted the first option, a leveraged but broad portfolio of equities. He eventually triumphed in the heated internal debate, to the consternation of the normally phlegmatic Black, who stormed out of the pivotal meeting in a rare fit of anger.[17]

As it turns out, the Stagecoach Fund was eventually killed anyway by the fallout from a 1971 Supreme Court ruling that the Depression-era Glass-Steagall Act prevented commercial banks like Wells Fargo from marketing mutual funds to ordinary investors. Wells Fargo's trust department had already secured commitments from the pension funds of Greyhound and Illinois Bell. But given that the hope of also attracting retail investors alongside them was now stymied, and otherwise tepid interest from institutional investors, the Stagecoach Fund initiative wound down. "There were a lot of barnacles attached to the ship, which eventually sunk it," recalls Booth, Fama's onetime protégé who worked on the fund.

This turned out to be fortunate. A leveraged fund would have been hammered in the subsequent 1974 stock market rout—likely setting back the development of passive funds by years. Instead, it was a less glamorous side effort run by McQuown's Management Sciences unit that ultimately became the first-ever index fund. And once again, Chicago provided the spark.

In 1970, Keith Shwayder graduated with a degree in economics from the University of Chicago, and returned home to Denver to work at the family business, the luggage maker Samsonite. He had drunk heavily from the well of financial academia at his alma mater, and was horrified to realize that the company's pension fund was invested in a bunch of poorly performing mutual funds. For someone steeped in the theory of efficient markets, it was anathema.

Shwayder called up his former teachers and asked whether there was anyone out there who was managing money in a more modern, theoretically sound fashion.[18] They put him in touch with Mc-Quown, who promptly flew to Denver to thrash out what Samsonite wanted to do. "I had no budget constraints, so if I wanted to get on an airplane and go someplace, I got on the airplane," McQuown recalls.

Wagner and Cuneo, McQuown's main lieutenants at Management Sciences, did the basic design and development,[19] but the skunk works wasn't allowed to manage money itself. So a new unit called Wells Fargo Investment Advisors (WFIA) was set up to house this weird new product. Vertin's department handled the day-to-day operations, and the fund itself would be managed by Fouse. Although little remarked upon at the time, WFIA would end up becoming the kernel of the biggest investment empire in the world several decades later.

The plan was to invest an equal amount of money in each of the fifteen hundred or so stocks listed on the New York Stock Exchange, as this was the closest approximation to the entire US equity market. And in July 1971, the first-ever passively managed, index-tracking fund was born, courtesy of an initial $6 million investment from Samsonite's pension fund.

Unfortunately, tracking an "equal-weighted" index of NYSE stocks proved a nightmare. Stocks move around all the time, so the Samsonite fund had to be constantly rejigged so that an equal amount of dollars would be invested in each stock. As a result, the trading costs were high and record-keeping was arduous.

The theory—backed by data—was that an equal-weighted fund would over time outperform more traditional measures of the stock market. Yet in practice it proved frustrating. "Mac had a bug about beating the market with Samsonite, and equal weighting was the way to do that," Fouse later recalled. "But it was virtually unmanageable."

However, inspired by the fund, WFIA in November 1973 launched a simpler fund open to all the bank's institutional clients—seeded with $5 million from Wells Fargo's own pension fund and an equal amount from Illinois Bell's retirement system—that would simply seek to mimic the performance of the S&P 500.* At the time, this accounted for about two-thirds of the entire US stock market anyway,[20] and the index was "capitalization-weighted"—in other words, the weighting of each company was according to its overall stock market value, and the fund would just have to buy an equal number of shares in each company. By 1976, Samsonite folded the money in its original vehicle into WFIA's S&P 500 index fund.

Its first manager was Thomas Loeb, a young former Eastman Dillon investment banker who had joined the trust department in early 1973. This fund was much easier to manage than its first iteration. Negating the need to constantly rebalance helped keep the tracking error—how much the fund diverges from the index it is supposed to mimic—to about 1–2 percent.† Finally, Wells Fargo had something compelling to show for its years of expensive, arduous research.

---

* The initial $10 million was also insufficient to buy a thousand shares in each of the S&P 500's members, so they had to try to approximate the index only until it had reached $25 million, according to Bernstein.

† A groundbreaking invention by Loeb in 1975 helped bring down trading costs as well, and was an early sign of how the invention of index funds would over time alter the financial industry ecosystem.

Loeb realized that Wells Fargo was paying too much to Wall Street brokerages when it bought and sold stocks for its index fund, when Standard & Poor's rejigged its benchmark every quarter, or when dividends needed to be reinvested. Dealers typically assume that anyone buying or selling is doing so for a reason—they have an informational advantage—and therefore charge a "spread" between the price they are willing to pay for a security, or buy at, to protect themselves. This comes on top of trading commissions.

But since Wells Fargo's index funds were not trading on any sort of informational edge, and trying only to cheaply track the market, maybe something could be worked out? And since index funds wanted to hold the whole market, perhaps brokers could arrange

▲

SUCCESS ALWAYS HAS MANY PARENTS, and there are many people who can make a plausible claim to have launched the first index fund, depending on one's definition. Wells Fargo arguably got there first with its venture for Samsonite. Yet it was a small, unwieldy account rather than a formal fund, and it tracked a cumbersome, equal-weighted NYSE index, leading some of its rivals to claim they got to the promised land first.

American National Bank can say it had the first publicly marketed S&P 500 index fund, but only after it converted an existing investment vehicle on September 4, 1973.[21] After months of arduous testing to ensure that they could replicate the S&P 500 index, Sinquefield simply sent a letter to investors in a $30 million "growth" trust announcing that the objective remained the same, but the strategy for doing so would be to match the S&P 500. Not one client objected. Still, it was tough to get new clients the first two years, with Sinquefield often telling colleagues that John the Baptist had an easier job than the early indexing proselytizers. Batterymarch started offering its S&P 500 index product in 1972–73, but found no takers until the final days of 1974, when the New York City Teachers' Retirement System invested $10 million.[22]

The three pioneering efforts weren't perfect index funds, in that

---

simultaneous trades of individual stocks in "baskets" instead of one at a time, at a lower overall cost?

He called up Stanley Shopkorn, the larger-than-life head trader at Salomon Brothers, one of the biggest and bolshiest Wall Street firms, who flew out to San Francisco to discuss the issue. Over dinner at the Canlis restaurant in the Fairmont Hotel, Loeb described his idea. "Well, Tom, what you've described is a program!" Shopkorn exclaimed. They worked out the details, got the approval from the trader's boss at Salomon—future New York mayor Michael Bloomberg—and the concept of "program trading" was born. "Taking cash and putting it into the equity market seamlessly, that was the ultimate idea," Loeb says. At first, program trades were still arduous. They were manually written up and faxed with the most competitive quote to the dealer, which would then distribute the trades to its brokers on the floor of the New York Stock Exchange. Today it can be done electronically and in nanoseconds, and program trading accounts for a huge chunk of all stock market activity.

they didn't buy every single stock in the S&P 500. Doing so would be too costly at a time when Wall Street firms still charged fixed commissions, and the tradability of smaller stocks in the blue-chip index was still poor. They were also simply too small to be able to buy all the stocks. To varying degrees, they replicated the benchmark through a process known as sampling—picking a broad but smaller subset of stocks that would best match the overall index.

Nonetheless, together the Wells Fargo, American National, and Batterymarch initiatives indisputably represented one of the biggest and most influential innovations of the modern era, the enormity of which would dawn only slowly on most in the industry.

"What we are witnessing today is the slow, almost imperceptible motion of a growing deep ocean swell that will form into a massive wave as it hits the investment beaches," LeBaron told a conference of financial analysts in January 1975. "Just as the surfer looks outwards to the sea to observe the swells so that he may judge the wave to come and does not look at the beach to see what has already gone by, so should we become sensitive to the buildup of a wave of mechanical strategies that is in progress today."[23]

Not everyone was successful in anticipating and surfing the coming wave, however. American Express Asset Management had in February 1974 filed a registration statement for what it called the "Index Fund of America"—initially aimed at institutional investors, yet with the potential of becoming the first widely available index fund, open to ordinary investors as well—but the company later withdrew the application.[24] Nonetheless, the parallel efforts to develop and spread the indexing gospel were vital. "We were always fighting and hating each other, but eventually we grew up and realized that the presence of [all of] us was an advantage to each of us, because it added credibility to the marketing," Sinquefield says.

By the end of 1975, Wells Fargo, Batterymarch, and American National Bank of Chicago were all successfully running cheap, index-based strategies for a clutch of forward-thinking pension funds and endowments. At that point, Batterymarch was managing about $100 million in its index strategy, American National roughly $120 million, while WFIA managed $150 million, according to estimates at the time.[25] The fees were in the range of 0.3–0.6 percent—a far cry from the lofty fees charged by most traditional fund managers.[26] In a small but important way, the benefits were finally starting to accrue to American pensioners, even if index funds weren't yet available to ordinary investors.

Nonetheless, it was Wells Fargo that *Institutional Investor* magazine already in the summer of 1972 dubbed "The Temple of Beta."[27] The first-ever advertisement for its inaugural index fund ran in early 1974, with the sober marketing tag "Wells Fargo presents important news for every corporate pension manager interested in approximating the long-term performance of the S&P 500":

> *Through the years, many managed funds have not approached the long-term growth record of the S&P 500. The objective of the Wells Fargo Index Fund for Employee Benefit Trusts is to replicate the S&P 500 itself and thus approximate the risks and returns of the index. Wells Fargo subjects its Index Fund and the Market to continuous comparative analysis by a unique computer process designed to help achieve this replication at an unusually low turnover cost. This is an oversimplification, of course, but we have some impressive details to support our story. We think you'll want to hear them.[28]*

As we shall see in the coming chapters, WFIA—or subsequent iterations at least—also enjoyed the greatest longer-term success of the first three pioneers. Sinquefield shortly followed up with two more index funds, this time focused on smaller companies that didn't qualify for the S&P 500 and international stocks, and eventually became the overall head of American National Bank's trust department. But he left in 1981, and American National Bank was subsequently subsumed by local rivals First Chicago and Northern Trust.

Meanwhile, LeBaron closed down Batterymarch's index-tracking strategy in the mid-1980s. Some rivals said it was because it did a poor job of tracking the market, yet the resolutely contrarian, be-first-not-best financier insists the reason was more unorthodox. After reading that there were by then seventy-five index fund providers, LeBaron decided that it had become such a commoditized industry that it made no sense for Batterymarch to continue it. Instead he turned his attention to the nascent interest in exotic stock markets in the developing world.

Frustrated by the travails of the Stagecoach Fund, and keen for a change of scenery, McQuown left Wells Fargo on March 17, 1974—exactly a decade after he first joined the San Francisco bank. But at that point, Fouse was firmly ensconced, and Vertin's conversion was complete. "By the end it was a love affair. Vertin and McQuown rode off into the sunset together," quips Booth.

McQuown confirms that toward the end of his stint the hostilities had thankfully ended, with what was once intense enmity becoming grudging respect and friendship. "Jim was a staunch enemy and turned into a staunch advocate," he says. "In the final analysis, he was a fantastic guy. But boy was he an argumentative son of a bitch."

Of course, many who knew both men would say the same about McQuown. Loeb, an amateur painter and the son of two artists who grew up reading biographies of all the greats, argues that there were uncanny parallels between the world of high art around the turn of the century and Wells Fargo in the 1970s. "The personalities were extremely strong, they had extremely strong beliefs, and they argued extremely strongly about it," he says. "The structures are totally different, but the personalities were all pretty fervent." In a sign of how completely the new way of investment thinking had won the argument, Wells Fargo's softball team was renamed the Efficient Frontiersmen, in a nod to Harry Markowitz's pioneering work two decades earlier.[29]

▲

THE INVESTMENT INDUSTRY REACTION TO all this was a mix of indifference, snickering, snark, and outright hostility. Even though the 1974 bear market—at the time the biggest since the Great Depression—had humiliated many professional money managers, they largely scoffed at the idea that any investor would actually settle for being average.

The investment manager turned historian Peter Bernstein recounts that at the time one former colleague sputtered that he wouldn't buy the S&P 500 even for his mother-in-law.[30] The Leuthold Group, a Minneapolis-based financial research group, famously distributed a poster where Uncle Sam declared, "Help stamp out index funds. Index funds are un-American!" Copies continue to float around the offices of index fund managers as mementos of the hostility they initially faced.

Of course, as the writer Upton Sinclair once observed, it is difficult to get someone to understand something when their salary depends on them not understanding it. "If people start believing this random-walk garbage and switch to index funds, a lot of $80,000-a-year portfolio managers and analysts will be replaced by $16,000-a-year computer clerks. It just can't happen," one anonymous mutual fund manager griped to the *Wall Street Journal* in 1973.[31]

Some in the industry argued that the academics were motivated by jealousy, not hard data. "The random-walk theory is merely the creation of a lot of business-school professors who are frankly envious of money managers because they make more money than the professors do," complained one investment manager.[32] Edward Zinberg of Prudential Insurance Co. opted for more honesty. "Like anybody, we like to think that we're getting more intelligent and better in our stock selection. You know how it is, hope springs eternal."

One early point of criticism—which would be echoed many times over the coming decades—was that if too many people turned to indexing, it would make markets less efficient and stunt their vibrancy. "The entire capital allocation function of the securities markets would be distorted, and only companies represented in indexes would be able to raise equity capital," Erwin Zeuschner and Mary Onie Holland of Chase Investors Management Corp. warned in a letter to the *Wall Street Journal* in 1975.[33]

It is no coincidence that their invention came out of lower-tier, smaller financial institutions rather than any of the traditional giants of Wall Street. Some early support came from unlikely corners, though, such as from Warren Buffett and Benjamin Graham, his redoubtable mentor and a famed investor in his own right.

However, the most important direct boost came from the so-called Baby Bells. At the time, the giant AT&T telephone company—"Ma Bell," which traced its lineage back to the company founded by Alexander Graham Bell—was made up of several regional companies. Together the Bell System had a near monopoly in the United States, until it was broken up in the 1980s, but each regional Baby Bell already had its own pension plans.

They became early and important adopters of index investing, after studying how their swelling investment plans were faring in the early 1970s. "They found out that their active managers were basically swapping bananas. One part of the system would be selling IBM stock, and another part would be buying IBM stock at the same time," Loeb says. "Their simple deduction was that they could cut down costs by indexing."

Moreover, some pension executives began to slowly realize that many of the fund managers they had hired were in reality little more than "closet indexers." In other words, they essentially just mimicked the performance of the stock market as a whole, but charged fees as if they were engaged in an expensive hunt for the best securities. That spurred many to shift their allocations. "We figured we should pay index fees for index management," George Williams, the head of Illinois Bell, told the *Wall Street Journal* in 1979.[34] He became a particularly sizable backer of the first batch of index funds.

By the end of 1977, there was about $2.9 billion of pension fund money in the smattering of index strategies that had been launched.[35] The 1974 bear market was a big impetus, but the longer-term picture slowly becoming clearer at the time was also grim. AG Becker, a prominent finance industry consultancy, found that 77 percent of US pension managers had trailed behind the S&P 500 in the decade ending December 1974.[36] As a result, the amount of pension money invested in index funds, or internally managed strategies, soared to about $91 billion by 1985,[37] with a flurry of big new entrants into the nascent index fund industry, such as State Street and Bankers Trust.

Nonetheless, these early index funds were solely the preserve of big institutional investors, like pots of pension money and insurance companies. Ordinary people still didn't have access, even if many were starting to benefit indirectly via their pension plans. And even their support was initially tepid. By 1977, *Institutional Investor* declared that "indexing is likely to be an idea whose time will pass."[38] At any rate, there was widespread skepticism that ordinary investors would ever adopt index funds. After all, they were completely unaware of the research being pumped out by academia on the poor average performance of their mutual fund managers, and anyway, who would want to just settle for mediocrity? "It seems unlikely that the public will ever embrace buying the averages in this way, since

individuals usually seek dramatic gains, not a market-linked performance many equate with mediocrity," the industry magazine
wrote.[39] Fouse later jokingly quoted the Nazi propagandist Joseph
Goebbels to explain why the general public was slow to cotton on:
"Only small secrets need protection. Big secrets are protected by the
public's incredulity."[40]

That this secret would burst free into the public domain was the
hope of Paul Samuelson, the doyen of American economics. In a
1976 column for *Newsweek*, he noted that pension funds could finally choose "prudent, across-the-board market index investing,"
but lamented the dearth of similar products for ordinary investors.[41]

"As yet, there exists no convenient . . . fund that apes the whole
market, requires no load, and that keeps commission, turnover and
management fees to the feasible minimum. I suspect the future
will bring such new and convenient instrumentalities," Samuelson
wrote. Indeed, the future delivered faster than the famous economist dared hope. In Valley Forge, there was already someone
preparing to end the public's incredulity and bring the "big secret"
discovered by many pension plans to the masses.

Chapter 6

THE HEDGEHOG

IN 1960, AN UNKNOWN FINANCIER named John B. Armstrong wrote a strident paper ridiculing academic research that purported to show that fund managers did a poor job of investing and should somehow strive to just mimic the market rather than beat it.

"Leading common stock funds have shown better long-term results than the Dow Jones Industrial Average," Armstrong wrote in the august *Financial Analysts Journal*. It was a direct riposte to the radical paper published in the same journal earlier that year by University of California professor Edward Renshaw, where he made the case for an unmanaged mutual fund that simply tracked a stock market index. To Armstrong it was a laughable idea.

While Armstrong conceded that some studies of mutual fund performance were "not so favorable," "The Case for Mutual Fund Management" highlighted how the four leading stocks-focused mutual funds—accounting for 15 percent of the entire industry at the time—had on average soundly beaten the Dow in the 1930–59 period. The article so impressed others in the investment industry that they gave the writer an honorable mention in the Graham and Dodd Awards, a prestigious prize in the field of investment writing and research.

The paper stated that Armstrong was the pen name of "a man who has spent many years in the securities field and in the study and analysis of mutual funds," but offered two vital clues to his real identity: The author was a graduate of Princeton University, and had written his thesis on the economic role of investment companies. In fact, as was later revealed, the anonymous writer was none other than John Clifton Bogle, who ironically would go on to found Vanguard and become the leading proselytizer for passive, cheap, market-mimicking index funds—the very idea he had sought to abort in 1960.

It is hard to whittle down a person's essence to one single characteristic, especially when they lived nearly nine decades and reshaped their industry, and, in some minds, perhaps even capitalism itself. Many acquaintances called Bogle "messianic" over his titanic crusade on behalf of index funds and the cultlike environment he inculcated at Vanguard. Others preferred "iron-willed," recalling how he would rarely yield in an argument. He preferred "determined," the word his family and friends used to describe him when he curiously inquired. "I think they are likely on the right track, even as I recognize that while determination is necessary to achieve one's goals, it can sometimes result in a single-mindedness that is not particularly attractive," he admitted.[1]

As the article written under his nom de plume reveals—borrowed from his admired great-grandfather Philander B. Armstrong, an insurance executive who railed against the industry's anticonsumer practices in the nineteenth century[2]—Bogle was not always the index fund zealot he ultimately became.

Initially, he was entranced by the professional investing industry that was blossoming as he entered adulthood. At the time of writing the *Financial Analysts Journal* article, Bogle was a young hotshot executive of Wellington, one of the oldest and largest mutual fund managers in America. But an odd combination of disaster and serendipity in the mid-1970s set him on the path to upending the industry he once venerated. "There's nobody more religious than a convert," observes Jim Riepe, one of Bogle's closest colleagues in the founding of Vanguard, as a way of explaining the remarkable metamorphosis.

The Greek poet Archilochus once observed that the fox knows many things, but the hedgehog knows one important thing—a phrase later made famous by the philosopher Isaiah Berlin. Bogle was the quintessential hedgehog. He always believed in one big thing with a fiery passion. He had the integrity and intellectual suppleness to shift positions, though. When he was later confronted with his change of heart on the merits of active investing, he quoted the economist John Maynard Keynes: "When the facts change, I change my mind. What do you do, sir?"[3]

▲

JACK BOGLE'S EARLY LIFE WAS profoundly shaped by the destruction wrought by the Great Crash of 1929 and the subsequent Depression. His father, William Yates Bogle Jr., was a dashing, wealthy businessman who had in 1916 crossed the border to Canada and volunteered to fly fighter planes for the UK's Royal Flying Corps during World War I, while his mother, Josephine Lorraine Hipkins, was a glamorous, charismatic, and forceful heiress from a venerable Scottish American family. Bogle's grandfather had founded the American Brick Corporation and cofounded the Sanitary Can company, which was later acquired by the American Can Company in 1908. His father worked at both after returning from the war.

William and Josephine's first twins died in childbirth, but in 1927 they welcomed William Yates Bogle III, and in May 1929 twins John Clifton and David Caldwell. Together the children became Bud, Jack, and Dave, the "Bogle Boys" of Montclair, New Jersey.

Unfortunately, their upper-class lifestyle was shattered in October 1929, when the Bogles' inherited wealth evaporated in the stock market crash. It left Bogle's father broken and pushed him into alcoholism, and forced the boys to move in with their grandparents in rural New Jersey, and ultimately to a two-room apartment on the third floor of a small house in Ardmore, a suburb of Philadelphia. All three boys had to start working from a young age to support the family, but their father's gradual descent was the biggest trauma. Bud Bogle once recounted to Lewis Braham, the biographer of Vanguard's founder:[4]

It always fell upon me to be the leader and to protect my younger brothers and myself against whatever kind of bad things my father got into, which was too much wine, women, and song. I could see the damage way before they realized what was going on. And I was the guy who had to find the damn bottles of booze and break them in front of him and cry. It was horrible. It affected my mother, and it affected everybody. My father was a wonderful sentimental man, and he would cry when I'd do that, but I didn't realize that alcohol is a disease.

However, it inculcated a strong work ethic in the Bogle boys, and their mother channeled her considerable energy into ensuring a good education for her sons at the Blair Academy, a prestigious boarding school in New Jersey. For the young Jack, it proved transformational. He later recounted with pride how he turned an initially dismal grade in algebra into a perfect one on his final exam, and how exacting English teachers taught him the art of writing.[5]

"Being away from our stressed home was the best thing for us,"

Bogle later said. "This fine New Jersey boarding school was—and remains—among the principal cornerstones of my long life."[6] To pay for the school fees the Bogle boys won scholarships, and Jack Bogle worked as a waiter in the dining hall. He graduated summa cum laude in 1947, and was named the student most likely to succeed by his peers. However, he narrowly failed to become the class valedictorian, something that vexed him so greatly that he (unsuccessfully) lobbied for some of his teachers to change his grades—an early sign of his utter inability to accept defeat.[7]

The Bogles could afford to send only one of the boys to college, with two needed to support the family. Given Jack's grades, he was the one who was chosen—an awkward fact that further fueled his determination to do well. He decided on nearby Princeton because of a generous scholarship and an abundance of jobs he could take to pay for expenses while earning his degree.

He majored in economics, and in his first year tackled Paul Samuelson's *Economics: An Introductory Analysis*, a recently published textbook written by the famous academic, which would go on to be the seminal introduction for generations of economists and financiers. He loved the subject, but found it tough at first. Midway through his first year he had only a D-plus grade—which would have cost him his scholarship if it had persisted—and only managed to scrape a C-minus through intensive study.[8]

At home the situation was also deteriorating. Josephine Bogle started to suffer the symptoms of what would ultimately be diagnosed as cervical cancer, and his father's drunkenness spurred Bud Bogle, recently discharged from the Marines, to throw him out of their modest family home. Their idolized mother got progressively worse, and by the end she was bedridden and injected with Demerol to help her deal with the pain. In February 1952, Josephine Bogle passed away. Later that same year William Yates Bogle Jr. also died, from a stroke at Bellevue Hospital. "I think he was a man who was not very strong, but who did his best," Bogle phlegmatically observed.[9] He later kept a model of a World War I Sopwith Camel biplane in his office as a memento to his father's finest hour.[10]

Luckily, Princeton proved a good environment for the driven young man, and his grades improved. But his early attempt to find an imaginative senior thesis in economics proved tricky, until one day he was browsing through magazines in the university library and came across an article titled "Big Money in Boston" in the December 1949 copy of *Fortune*. The piece focused on the Massachusetts Investors Trust, the first "open-ended" mutual fund in America. It had been founded back in 1924 with $50,000 to give ordinary investors access to the burgeoning US stock market. Until then most investment vehicles had been "closed-ended" trusts, in that they offered only a fixed number of shares when they were sold and could not take in new money, and the Bostonian innovation proved a big hit. By 1949, the Massachusetts Investors Trust managed $110 million.

At the time, the entire mutual fund industry consisted of only ninety funds that managed about $1.8 billion, and was overwhelmingly based in Boston. Yet the *Fortune* article noted that it was a "rapidly expanding and somewhat contentious industry of great potential significance to US business."[11] This piqued Bogle's interest, and he resolved to write his thesis on the topic.

In his later years, Bogle was keen to highlight how his thesis stated that "funds can make no claim to superiority over the market averages," foreshadowing his index fund messianism. But in truth "The Economic Role of the Investment Company"* is overwhelmingly positive on the merits of mutual funds. "Most funds do use sound judgment in diversifying their portfolios, and the criticism

---

* The term "mutual fund" was not yet common, and was never mentioned in the 1949 *Forbes* article.

that the funds merely 'buy the averages' is seen as invalid," Bogle wrote.[12]

However, his analysis of the industry's growth potential was spot-on; his exhortation for it to operate in "the most efficient, honest, and economical way possible" and the prescription to fuel further growth by reducing initial sales fees (the "load" in industry parlance) and management costs were a harbinger for Vanguard's later growth. The 123-page thesis earned an A-plus, helped Bogle graduate magna cum laude in 1951, and caught the eye of another former Princeton man, Walter Morgan, the founder of Wellington Management Company.

▲

ORIGINALLY AN ACCOUNTANT who offered clients investment advice, Morgan in 1928 raised $100,000 for his own mutual fund and later named it after Arthur Wellesley, the "Iron Duke" of Wellington who had bested Napoleon at the Battle of Waterloo.[13] Morgan was innately conservative after his family had lost money on speculative stock bets, and Wellington was one of the first "balanced" mutual funds, which invested in both stocks and bonds and eschewed juicing its bets with borrowed money.

Morgan's caution served him well in the Great Crash of 1929, and a series of astute bets during World War II propelled it into the industry's upper echelons. By 1951, Wellington managed about $190 million, making it the fourth-biggest mutual fund in the United States.[14]

The freshly graduated Bogle was weighing job offers from the Philadelphia National Bank and Boening & Company, a local stock brokerage, when Morgan was introduced to him. Wellington's founder was initially reluctant to hire from Princeton, as he thought its students were spoiled. But he was intrigued by Bogle's thesis, which he annotated and sent to Wellington's staff for them to read, and liked the cut of his jib when Bogle was interviewed. Morgan convinced the young man that he should join a fast-growing, emerging industry rather than a fusty bank, and on July 8, 1951, Bogle went to work for Wellington.

He immediately threw himself into every task handed to him, showing off a prodigious work ethic, his skills with a slide rule, and an ability to quickly grasp every aspect of an investment company's operations. By 1955, he was made Morgan's personal assistant, with a wide remit to explore various parts of Wellington. His personal life also thrived. In 1956, he married Eve Sherrerd, the sister of his good friend and Princeton schoolmate Jay Sherrerd, and the first of their six children was born the following year.[15]

Professionally, Bogle's biggest achievement at the time was convincing Morgan to launch the company's second fund in 1958, which would invest purely in stocks. Initially it was unimaginatively named the Wellington Equity Fund, but in 1963 it was rebranded as Windsor and subsequently managed by John Neff, one of the all-time great mutual fund managers. Its success helped make Bogle become Morgan's heir apparent and an industry wunderkind. He was named to Wellington's board in 1960, and made administrative vice president in 1962 and executive vice president in 1965.[16]

However, the 1960s were not without their tribulations. Bogle had always appeared strong as an ox, but he suffered a sudden heart attack while playing tennis with his brother-in-law on the Labor Day weekend of 1960. In the middle of the first set, he suddenly felt a flashing pain, and after catching his breath he told Sherrerd, "You're not going to believe me, but I think I just had a heart attack."[17] Both laughed at the idea. Bogle was just thirty-one, after all, and seemingly fit as a fiddle. So they resumed the game—with Bogle even winning the set—only for the pain to resume. His wife, Eve, took him to a doctor, who diagnosed it as a heart attack and hospitalized him for six weeks. It proved the first of six heart attacks for Bogle over the years, and many more hospital visits for irregular heartbeats. He was later diagnosed with a genetic disease called arrhythmogenic right ventricular dysplasia, which ultimately forced him to get a heart transplant in 1996.[18]

Bogle never stopped working at full throttle, even at times from his hospital bed. And his love of tennis and squash remained undimmed. Jeremy Duffield, a former colleague, remembers having to call an ambulance after one tough game, but when the paramedic offered an anesthetic ahead of administering a defibrillator shock, Bogle declined, saying, "I want to see what it feels like." Later, he kept a defibrillator at the front of the squash court in case it was needed, he'd say. However, his regular opponents felt it was mostly done to gain a competitive advantage by deterring them from giving him a tough game, rather than for any medical purpose.

Moreover, although his personal career was rocketing, the 1960s were a tough time for Wellington. The company's conservatism was out of sync with the ebullience of the "go-go" bull market and a new generation of star money managers emerging from it. Although Wellington's assets under management hit $2 billion by 1965, its market share of the US mutual fund industry was sliding. Morgan tasked Bogle with turning the ship around.

Unfortunately, Bogle's strategy for doing so proved disastrous, both for him and for the venerable investment company. Rather than attempt to set up a new racier "growth" fund from scratch, he decided that Wellington should instead merge with one of the trendy investment groups. He explored several potential partners—including Capital Group in Los Angeles and Franklin Custodian Funds—but was turned down.[19] So in late 1965, he began courting Thorndike, Doran, Paine & Lewis (TDP&L), a young management company started by a bunch of patrician Bostonians who managed the Ivest Fund, one of the industry's best stock fund performers at the time.[20]

It was a clash of personalities. Bogle was loud, confident, and forceful, while Robert Doran was quiet and introverted, and Nicholas Thorndike was a big-picture man who eschewed the nitty-gritty operational aspects Bogle thrived on. Both of the Boston men believed in a more modern, consensual form of leadership, while Bogle subscribed to what might be termed an "Ankh-Morpork" democracy, coined by the late fantasy writer Terry Pratchett: one man, one vote. Bogle was the man and he had the vote.

Astonishingly, they actually hit it off at first, and Morgan himself endorsed a deal. Wellington's founder wanted to keep temporary control of the company in the early years of the merger, but if everything went to plan, the four members of the "Boston group," as they became known, would after five years take control of 40 percent of the merged group, Bogle 28 percent, and the balance owned by public shareholders (after the company had listed some of its shares in 1960). On June 6, 1966, the agreement was signed,[21] with Bogle presenting each of his new partners a small silver tray on which he had cemented a $1 "peace dollar" coin.[22] In November 1967, Bogle was named president and chief executive of Wellington, and in 1970 he was named chairman of the Wellington funds.

On paper, the merger seemed sensible to both insiders and outsiders. "Wellington gets a hot research group deep with young investment management and analyst talent, and Ivest gets the benefit of Wellington's prestigious name, its powerful distribution organization, and the administrative and marketing talents of John Bogle," *Institutional Investor* wrote in a cover story on the merger, titled "The Whiz Kids Take Over at Wellington," illustrated by Bogle as a multi-armed quarterback handing balls of financial securities to the four Boston partners.[23]

Initially, the merger appeared a runaway success. Buoyed by the marriage of its strong returns with Wellington's powerful distribution network, Ivest's assets vaulted from almost $50 million at the end of 1966 to $340 million by the close of 1968. Inspired by its new young hotshots, Wellington churned out several new funds aimed at capturing the zeitgeist, managed out of TDP&L's Boston office, rather than its Philadelphia headquarters. They also picked up the reins of the struggling flagship Wellington Fund itself. Doran said that the five men had "an extraordinary personal relationship," while Bogle gushed that the merger had "worked better than anyone had expected."[24]

However, the bonhomie quickly soured. The go-go era died soon after the merger, with the S&P 500 between November 1968 and May 1970 slumping into its first bear market since the Bay of Pigs debacle in 1961. The "Nifty Fifty" stocks that had helped propel Ivest's performance were among the worst hit, and tensions between Wellington's top executives were rising. Bogle's hopes to start a bond fund had initially been stymied, leading to some ructions, and he was irate over their poor management of the Wellington Fund. Meanwhile, TDP&L was frustrated over poor administrative work on its Ivest Fund.[25]

But the main core problem was the clash of personalities that caused a festering animosity between Bogle on one hand and the four Bostonians on the other. None of them had suffered any major professional setbacks until then, magnifying the differences. Eventually Morgan had to step in to play peacekeeper. "I taught Jack to be pretty tough—like I had been, because I owned all the stock and could do any damn thing I wanted," Wellington's founder said at the time. "But you can't quite do that when you have four or five guys who are virtually equal to you."[26]

By 1972, the conflict had become public knowledge, forcing the five partners to more clearly define their responsibilities and declare a truce. "When the conflicts reached the crisis stage, it forced all of us to look at ourselves and I think this introspection was good,"

Bogle told a journalist at the time.[27] "I know I am less egotistical than before and probably more tolerant too."

It didn't stick. US equities dived into a new bear market in January 1973, which ended up being the worst since the Great Depression. The impact was severe. The once-conservative Wellington Fund, which had managed as much as $2 billion prior to the merger, shrank to under $1 billion, Ivest saw its performance collapse, many of the company's newer, trendier funds were shuttered, and the stock of Wellington Management Company itself plunged from a high of $50 in 1968 to a low of $4.25 in 1975.[28]

In this crucible, the mix of the starkly different personalities of the five men atop Wellington began to mix in even more toxic ways. "It was awful," recalls Jan Twardowski, Bogle's assistant at the time. "The elephants were fighting, and we mice were scampering trying not to be trampled. It got quite vicious." Clearly, a reckoning was looming.

▲

JIM RIEPE PACED ANXIOUSLY AROUND the billiard room of the Union League Club on the corner of Park Avenue and 37th Street in New York, a venerable gentleman's club once frequented by the likes of John Pierpont Morgan and Teddy Roosevelt. It was too early for a drink, so he settled his nerves by playing a few solo racks, while awaiting the verdict from the Wellington board meeting taking place next door.

In it, his boss Bogle was fighting for his professional life. By then, the Boston group outnumbered the old Philadelphia contingent on Wellington's board, and the relationship between Bogle and his colleagues had broken down completely.

In November 1973, Doran visited Bogle and told him point-blank that the situation was dysfunctional and had to end. "I've talked to the others, and we think it would be best if you left the company," Doran told Bogle, with unusual emotion for the normally introverted money manager.[29] He offered a financial settlement—a $20,000-a-year annuity for the next fifteen years—for Bogle to leave quietly, but Bogle refused with his usual tact. "I've heard of few stupider things than that," Bogle told Doran.[30] He then called up the directors on Wellington's board, and realized to his horror that Doran had the votes needed to fire him. He still refused to go quietly. Four days later, he once again refused to resign. The situation was clearly coming to a boil.*

The next board meeting—held in "neutral" New York, rather than Boston or Philadelphia—on January 23, 1974, looked like it might be where the axe would finally fall. Yet to aghast confidants, it seemed that Bogle still assumed it simply couldn't happen, whatever the tensions between Boston and Philadelphia. He so obviously knew more about the investment business than his rivals—he was so obviously *smarter*—that he couldn't really contemplate that such a travesty could ever occur, was Bogle's apparent reasoning. "It was this sort of blind confidence in himself, which convinced him that everybody else would eventually understand that he really is the best person to do this job," Riepe later recalled.

At the board meeting, Bogle presented a radical twenty-page memo that he hoped would save his job. He argued that Wellington should mutualize itself, with its funds acquiring the company, and Wellington would in practice become a subsidiary of the funds that would operate "at cost." The Thorndike, Doran, Paine & Lewis merger would be dissolved, with the Boston company once again

---

* The growing turmoil was starting to worry some of the independent directors on the separate boards of Wellington's funds, according to Braham's Bogle biography. "I am concerned about the possibility of reports of Wellington dissension causing damage to the shareholders," Barbara Hauptfuhrer wrote to her colleague Charles Root on January 3, 1974. "For example, such reports could conceivably trigger panic redemptions which would not permit orderly liquidation and therefore would be very harmful to the shareholders. Can this be avoided?"

becoming independent, and Bogle would remain the head of Wellington.[31]

Although seemingly self-serving, it was an idea Bogle had been mulling for some time.[32] He had long been concerned that investment companies serve two often conflicting masters, the owners of the money manager, and the clients. Clients ideally want the best performance possible for the lowest fees. The investment manager also wants premier performance—after all, it helps attract new investors—but also wants to pay its people high salaries and its owners hefty profits, a thorny contradiction. The Gordian knot tying the two together could be severed only with a sword of full mutualization, where funds own their managers, he believed.

Nonetheless, the proposal bombed. The board voted 10–1 to request that Bogle resign (he recused himself, and the one vote in his favor was John Neff's). When he once again refused to do so, ten members of the board voted to fire him outright, with Neff and Bogle abstaining. Doran was then duly elected the new president of Wellington Management Company.[33]

When Bogle walked, ashen-faced, out of the board meeting at the Union League Club he strode over to Riepe and they drafted what the press release of his defenestration should say. Their afternoon train ride back to Wellington's headquarters in Valley Forge was somber, quiet, and tense. "He was devastated," Riepe recalls.

Yet Bogle, determined as ever, quickly decided to launch an audacious countercoup. By law, US mutual funds must have their own boards of directors, a majority of which must be independent from the investment managers who actually control the money. In theory, they can even select a new investment manager for the funds. In reality, investment managers often handpick the same nominally independent but in reality supine directors to sit on fund boards, both to cut costs and to maintain control, and even for truly independent boards removing a fund's investment manager would be extraordinarily difficult to justify. As a result, a fund's board's primary role is to ensure that its administration is effective, review expenses and fees, and monitor for any potential conflicts of interest.

The Boston group was not as familiar with the details of fund boards as Bogle was, and had spent little time getting to know the Wellington fund directors. At the time of the merger, the Bostonians had added a few Ivest Fund directors to the eleven Wellington funds' boards, but they did not enjoy a clear majority of the seats. This opened up a crack for Bogle to exploit. "I was determined to win at the craps table what I had lost at the roulette table," he later recounted.[34]

The very next day Bogle took the 6 a.m. train back to New York to make his case directly to the funds' boards. "You don't have to fire me," he told them.[35] "This is your corporation. You oversee these mutual funds on behalf of their shareholders. Wellington Management Company doesn't own the mutual funds. This is a great opportunity for us. The funds ought to have their own voice." He then presented his radical mutualization idea again.

This was still a bridge too far for the independent directors of the eleven Wellington funds, but Charles Root, their chairman, didn't care much for the Bostonians, and resented their assumption that they would simply rubber-stamp the corporate coup. So the board tasked Bogle with conducting a "Future Structure Study" to explore various options around the relationship between the funds and Wellington Management Company, ranging from the status quo to Bogle's outrageous mutualization proposal. Suddenly, Bogle had a chance to stage a stunning comeback.

After months of furious negotiations, memo-writing, rebuttals from the Bostonians, and lengthy, combative board meetings at the stuffy Union League Club—during which Bogle's younger colleagues would take on their Boston counterparts at pool—Bogle finally presented three options for "The Future Structure of the Wellington Group of Investment Companies" at a March 20 board meeting, a 250-page tome authored by Bogle, his lieutenant Riepe, and assistant Twardowski.[36] Despite its length, Bogle had whittled down the options to four:

1. The status quo with Wellington Management Company controlling all of the fund-related activities.
2. Wellington would continue to handle all fund operations except administration—which included fairly mundane tasks like shareholder record-keeping and communications, legal and compliance, fund accounting, and handling share purchases and redemptions.
3. Wellington would continue to handle all fund operations except administration and underwriting—which meant the funds would also control Wellington's sales organization, advertising, and marketing activities.
4. The Wellington funds would acquire all fund-related activities from Wellington Management Company, including investment advisory services—de facto full mutualization.

Bogle himself naturally favored the last option, which would hand him full control of the three main legs of a money management company. But the fund directors had hired former SEC commissioner Richard Smith to advise them, and for the sake of avoiding lengthy legal battles, Smith counseled the board that any decision would have to be unanimous. That killed the likelihood of the most revolutionary option, Bogle feared.

He was right. On June 20, 1974, the board finally made its decision, settling on the second, least ambitious option. The Wellington funds would set up a new subsidiary jointly owned by them, which would handle all administrative tasks. Although it was a very small step toward independence, Bogle and Riepe believed it was the proverbial camel's nose under the tent.

In later years, Bogle would often recount how he left Wellington the same way he was hired: "Fired with enthusiasm!" In truth, his closest colleagues said Bogle long felt humiliated, angry, and bitter about the "great bifurcation," as it became known. It gnawed at him. Until recently, he had been the head of one of the biggest and oldest money managers in America, after suffering nary a single setback in a remarkable career. Now he was a glorified clerk—albeit a well-paid one.

But the profound sense of injustice poured rocket fuel on the already raging bonfire of Bogle's determination, driving him to transform what could have been a monument to his biggest humiliation into something truly special.

"He was bitingly angry," recalls LeBaron of Batterymarch, an acquaintance of Bogle's who met him for lunch around the time. "I think these guys [Thorndike, Doran, Paine, and Lewis] were essentially the founders of Vanguard, because they made him angry enough that he wanted to prove that what they thought was just the tail of the dog was going to wag the dog."

Chapter 7

BOGLE'S FOLLY

ONE LATE SUMMER DAY OF 1974, a dealer in antique prints came calling on Jack Bogle in Valley Forge. It proved a serendipitous visit.

The fund directors had pressured Wellington into letting Bogle keep his old office, but the prints on his wall were the property of the investment management company, and had been carted away in the great bifurcation. So Bogle bought a dozen prints depicting the Napoleonic Wars, including the land campaigns of the Duke of Wellington, after whom the company had originally been named, and Lord Horatio Nelson's naval battles, to decorate his now-spartan office.

Grateful for the business, the dealer gave Bogle a copy of the original book, *Naval Battles of Great Britain 1775–1815*, from which the naval prints had been lifted. Leafing through it, Bogle came across something Admiral Nelson had written after the Battle of the Nile in 1798: "Nothing could withstand the squadron under my command. The judgment of the captains, together with the valor and high state of discipline of the officers and men of every description, was irresistible."[1] This resonated immediately with Bogle, who then spied below Nelson's signature, "HMS *Vanguard*, off the mouth of the Nile."

The new fund administration company being set up was just weeks away from being formally incorporated, but after losing yet another bruising battle with his enemies in Boston, Bogle had been told that he couldn't use the Wellington name. After first threatening to quit in a fit of pique,[2] he hunkered down with Riepe and Twardowski to discuss what to call the new venture, with options ranging from Victory (too grandiose) to Mutual Fund Management Company (too bland). Once Bogle had spied the name of Nelson's flagship—and hung what he thought was the print of it in his office— he was enamored with it.*

The Wellington fund directors were less thrilled, correctly realizing that the name indicated that Bogle had grander visions for the new company than mere clerical work. But they grudgingly relented.[3] As a result, the company culture eventually became suffused by nautical references—such as staff being called crew, the cafeteria going by the Galley, and the hallways adorned with maritime paintings.

It was an odd, chaotic period for the newly christened Vanguard Group of Investment Companies. The messy practical process of the bifurcation was still under way, with some Wellington staff being sent up to Boston and others staying in Valley Forge, where they would work cheek-by-jowl with their old/new colleagues at Vanguard. The core business was also challenging, with Wellington funds by then having suffered forty consecutive months of investor outflows—a grim streak that would continue until January 1978.[4]

Most of all, Bogle was still venomously bitter about his defenestration. He later confided to Riepe that he had seen a therapist to help work through it. The therapist had told Bogle that he didn't

---

* Riepe had talked to some advertising executives, who had told him that some letters are considered "strong," and *V* was among them, which helped the deal.

need to get rid of his bitterness entirely, because doing so would go against human nature. But he advised him to try to lock it away in a mental box, and go about his business and focus on other things. Occasionally, he should lift the lid and feel the bitterness again, but then tuck it away again and refocus on more important matters. Something about the imagery appealed to Bogle, and the advice appeared to help him. "But I knew the box was always there, and it would at times come out in some funny ways," Riepe recalls.

Against this messy backdrop, Vanguard was finally incorporated on September 24, 1974. It initially had a staff of fifty-nine people—nineteen executives and forty in the accounting and operations group—and was owned by the funds it administered, such as the original flagship Wellington, Ivest, and Windsor, which in total managed about $1.4 billion.[5] Bogle was its first president, paid $100,000 annually—the same as his salary at Wellington. Vanguard was responsible for bookkeeping, filing tax returns, government reporting duties, and handling shareholder records. The company would operate at cost, returning any profits to its constituent funds, which soon helped them reduce the annual fee they paid to the Wellington Management Company by $1 million to $6.4 million.[6]

The press was not kind. In May 1975, *Forbes* published a scathing piece on the corporate shenanigans surrounding the bifurcation, titled "A Plague on Both Houses?"[7] This infuriated Bogle. But on the whole, the public reaction to the groundbreaking establishment of Vanguard was one of obliviousness—something that seemed to pain Bogle even more.

He clearly had grander designs for Vanguard and started plotting how he could gain control of distribution and investment management as well. "While a third of a loaf was better than none, I concluded that we should promptly set about seizing the other two-thirds," he later wrote.[8] He needed to find a way to unclench Wellington's grip over its funds for Vanguard to truly declare its independence. The first opportunity to do so struck like a thunderbolt.

▲

IN THE FALL OF 1974, Paul Samuelson, who had a few years earlier become the first American to win a Nobel Prize in Economics, published a seminal column in the inaugural edition of the *Journal of Portfolio Management* titled "Challenge to Judgment." It landed like a call for atheism published in the Vatican's *L'Osservatore Romano*.

Samuelson raised the mounting academic evidence that most professional investment managers did a poor job relative to the market's returns. While stressing that there was nothing in the efficient-markets hypothesis that necessarily precluded some uncommonly brilliant fund managers from consistently beating the market, he pointed out that such skill was clearly scarce, and the few who possessed it were unlikely to rent their talents out cheaply to the hoi polloi. Meanwhile, much of the hyperactive trading caused by the vast majority of mediocre fund managers attempting to beat the market was a waste, given the costs of trading.

"I would like to believe otherwise. But a respect for evidence compels me to incline towards the hypothesis that most portfolio decision makers should go out of business—take up plumbing, teach Greek, or help produce the annual [gross national product] by serving as corporate executives," he scathingly wrote.[9]

Samuelson briefly noted the index funds launched by Wells Fargo and Batterymarch, but urged more big institutions to set up a large passive fund that tracked the S&P 500, "if only for the purpose of setting up a naive model against which their in-house gunslingers can measure their prowess."

To Bogle—who had years earlier battled with Samuelson's textbook at Princeton—the column was electrifying. It inspired his future mantra that "strategy follows structure," and this was a strategy that arguably suited Vanguard's hamstrung structure perfectly. The few existing index funds were almost solely the preserve of pension funds, and while they were beginning to gain traction, none of Vanguard's competitors in the mutual fund industry—mostly aimed at ordinary investors—would want to start a low-cost product that might show up its pricier, traditional actively managed funds. Meanwhile, Vanguard's at-cost structure was the perfect match. Plus, he obviously knew a few gunslingers in Boston whom he wouldn't mind humbling.

"Dr. Samuelson's challenge struck me like a bolt of lightning, igniting my conviction that upstart Vanguard had a remarkable, even unique, opportunity to operate a passively managed, low-cost index fund and have the market to ourselves for at least a few years," he wrote in his autobiography.[10]

Bogle would later claim that he was ignorant of academic ideas like Markowitz's modern portfolio theory and Fama's efficient-markets hypothesis, and was at the time unfamiliar with the pioneering efforts of Wells Fargo, American National Bank, and Batterymarch. Given the coverage that they received in the industry press and Bogle's wide-ranging intellect, voracious news consumption, and visits to Chicago, this simply isn't credible. He would often point to his 1951 thesis and its observation that "funds can make no claim to superiority over the market averages" as the intellectual genesis of Vanguard's first index fund, conveniently ignoring that the thesis actually broadly advocated for actively managed portfolios, and his anonymous attack on the idea under the pen name John B. Armstrong.

Nor was he quite as zealous about the inability of skilled managers to be able to beat the market over time as he later sometimes appeared. He had grown close to Neff, who over the years had racked up an astonishing track record managing Wellington's Windsor Fund. They were only two years apart in age, sported matching efficiency-first crew cuts,[11] and Bogle always appreciated Neff's having stood up for him in the Bostonian coup.

It is true that Bogle had always thought that most investment managers charged too much, which was a headwind for their clients—the "cost matters hypothesis," as he called it. Index funds were therefore appealing. Several friends and colleagues note that he was an outrageous cheapskate personally as well, and the idea of a cheap, simple product for the masses undoubtedly resonated.

Nonetheless, despite Bogle's later emergence as the leading champion of passive investing, the birth of the first index fund for ordinary everyday investors—an innovation that would ultimately upend the entire investment industry—was simply a result of Vanguard's hamstrung circumstances and his burning desire to get out from under the thumb of his erstwhile partners. Whatever Bogle's latter-day protestations, it was no grand mission, merely a strategic gambit in his ongoing war with the Bostonians. "It was his foot in the door of independence," says Twardowski, Bogle's assistant at the time. "In the later years, he would say that he understood all these things and he planned all this. Not so much. Who could have predicted the indexing revolution? But it turned out quite well," he observes.

The work of setting up Vanguard, getting the reorganization formally approved by the Securities and Exchange Commission, and arranging a confirmatory vote by the Wellington fund shareholders consumed most of the crew members' time. But sometime in early 1975, Bogle walked over to Twardowski—who had studied computer programming at Princeton before taking an MBA at Wharton—and asked him whether he could run an index fund. "Umm, give me a few days," Twardowski replied.

Twardowski set about researching the concept, and wrote some programs testing it out in APL, a now-obsolete coding language, on a timeshare mainframe, using a public database of stock prices and simple capitalization-weighted algorithms. After a few days of work, he was confident enough to say that it could be done fairly easily, and gave Bogle the thumbs-up.

Bogle's desire was then further whetted by the publication of an incendiary article in the *Financial Analysts Journal* in July 1975 by Charles Ellis, then the president of Greenwich Associates, a financial consultancy the former banker had founded after leaving Donaldson, Lufkin & Jenrette. Ellis provocatively argued that investment management had become a "loser's game." He pointed out that given the average fund's annual turnover of stocks in its portfolio, the trading costs incurred as a result, and the fees it charged investors, money managers had to outperform the stock market by a wide margin for their clients to come even close to doing so on a net basis. "If you can't beat the market, you should certainly consider joining it," Ellis wrote.[12] "An index fund is one way. The data from the performance measurement firms show that an index fund would have outperformed most money managers."

Emboldened, Bogle, Riepe, and Twardowski set upon the task of making a formal presentation to the Vanguard board. Given his fame and stature, Samuelson's article was exhibit A. The second part was Bogle essentially repeating the exercise he did under the name John B. Armstrong—but this time with very different results.

Bogle found that over the three decades prior to 1975, the average US equity mutual fund had returned only 9.7 percent, compared to the S&P 500's 11.3 percent return. Given the impact of compounding returns, this had a huge impact in pure dollar terms. Someone who invested $1 million in the average equity fund at the start of the thirty-year period would be sitting on $16.39 million in 1975—a tidy sum. But someone who had just tracked the S&P 500 would be holding over $25 million.[13]

The proposal to set up a passive, index-tracking mutual fund was presented at the September 18, 1975, Vanguard board meeting. The directors were skeptical, pointing out to Bogle that its mandate precluded Vanguard from engaging in investment management activities or any marketing. Bogle disingenuously argued that since the fund would be unmanaged, it didn't breach Vanguard's narrow mandate, and a public sale of the fund could be done by an outside club of brokerages and investment banks. Astonishingly, the board accepted this tenuous logic and approved the proposal. The game was on.

▲

TO GET A BETTER UNDERSTANDING of what was needed to run an index fund, Twardowski reached out to John McQuown at Wells Fargo, Rex Sinquefield at American National Bank, and Dean LeBaron at Batterymarch. Sinquefield proved particularly helpful to Twardowski. But an index-tracking open-ended mutual fund—with money often flowing in and out daily—confronted very different challenges than did passive funds used by big institutional investors like a pension plan.

The first index funds had all been pooled trusts or individual accounts for pension funds, which tend to write big investment checks and not move money around much. Dealing with hundreds, thousands, potentially even hundreds of thousands of individual shareholder accounts where money can flow in and out daily was more complex, especially at a time when computers were still rudimentary. Regulators also impose more stringent conditions and reporting standards on funds that are open to the general public, as opposed to big, sophisticated institutions.

By December 1975, Vanguard had filed a registration in Delaware for the "First Index Investment Trust." By April of the following year, Bogle, Twardowski, and Riepe had prepared a draft prospectus for FIIT, which projected that the cost of managing an index fund would be 0.3 percent annually in operating expenses, and 0.2 percent in transaction costs—roughly a tenth of the all-in cost of an actively managed fund.[14] After they answered follow-up questions from the Vanguard board, the prospectus was formally filed with the SEC in May 1976.

Vanguard signed a deal with Standard & Poor's to be able to license their index for a nominal sum, reflecting how the company didn't yet recognize its indices as a potential revenue stream.* The next step was to assemble a team of brokerage firms to manage the sale of shares to their clients, given that the fund needed some money to get started and Vanguard had no distribution itself. Bogle confidently told the board that he expected them to be able to raise as much as $150 million in the initial offering, more than enough to buy all the shares needed to replicate the S&P 500.[15]

Bache Halsey Stuart, Paine Webber Jackson & Curtis, and Reynolds Securities signed up on the condition that Vanguard could enlist one of the big Wall Street firms to lead the offering. To Bogle's delight, Roger Wood of Dean Witter—one of the biggest US brokerages before being subsumed by Morgan Stanley in 1997—agreed to do so. Fate helped Vanguard assemble a prestigious group of underwriters: On May Day 1975, US regulators had abolished the practice of fixed commissions for stock trades, and as a result brokers were desperate to hang on to their clients.

Bogle's optimism was stoked by two well-timed pieces in the press. In June 1976, *Fortune*—which had inspired his thesis on mutual funds a quarter century earlier—published a big six-page article titled "Index Funds—An Idea Whose Time Is Coming." It explored the intellectual underpinnings, detailed the poor performance of most fund managers, explained the initial pioneering efforts, and

---

* Today, the three big index providers S&P Dow Jones Indices, FTSE Russell, and MSCI are wildly profitable thanks to licensing revenues from their benchmarks, as will be explored in later chapters.

presciently argued that "index funds now threaten to reshape the entire world of professional money management."[16] In August, Samuelson in *Newsweek* noted with delight the response to his challenge two years earlier: "Sooner than I dared expect my implicit prayer has been answered," he wrote. "There is coming to market, I see from a crisp new prospectus, something called the First Index Investment Trust."

However, the initial optimism faded when the brokerages took Bogle and Riepe on a roadshow to talk to their clients around the country. Index funds might have been trendy among the financial cognoscenti of Chicago, but financial advisors and ordinary investors in Buffalo or Minneapolis were noticeably less enthusiastic. By the end of it, the underwriters gloomily warned that they might be able to raise only $30 million, not nearly enough to buy the entire S&P 500. Riepe asked Twardowski whether he could still replicate the index with a smaller haul. After testing his program, Twardowski said yes.

Bogle was an avid betting man, fond of slamming his wallet down on the table to signal that a wager was on whenever he argued about some fact or figure with his crew. He therefore started a betting pool on how much they would raise. Ever the optimist, Bogle said $150 million (though he later hedged his bet with another call of $45 million). Dean Witter's Wood said $125 million. Riepe and Twardowski were more pessimistic, and said about $30 million each. In the end, FIIT raised only $11.32 million on August 31, 1976.

It was an abject failure. That wasn't nearly enough to buy the entire index. The underwriters asked Bogle if he wanted to scrap the whole thing, but he insisted they go through with it. "No," he told them, "we now have the world's first index fund, and this is the beginning of something big."[17] But with just $11 million, Twardowski could buy only 280 stocks of the S&P 500—the 200 largest, which represented almost 80 percent of the index by weighting, and another 80 stocks of smaller companies chosen carefully to best mimic the rest of the index.

The pool was won by Bob Lippman, a relatively new executive at Vanguard, who had entered several bets, but whose lowest number—the lowest in the pool by some distance—was $11,111,111. Twardowski promptly sent him a memo, saying he had some good news and some bad news:

> *First, the good news: Congratulations! Your estimate of $11,111, 111 was unnervingly accurate on the final size of the underwriting; we received the check for $11,320,00 this morning. The list of all the various estimates is attached. I'm sure that your $27 winnings will warm your evening.*
>
> *Now, the bad news: The fact that your estimate was by far the lowest has not escaped Mr. Bogle's attention. In view of your lack of confidence in our organization, he has asked me to thank you for your valuable services during your relatively short tenure with Vanguard. Chuck Williams has some old Bekins boxes you can use when cleaning out your desk. (Note: Anticipating your protest, Mr. Bogle says that your two other estimates—both considerably higher—do not change the situation. As he put it, your estimates "were still well below average with respect to the standard deviation of the means of the competitive group of estimates." I trust that's perfectly clear.)*

Twardowski confirms that the memo was a joke, and typical of the joshing among Vanguard's tight-knit crew. Nonetheless, despite the bonhomie, the offering had clearly bombed, and FIIT was swiftly dubbed "Bogle's Folly" by the press.

The debacle was so severe that it killed the chances of anyone else thinking of following in Vanguard's footsteps. Indexing might enjoy growing appeal among pension funds, but the general public appeared indifferent, and to many mutual fund groups it was anathema. "The jury is still out, but you have to keep costs so low that there's very little profit in indexing for conventional mutual fund management companies," Michael Lipper, a prominent mutual fund industry analyst, said at the time. "Besides, most money managers have a hard time swallowing the idea that you can't beat the market. It's a paradox they're not willing to accept yet."[18]

Rivals were not above some sniping. Fidelity's chairman, Edward (Ned) Johnson, snootily told the *Boston Globe* that the investment group he led would certainly not be dabbling in the field. "I can't believe that the great mass of investors are going to be satisfied with just receiving average returns. The name of the game is to be the best," he said.[19] Bogle later recounted with relish how another competitor put out a flyer asking rhetorically, "Who wants to be operated on by an average surgeon, be advised by an average lawyer, be an average registered representative, or do anything no better or worse than average?"[20] Riepe's retort was always to ask whether they would be happy shooting "just par" in golf.

THE FIRST INDEX INVESTMENT TRUST was a symbolically and strategically important milestone for Vanguard—the first time it managed money independently of Wellington—but financially it was a dud. Performance-wise, FIIT did its job of matching the S&P 500, but it continued to prove a tough sell for ordinary investors. By the end of 1976, it had managed to gather only $14 million of assets, and growth was slower than treacle. Selling a passive fund to everyday investors still mostly keen on fund manager gunslingers who promised to shoot the lights out was clearly going to be a herculean task.

One prominent fan was Burton Malkiel, the Princeton economist who had first popularized some of the academic investment theories through his book *A Random Walk Down Wall Street*. He left President Gerald Ford's Council of Economic Advisers in 1977 when Jimmy Carter took over the White House, and promptly joined Vanguard's board. He often joked with Bogle that the two of them must have been the only investors in FIIT. It didn't cross the $100 million mark until the end of 1981—and that was only after merging it with another $58 million fund.[21] Bogle would often describe his index fund as "an artistic, if not commercial, success."[22]

In the subsequent years, Vanguard depended far more on the success of a money market fund introduced in 1975. Money market funds invest in short-term, high-quality debt, such as US Treasury bills or commercial paper issued by the likes of IBM or General Electric, typically maturing in less than nine months. Their popularity soared as the Federal Reserve jacked up interest rates in the 1970s to finally stamp out the inflation that had plagued the US economy for decades. This helped counteract the seeping outflows from struggling equity mutual funds. By the end of 1981, Vanguard's money market funds—managed by Wellington—managed $1.4 billion, roughly 40 percent of the company's overall assets. That was a lifesaver after its years of turmoil.[23]

But FIIT did help Bogle seize back another "third of the loaf" of investment management from Wellington. Distribution—essentially the marketing and sales of mutual funds—is less glamorous than the front line of investment management, but it is vital to an investment company's health. As long as Wellington Management Company controlled distribution, Vanguard would be utterly beholden to it, and unable to seize back investment management—where the money is actually made.

One of the challenges that Vanguard's new index had confronted was the reluctance of many investors to pay an initial sales fee to buy the passive fund, on top of the ongoing management fee. So-called loads—up-front charges paid by an investor to an intermediary broker—were common at the time, often amounting to 8 percent up front of the sum invested. Paying one is more palatable if you can at least hope that the fund manager can claw that back through their expertise. Most of the money went to the broker doing the selling, with some passed on to the management company to help pay for the cost of distribution. While FIIT might charge only a modest 0.3 percent a year, anyone wanting to buy it would still have to pay a load of about 6 percent to a broker.

In the 1960s, when the stock market was buoyant and returns were healthy, most investors were happy to pay the load. But in the tougher 1970s, the tide began to shift. Some mutual fund groups had started to convert to no-load, and Bogle believed that this was a long-term trend that Vanguard had to jump on. It suited Vanguard's low-cost structure, and would force Wellington to defend its underperforming distribution. Bogle also wanted to attract some institutional investors to its index fund, and they were typically loath to pay any load fees.

Immediately after the launch of Vanguard's index fund, Bogle in a letter to directors therefore proposed that the Wellington funds terminate the distribution agreement with Wellington Management Company and go no-load, in effect scrapping the distribution system that had supported it since 1929 and begin marketing directly to investors. He argued—again somewhat disingenuously—that this didn't breach Vanguard's mandate, as it wasn't strictly speaking doing any distribution, only eliminating it.[24]

Bogle's old nemeses Doran and Thorndike were still on the board, and vociferously fought the proposal. But in light of four years of investor outflows and no light on the horizon, their arguments foundered. After yet another tense, combative evening board meeting in New York on February 8, 1977, the board voted 7–4 to go no-load.[25] Bogle was thrilled, but the brokerages that Wellington had built a relationship with and depended on to distribute its funds for nearly half a century were incensed. The salvation for Vanguard proved to be Neff's Windsor Fund, which was doing so well that many brokers were reluctant to recommend that clients ditch it. By 1979, Windsor's size had even outstripped Wellington, the flagship fund once managed by the company's founder Morgan.*

Vanguard took another momentous step toward independence in September 1977, setting up a fund that would invest in US municipal bonds. It was that year, for the first time, that mutual funds were allowed to pass through to their investors the tax-free income provided by municipal bonds. In addition to being no-load, the Warwick Municipal Bond Fund would be managed by Citibank—the first time any of the funds in the Vanguard/Wellington fund complex had been handled by a third party. "That decision was significant, because it set in motion the possibility that Vanguard would be restructuring itself and making its own decisions," according to Phil Fina, one of Vanguard's attorney's at the time.[26] Indeed, Bogle's next gambit was to seize the final, third piece of the loaf of investment management.

In 1980, the Vanguard board was discussing stripping Citi of its mandate to manage Warwick due to its poor performance. Pouncing on the opportunity, Bogle proposed that Vanguard set up its own internal fixed-income group that would manage both the municipal bond funds and also the money market funds managed by

---

* Going no-load ended up taking longer and being more complex than Bogle had envisaged, though. Vanguard needed SEC approval to use fund assets to pay for distribution directly, rather than indirectly through management fees paid to Wellington Management Company. To Bogle's incandescent fury, a judge initially nixed his proposal, but eventually he won through. Although unintentionally, this had far-reaching consequences for the industry. Eventually the SEC let all mutual funds charge distribution fees of investors. To a large extent those asset-based fees have now substantially reduced or replaced front-end loads, which used to dominate the industry.

Wellington Management Company. After all, Vanguard's at-cost business model made it perfect for the task of managing lower-returning, steadier income funds like that at a much lower cost to investors, he reasoned.[27] By this time, Doran and Thorndike had both left the board, and in September 1980 the directors almost unanimously blessed the proposal.*

Finally, Vanguard was no longer a mere clerical outfit, a symbolic sop by a sympathetic board to an ousted chief executive, but a full-service investment company in its own right. It was ready for Bogle to take on the world and start exorcising some of the ghosts of 1974.

Beyond transforming a painful memory of abject personal failure into a humorous genesis story retold countless times with relish by Bogle, Vanguard would go on to help millions of people secure more comfortable retirements—and become one of the most disruptive forces in the annals of the investment industry.

---

* Bogle and Riepe then hired Ian MacKinnon, a promising bond fund manager at Girard Bank in Philadelphia, who quickly built up what would become an enviably successful fixed-income group at Vanguard.

Chapter 8

VANGUARD RISING

IN AUGUST 1979, *BUSINESSWEEK* PUBLISHED one of the journalism industry's hall-of-fame covers, declaring "The Death of Equities" in arguing that "inflation is destroying the stock market." However, led by Fed chairman Paul Volcker, the US central bank was finally getting on top of the problem. After a brief but painful recession in the early 1980s, both the bond and stock markets embarked on what would prove to be one of the biggest bull runs in financial history.

Coupled with the birth of the 401(k) retirement plan—which sprung almost accidentally from the 1978 Revenue Act, and encouraged Americans to save for their own pension through stock funds—this buoyed virtually every investment company. But few more so than Vanguard. In September 1980, Vanguard reached $3 billion of assets under management, an occasion Bogle celebrated by throwing a champagne party for all three hundred Vanguard employees and clambering onto a table to give a speech to the assembled crew members.[1] This ritual continued for each billion-dollar milestone, and quickly turned into $10 billion celebrations. The company jumped into the 401(k) business in 1983, and by the end of the decade it managed over $47 billion.

Positioning Vanguard as a low-cost provider in a high-cost industry proved astute, with the growth of 401(k) plans powering its rise. Moreover, the faster it grew, the more it could cut costs. Vanguard's unique structure meant profits were returned to shareholders in the form of lower fees. In 1982, the average expense ratio of its then twenty-one funds—the all-in cost of its funds, weighted by their size—was a mere 0.6 percent. By 2000, that had fallen to 0.27 percent for nearly a hundred funds.[2] Over the same time, the average costs of mutual funds actually increased.

Bogle's distaste for swish advertising campaigns was more than negated by his relentless, skillful courting of the press. The onetime *Philadelphia Bulletin* night reporter knew what journalists wanted—controversial, quippy, and comprehensible quotes—and proved a wizard at producing them. If someone in the media wanted an acerbic take from an industry insider, they knew exactly where to go. He was approachable in an industry where public relations often meant a bland statement or guarded conversations with journalists, and no one else could spin a tale like he could.

Over the years countless journalists got to know Bogle's booming baritone—even colleagues would occasionally jokingly call it "the voice of God"—through long interviews and phone calls. He gradually became known as Saint Jack, the titanic, self-ordained moral voice of the asset management industry. Initially it was a moniker used by critics riled by his moralizing tone, but his growing number of fans co-opted it as the best way to describe Vanguard's founder.

As a result, Vanguard naturally started getting glowing press for its low costs and transparency. "Bogle's relationship with the press, being the first to be called on a lot of subjects, is a tremendous asset,"

Jack Brennan, Bogle's protégé and eventual successor as CEO, later said.[3] "It's worth millions of marketing dollars every year to us."

He could be prickly at times, however. When Daniel Wiener, a former journalist who had in 1991 started a newsletter called *The Vanguard Adviser*, estimated Bogle's salary at about $2.6 million for the year—well below the industry average even at the time—it caused the founder to go ballistic. Vanguard subsequently sued Wiener's company for using its name.[4] Bogle had carefully cultivated a David-versus-Goliath image in his press battle against the bigger, rapacious money managers, but Vanguard launching a lawsuit against a tiny independent business—which actually helped steer customers to the money manager—made David seem like a bully himself.

The lawsuit was eventually settled when Wiener changed the name to *The Independent Adviser for Vanguard Investors*. Nonetheless, it left "a few smudges on the white knight's armor," an otherwise laudatory *Philadelphia* magazine profile noted at the time. "Holding yourself up as a model of purity and integrity is all well and good, but if you ever seem to be involved in anything that looks bad, it looks really bad," the writer noted.[5] Bogle later admitted that Wiener's estimate was accurate. In fact, in retirement he would reverse himself completely and urge his former company to be more forthright on how its senior executives are paid.

Yet the smudges disappeared fast, and the growth enjoyed by Vanguard was remarkable. At the end of 1980, Bogle's ship accounted for less than 5 percent of the US mutual fund industry. By the turn of the millennium, its assets under management had crossed $562 billion, and made up more than a tenth of the rapidly expanding US mutual fund market.[6] Most of its funds grew by leaps and bounds, but it was an initially maligned product that really started supercharging Vanguard's expansion in the 1982–2000 bull run.

After languishing, the First Index Investment Trust—rechristened the Vanguard Index Trust in 1980, and later the Vanguard 500 Index Fund—gradually became an astonishing money-gathering machine. At the end of 1982, its assets were just $100 million, making it the 104th biggest of 263 equity-focused US mutual funds. It reached the $1 billion milestone in 1988, ranking 41st among 1,048 funds.[7]

By then, a smattering of rivals had launched similar index funds for ordinary investors, but they were either shut down or struggled for traction.[8] Investment groups that could have competed more aggressively with Vanguard—Wells Fargo Investment Advisors, State Street, and Bankers Trust, whose index strategies were all growing strongly among institutional investors like pension funds—were precluded from entering the retail arena. The Depression-era Glass-Steagall Act still banned bank-owned money managers from selling products to ordinary investors, and due to this regulatory quirk, and the reluctance of retail-oriented investment groups to cannibalize their own traditional funds, Vanguard for a long time enjoyed an unimpeded run selling index funds to ordinary investors.

As a result, the Vanguard 500 in April 2000 vaulted past Fidelity's famed Magellan Fund to become the biggest mutual fund on the planet, with $107.2 billion in assets.[9] It was largely a symbolic passing of the baton, as Magellan had been closed to new investments for a few years, but an undeniably powerful one. "The Vanguard portfolio's ascendancy reflects a gigantic shift in investment strategy by millions of Americans," the *Wall Street Journal* noted at the time.[10] "By putting so many stock pickers to shame, Vanguard 500 helped spawn dozens of index funds—and many more are on the way—tracking nearly everything."

Finally, ordinary savers were following in the footsteps of pension funds and directly benefiting from the cheapness—and better average performance—of index funds. The billions of dollars that had historically flowed into the pockets of Wall Street's well-heeled denizens were finally staying a little more in the bank accounts of people saving up for their kids' college accounts or their retirement pots. Samuelson would later rank the birth of the Vanguard 500 fund alongside the invention of the wheel, alphabet, Gutenberg printing press, wine, and cheese.[11] Yet even the mighty Vanguard 500 fund would eventually be toppled by another member of Vanguard's fleet.

▲

EARLY IN 1992, BOGLE WALKED into the office of George Sauter, who ran the company's equity funds, and said, "Gus, let's stop messing around, and let's do a total stock market fund." To some pedants, this was the day *real* index investing began.

Sauter was steeped in the financial theory of Markowitz, Sharpe, and Fama, having earned an MBA at the University of Chicago. After dabbling in various business ventures—including buying a small gold mine—he ended up at Vanguard in 1987. It proved the proverbial baptism by fire. Just two weeks later, the US stock market suffered its biggest one-day collapse in history, a crash that quickly became known as Black Monday. Yet Sauter proved an inspired, timely hire.

At the time of his arrival, Vanguard had only two index funds, the Vanguard 500 and a bond fund started the previous year, which combined still managed just $1.2 billion.[12] While Vanguard's funds were much cheaper than its rivals, thanks to its at-cost structure, word simply spread slowly. The internet was still in its infancy, Vanguard refused to do much marketing, and there were few brokers clamoring to push their funds, given the lack of sales fees. Even Bogle was still primarily focused on building up Vanguard's raft of actively managed funds. The biggest win was Brennan's success in courting PRIMECAP, an investment group set up by three fund manager stars who split from Capital Group in 1983.

But Sauter set about writing new trading programs in his spare time that reduced trading costs and improved how well the index funds tracked their benchmarks. When index funds finally started to grow dramatically in the early 1990s—accounting for over a tenth of Vanguard's assets by 1991[13]—Bogle refocused on Vanguard's maiden strategy.

Jeremy Duffield, who oversaw the Vanguard 500 fund until Sauter joined, said that in the early years Bogle was "a fan of indexing, but he wasn't a raving fan." It was only by the late 1980s–early 1990s that he began his relentless crusade on behalf of indexing. "He then realized he had something. And then set himself up to build it up," Duffield says. Vanguard had launched an "Extended Market Index Fund" at the end of 1987, which invested in mid-sized companies too small to qualify for the S&P 500, but in 1992 Bogle decided that they should construct one big fund that invested in the entire US stock market.

Although the S&P 500 accounts for the vast majority of the US stock market by size, it is still only a collection of the 500 or so biggest US companies, as chosen by the index committee of Standard & Poor's. According to the financial theory, an index fund should really try to encompass everything. The S&P 500 was just a convenient, practical shorthand for the early pioneers that morphed into the de facto definition of the stock market.

In 1992, Vanguard decided to capitalize on the improving trading conditions for smaller stocks to launch the Vanguard Total Stock Market Index Fund. "In my mind, that was the first index mutual fund," Sauter says. "If you're a purist on indexing, true mutual fund indexing started in 1992."

After another slow start, it became a smash hit. In October 2013, it vaulted past the Pimco Total Return Fund managed by "bond king" Bill Gross to become the biggest in the world. Today the Vanguard Total Stock Market Index Fund manages over $1 trillion.

Even alone it would rank as one of the biggest asset managers in the world, and that sum is more than the annual economic output of Saudi Arabia or Switzerland. Coupled with a slew of other fund launches and the rising popularity of passive investing in the 1990s, index funds accounted for nearly half of Vanguard's overall assets by 2000.[14] Today, that figure is about three-quarters.

The 1980s and 1990s were not without their challenges, as Vanguard's relentless growth stressed every sinew of the company. Despite priding himself on knowing every aspect of the investment industry, Bogle's strengths were not in details, organization, and process. His determination to keep costs low also meant that Vanguard long underinvested in technology, which often caused immense challenges. "We had incredible growing pains along the way," says Duffield. "We had some times in the mid-1980s where we nearly hit the wall on volumes."

Jim Norris, who joined Vanguard as a fund accountant at the end of 1987 and later became Bogle's assistant, recalls that the Black Monday crash in particular revealed the company's weaknesses. "We answered the bell, but barely. It really uncovered a lot of operational sloppiness." But thanks largely to the efforts of Brennan, Bogle's right-hand man and de facto chief operating officer, Vanguard gradually established a better organizational structure and a more modern technological backbone, which helped prepare it for the growth to come.

Bogle's ego—which even he would occasionally joke, with a dose of self-awareness, was considerable—grew in tandem with Vanguard's success. When all six top executives voted to let local contractors handle a major IT overhaul in the early 1990s, Bogle overruled them and gave the contract to McKinsey.[15] His mounting confidence was physically manifested at Vanguard's growing new campus in Malvern, where it moved in 1993 after the office park in Valley Forge proved too small to accommodate the swelling crew.

Soon after the new Malvern headquarters was opened, Bogle commissioned Maritza Morgan, an artist whose work he admired, to create a 25-by-5-foot, five-panel vividly painted mural of the Battle of the Nile, carved out of wood. Cheekily, Bogle asked that the name of the French ship *La Spartiate* being bombarded by HMS *Vanguard* in the central panel be changed to *La Fidelité*, a none-too-subtle barb at the Boston investment group whose patriarch had been so dismissive of Vanguard's first index fund.

Nothing seemed able to push Vanguard and its imperious captain off course. Every May, Bogle would take his senior "crew" to a management retreat. In 1993, they went to the Skytop Lodge in the scenic Pocono Mountains—a fifty-five-hundred-acre idyllic golf course resort coincidentally established in 1928, the same year as Wellington. Vanguard had just crossed the $100 billion of assets under management mark, and at the getaway, Bogle confidently predicted that Vanguard's heft would likely cross the $1 trillion mark by the mid-noughties, given the "tyranny of compounding." He was right, but Vanguard would get there under a different captain.

▲

COPYING HIS MENTOR MORGAN, Bogle always had a young assistant, typically a man in his midtwenties, sometimes with little business experience but a solid academic pedigree, whom he could mold in his own image. He demanded loyalty and a prodigious work ethic, but also independence of mind and integrity—sycophants need not apply.

His former assistants joke that one would measure service under Bogle in dog years, and liberally share anecdotes of his outrageous demands and acerbic comments about part-time workers if they came in much later than 7 a.m. But even Norris—who had one of the longest stints of anyone, with seven years under the lash—

says he would work all seven all over again. "He was incredibly demanding, but I learned so much," says Norris, who led Vanguard's international operations until retiring in 2020. "You were always sparring. But it's actually what we enjoyed." Bogle genuinely loved talking to everyone, from Vanguard's security guards and cafeteria staff to the board members and pension fund executives, and his bonhomie engendered ferocious loyalty.

Every Christmas, Bogle would host a lunch and in later years a dinner for his former assistants. It was a boisterous annual tradition for the people who had served under his command—many of whom had gone on to senior positions at Vanguard and elsewhere in the investment industry. The goal was always to ensure that the booze bill outstripped the food bill. At one point, Bogle would give a toast, and always included the line "You are all a tribute to my good judgment." The past assistants would humorously say "Hear hear!" and continue drinking, racking up a hefty bill for Bogle, normally a notorious cheapskate and self-styled Scotsman. (Professor Malkiel, the Vanguard board member, jokes that Bogle's favorite drink was an $8 bottle of cabernet sauvignon.)

There was plenty of verbal sparring at the dinners as well, especially between Bogle and Riepe, who had left Vanguard for a top position at rival T.Rowe Price in 1982, and Duncan McFarland, who rose to be the chief executive of the Boston-based Wellington Management Company, the onetime enemy. But everyone delighted in pricking their mentor's towering ego a little. At one dinner, Riepe and Twardowski presented him with a clerical collar, telling Bogle that as long as he was going to preach like a self-righteous evangelical, he ought to wear the appropriate costume. "He greeted it with mixed emotions," Riepe recalls. But the assistants loved it.

At another dinner, Norris presented a list of famous "Bogleisms," such as Bogle's tendency to dip his head and wave his hand in a salute when passing someone in a corridor, and his catchphrase, "The hell you say!" He also distributed a list of handy Bogleism translations:

Whenever Jack Says:	*What He Means Is:*
"I know it's not your fault."	*"It's your fault."*
"You decide."	*"Do what I would do."*
"I'm sure it's my own fault."	*"Well it sure isn't my fault."*
"I need it by 3:00."	*"I need it by 1:00."*
"Something doesn't look right here."	*"You screwed the whole thing up."*
"Don't spend too much time on it."	*"Stay as late as you need, make sure it's right."*
"Pick me up around 7:00ish."	*"Pick me up at 7:00 and not one second later."*

For the most part, it was good-natured joshing, fueled by wine, affection for Bogle, and the competitive nature of all the men involved. Yet with Brennan, Bogle's anointed heir, the tension later became palpable. And in the later years, Brennan stopped coming, after a rupture almost as dramatic and traumatic for Vanguard as Bogle's ousting from Wellington had been.

Brennan was one of Bogle's brightest protégés, and arguably enjoys a claim to Vanguard's success almost as great as his mentor's. The reserved, patrician Bostonian joined Vanguard as Bogle's assistant in 1982, after a degree in economics from Dartmouth, brief stints at the New York Bank for Savings and S.C. Johnson & Son, and an MBA from Harvard. Brennan came from a well-off family—his father, Frank, was the president of Boston's Union Warren Savings Bank, and a pillar of the city's financial and Irish Catholic establishments—but valued hard work just as much as Bogle. Frank Brennan's parents had been impoverished immigrants from

County Kerry, Ireland, and had toiled away as janitors to put their son through college.[16] Frank Brennan, a Bronze Star World War II tank commander, expected his children to work hard as well, and refused to give them any juicy internships at his bank. Jack Brennan therefore spent his summers mowing the grass of medians on the Massachusetts Turnpike.[17]

A herculean work ethic was the defining characteristic that Bogle demanded of his protégés, and Brennan and Bogle became inseparable, a closeness deepened through frequent squash games[18] and daily lunches in the Vanguard cafeteria.[19] As Brennan moved up the ranks of Vanguard, his organizational savvy and management skills complemented his mentor's more grandiose, visionary approach to running the company. "I don't think it is appreciated about Jack Brennan just how good he was as an executive," says Duffield. This was essential in the breakneck expansion that started in the 1980s, when Brennan forged order out of the near-chaos that sometimes reigned. By 1989, he was named Vanguard's president, and Bogle's heir apparent.

Their styles were radically different. Bogle was gregarious and adored the spotlight, while the taciturn Brennan shunned it. Where Bogle almost took pride in the shabbiness of his clothes, often coming to work in frayed shirts and ill-fitting suits, Brennan always looked immaculately turned out. Even when he worked on Saturdays he would turn up in pressed khakis and a dress shirt. Bogle enjoyed squash and tennis, but only recreationally, while Brennan was the complete athlete, playing rugby and hockey and running marathons.

Yet they both valued grit and complemented each other well. Bogle was the innovative visionary and motivator, who would rally the company through stirring speeches at town hall meetings and company picnics, while Brennan was the implementation man who ensured that Bogle's ideas were actually executed. Their competitive natures powered both men, as Bogle once confided to his brother Bud: "I used to get to work at 7:30 but then Brennan came to work at 7. So I started coming to work at 7. And then Brennan started to get there at 6:30, so I started being there at 6:30."[20]

In many respects, Brennan's rapid career trajectory and relationship with Bogle resembled the one that Bogle had enjoyed with Morgan at Wellington. "He quickly earned a reputation as a tough manager," Bogle wrote in his last book, published shortly before he passed away in January 2019. "Of all the people I've ever worked with, no one possessed Brennan's ability to get what he wanted."[21]

However, his carefully chosen words—which might as well have been written about himself—obscured an extraordinary fallout, a schism between mentor and protégé that reverberated through Vanguard for years and gnawed at Bogle until the day he died. Duffield, another former Bogle assistant who admired both men greatly, compared it to a Greek tragedy.

THE BEGINNING OF THE SCHISM can be traced to 1995, when Bogle's long-struggling heart began to give up. His health went downhill at an alarming rate, unnerving his colleagues. By the end, he couldn't cross a room without getting winded. Brennan, who had been named Bogle's successor in May, had to pick up more of the work, and was in practice running all of Vanguard ahead of his formal ascension to the chief executive job in January 1996. Eventually, Bogle had to be hospitalized in Philadelphia's Hahnemann Hospital in October 1995, and put on the heart transplant list. There he gradually wasted away on an IV for 128 days before, on February 21, 1996, receiving the donated heart of a thirty-year-old.[22]

Brennan was devoted to his mentor, visiting Bogle almost every day at the hospital and bringing work to keep him stimulated. While the transplant had been successful beyond belief, Bogle finally accepted reality, and on his return stepped back to be Vanguard's chairman. The list of companies where the founder is unable to relinquish the reins, or picks unsuitable successors, is as long as a bad year. Yet for a brief moment it looked like Bogle had managed a succession with as much aplomb as he had the founding of Vanguard. In a press release, he lauded Brennan as "the best person I could possibly have found . . . a man of extraordinary character, intelligence, diligence, and judgment."[23]

But then Bogle's relentless nature flared up again. After a period of recuperation, he returned to Vanguard's headquarters raring to go. He was the chairman, but acted like he was still the chief executive, barking orders at crew members despite Brennan by then having in practice managed the company by himself for several years. "Jack was born again, and basically came back to Vanguard and says, 'I'm back. I want to run the place again.' And, needless to say, both Jack Brennan and the board thought that was not a good idea," says Malkiel.

The board's concern was partly lingering fears over Bogle's age and health, but mostly the fact that Vanguard had by then become a big company and needed a different kind of CEO at the helm. "Brennan could never have been the founder, the innovator of index funds," Malkiel observes. "But Jack was not the person who could run a big institution."

Bogle, on the other hand, seemed to see Brennan's refusal to step back down as CEO, and the board's backing of his onetime protégé, as an insult. The result was an increasingly antagonistic series of clashes between the two men—with eerie echoes of how the headstrong Bogle had clashed with the more consensual leadership style of Thorndike and Doran decades earlier. This time it was compounded by the initial closeness of the two men, which seemed to make the schism particularly painful for both. Malkiel reckons that the big break came when Bogle indicated to a journalist that he regretted making Brennan CEO. For Brennan, who had studiously only sung Bogle's praises publicly and internally, it was devastating. "Brennan was just fundamentally hurt," Malkiel says.

The result was a series of boardroom clashes, over everything from Brennan's desire to invest more in technology to dabbling in some internet advertising. Ultimately, they even refused to speak to one another. Having a chairman and CEO at loggerheads to this degree was untenable, so the board made Brennan chairman in 1998 and appointed Bogle "senior chairman"—a move that he saw as another slap in the face. When asked about his relationship with his onetime protégé around then, Bogle simply answered, "That's an essay question," and declined to say anything else[24]—possibly the only time he ever held his tongue.

A rupture was looming. In early 1999, Bogle was approaching seventy, the mandatory retirement age for board members. He assumed that as the company's founder he would be allowed to stay, and was outraged when the board—mindful of the debilitating conflict with Brennan—decided to enforce the requirement. Even Malkiel, a friend of Bogle, agreed that it had to be done. "The board correctly decided you can't have two masters," he says.

The resulting power struggle was nasty, and spilled out into the press. While Brennan was little known externally, Bogle was the famous Saint Jack, the industry's moral voice, who was now being shoved aside by the company he founded to give investors a "fair shake." The Bogleheads—the online forum for fans of Vanguard's founders—were outraged. After the public spat, Vanguard and Bogle agreed that the founder would step down from the board, but become head of a new internal think tank, the Bogle Financial Markets Research Center.

Although this allowed him to keep playing the industry-advocate role and burnish his reputation as the investing world's conscience, it was a messy compromise that left plenty of bad blood lingering. When Bogle's brother Bud once asked about his decision to hand the reins over to Brennan back in 1996, Bogle told him, "It was the biggest mistake I ever made."[25]

The bad blood ran deep. Inspired by his discovery that former US presidents John Adams and Thomas Jefferson had later in their lives set aside a lifetime of political enmity and become fast friends, Bogle eventually made peace with his old Boston nemeses Doran and Thorndike.[26] But he never did with Brennan, telling his biographer that it would happen only "when hell freezes over." Riepe, a good friend of both men, tried several times to engineer some kind of reconciliation, especially toward the end of Bogle's life. He was unsuccessful. "It was something that was quite bitter," Riepe says.

In his later years, Bogle spent much of his time polishing the legend of Jack Bogle, in fact so much so that some friends felt he was writing others out of the picture. At one point, Jim Norris told Bogle that he should relax and enjoy his legacy, rather than spend every moment burnishing it. "In a hundred years from now, we'll only be talking about a handful of people from this era. They'll talk about Warren Buffett, and they'll be talking about you," he said. "You're not going to get written out of the history books. No one's going to rewrite history. But on the other hand, no one's going to write a history that isn't real." Malkiel had a similar conversation with his old friend during one of their regular breakfasts at the Nassau Inn in Princeton, when Bogle made a startling admission: "I'm really worried that people are going to forget about me," he quietly confided to Malkiel.

He needn't have worried. Bogle's fame became greater than that of almost anyone else in finance. Shortly before he passed away, the *Gawker* writer Hamilton Nolan wrote a strongly worded tribute to Vanguard's founder on the occasion of the fortieth birthday of the

Vanguard 500 Index Fund. "Che Guevara looks good in a beret, and Eldridge Cleaver had his moments, but today let us all take a moment to honor Real Motherfucking Hero of the People: John motherfucking Bogle, who has kept hundreds of billions of dollars out of the pockets of Wall Street greedheads," Nolan wrote.

Although he was taken aback by the language, the tribute still thrilled Bogle. In one of his last interviews before passing away in January 2019, he looked back at his life and had no regrets—including not having made much money from his baby. "What do I need a private jet for? I need my wife to drive me around. It doesn't do my psyche any good to know that I have more than someone else," he said.[27] "I'm very comfortable with what I've done for the world."

There are those who think the foibles of great people should be ignored, that highlighting their weaknesses is mean-spirited when stacked up against their achievements. But flaws don't detract from their greatness—they enhance it, by making them real, convoluted people. The characteristics that made Bogle such a titanic figure in the history of finance—his ferocious, all-consuming, thermonuclear drive, his towering ego and refusal to listen to naysayers—were the same ones that ultimately caused such a messy, acrimonious end to his captainship of Vanguard. To many of his friends, the tragedy was that Bogle didn't realize that by handing the reins over to Brennan and others who followed him, he actually ensured that his beloved ship would continue to thrive. And he was freed up to enjoy a hugely influential post-Vanguard career as the industry's moral voice—even if he occasionally directed his ire at the company he founded.

At Bogle's funeral at Bryn Mawr Presbyterian Church on January 21, 2019, Duffield read a poem, based on "In Flanders Fields" by John McCrae, he had composed for the occasion. It was a fitting epitaph to a zealous convert who arguably did more to popularize index investing than anyone else, and a promise from the remaining crew members to continue his legacy:

> *On Vanguard's seas, the waves still flow*
> *With foaming crests, row by row*
> *That cover his resting place; and in the sky*
> *The gulls, still bravely singing, fly*
> *Scarce heard amid the guns below*
> *Take up my quarrel with our foe*
> *To you from failing hands I throw*
> *The torch; be yours to hold it high*
> *If ye break faith with those who die*
> *I shall not sleep, though winds still blow*
> *O'er Vanguard's seas.*

Chapter 9

NEW DIMENSIONS

DAVE BUTLER WAS MISERABLE. He had fulfilled his ambition to make it to Wall Street in 1991, working for the mighty Merrill Lynch. But unlike many other strutting young bulls who enter finance and grow to love its combination of hard work and hefty rewards, he felt increasingly unhappy and restless. He longed to return to California, and even toyed with leaving finance altogether to become a high school basketball coach.

The lanky Butler, clocking in at over six foot six, had been a professional basketball player before entering the financial industry. After making his name as a skillful forward for the University of California's Golden Bears in the early 1980s, he was a fifth-round NBA draft pick by the Boston Celtics in 1987. However, he never got to play with Larry Bird.

An NBA strike that summer spurred Butler to practice with a team in Turkey, which promptly offered him a contract far more lucrative than the rookie deal extended by the NBA. Since he had no clue when the US game would restart, Butler thought a year in the Turkish league would toughen him up (and make him a decent wedge of money in the process). Unfortunately, halfway through the Turkish season he tore his calf, killing his chances of making it in the NBA. He played one more year in Japan, and then returned to Berkeley to finish an MBA. In 1991, he joined Merrill Lynch as a salesman in New York. The journey from NBA prospect to Wall Street might seem quixotic, but Butler had always had a good head for numbers, and had long found finance fascinating. To him it felt like a natural leap.

However, the mundane, grimier reality of Wall Street was a massive comedown. Butler's work mostly consisted of calling up banks and seeing if they had any dud debts they wanted to sell on. It gradually started becoming clear that he—and many of his colleagues— didn't really know what they were doing, nor did they care. It was all about drumming up fee-generating activity, regardless of what actually made sense for clients.

At the same time, Butler discovered just how terrible even industry insiders often are at dabbling in markets. He started placing his own stock market punts using a fancy system touted by *Investor's Business Daily* called CANSLIM, after the acronyms of factors used to sift through promising stocks. Butler's first eight picks were winners, but the ninth was awful. On the advice of his broker, he sank his previous winnings into Boston Chicken, and promptly lost all the money he had made. His colleagues seemed to do just as badly.

Despondent and increasingly frustrated with work, he decided to return home to California—whether in finance or not. Wall Street just wasn't for him. But one day he was at his desk scanning job advertisements in the *Wall Street Journal*, and spotted an ad for an unnamed "money manager" based in Santa Monica. Curious, he called up, but discovered little other than that the firm was called Dimensional Fund Advisors and managed less than $10 billion— respectable but still a minnow in the world of big asset managers.

He sent over his résumé, but remained unconvinced. Over the Christmas break of 1994, he swung by DFA's waterfront headquarters on 1299 Ocean Avenue to meet with Dan Wheeler, one of the firm's senior executives, but mostly because it was only an hour away from his folks and he needed to get his dry cleaning done anyway.

As he stepped out of the elevator into the building's eleventh-floor lobby, he ran into DFA's gruff but friendly founder, David Booth, the onetime Gene Fama protégé and former Wells Fargo Management Sciences gofer. Standing next to him was none other than Merton Miller, the Nobel laureate University of Chicago economist, who happened to also be a board member of the company. Booth had to run to an appointment, so Wheeler asked if Miller would join him and Butler for lunch. Miller was happy to oblige, and the three of them departed for the nearby Ocean Avenue Seafood.

At lunch, Miller dazzled the starstruck Butler with tales of efficient markets, the benefits of diversification, and the importance of low costs. It was an "Aha!" moment for the disillusioned young salesman, with Miller expertly pulling together a lot of different strands of Butler's experiences on Wall Street and suddenly making sense of them. That evening, Butler went home to his parents, pulled out his old economics textbooks from Berkeley, and spent the night rereading them. He resolved to accept any job offer that DFA might make. He joined the very next week, in January 1995, convinced that this was a very special company.

Indeed, DFA was on its way to becoming a quirky giant of the index investing revolution—even boasting actor and former California governor Arnold Schwarzenegger as an investor. Although not as well known or as big as Vanguard, the company had played a major role in spreading the indexing gospel—through a cultlike band of fanatical financial advisors schooled in the doctrine of efficient markets at DFA "boot camps"—and helping nurture its next evolutionary stage.

Nonetheless, like Wells Fargo and Vanguard before it, DFA initially also suffered a bumpy ride, rattled by herculean business challenges and corporate infighting that nearly threatened to tear it apart.

▲

DAVID GILBERT BOOTH WAS BORN on December 2, 1946, and grew up in Garnett, a tiny rural town of just three thousand people outside Kansas City. His parents, Gilbert and Betty Booth, later moved the family to the nearby town of Lawrence to ensure that their children could go to a good school. Lawrence was practically a big-city experience for the Booths after Garnett, despite boasting a population only narrowly over thirty thousand people at the time. The University of Kansas was there, and the local hotel was five stories high—the tallest building the young Booth had ever seen. It even had a pizzeria.

Booth excelled at school, especially math, played basketball despite his small frame, and worked as an usher selling popcorn at the local Memorial Stadium to make some money. Eventually he went to Kansas University to study economics. The Vietnam War was raging, and his university days were largely shaped by finding ways to avoid the draft, such as taking a master's.

He initially planned to take a PhD and teach at the school, but one of his professors—a University of Chicago alumnus—introduced him to the theories of Gene Fama and urged him to go there instead. Assuming that he would still eventually be called up anyway, Booth thought he might as well apply, on the grounds that the military had to put you back in the same position you were in before the draft.

On induction day, Booth tried to extricate himself on the grounds of virulent allergies. He was duly laughed off and assigned to the Army. But later that day, he by chance ran into the chief medical officer who had done the physical examination. Curious, the officer asked the young Kansan what he might have done if he had been rejected. Booth replied that he had been planning to take a PhD at the University of Chicago. "Let me see your file one more time," the medical officer said. He then scribbled out his previous comment and rejected Booth for active service. Booth soon packed his Valiant convertible[1] and headed to Chicago instead. "If it hadn't been for the draft, I probably would have just taken a job in Kansas," Booth recalls. "When I was standing there in my first year presenting a paper to Fama or [Merton] Miller, it felt good. I knew I could have been out in some swamp in Vietnam."

Booth enjoyed Chicago, especially Fama's classes. The professor would be so energetic in explaining how risks and returns were linked, and how market prices reflected the overall wisdom of thousands of investors, that he would often be drenched in sweat by the end of class. To cool down he would open a window even in the depths of the midwestern winter.[2] Sometimes the wiry Fama would join some of the students in a game of basketball, and proved more ferociously competitive than any of the young bucks playing. At Chicago, Booth also got to know another precocious student in the year below him—Rex Sinquefield. Both young students grew close to their professor and absorbed Fama's acerbic view of fund managers. "I'd compare stock pickers to astrologers. But I don't want to bad-mouth the astrologers," the professor once quipped.[3]

But Booth kept struggling with a gnawing sense that academia was not for him. He was the brightest student in Fama's class, earning a prized spot as the eminent finance professor's teaching assistant, but the attraction of a PhD and then teaching itself started to feel less appealing. A Christmas visit back to his grandparents in Kansas, who still worked the fields, hammered home how uneasy he was about a career in academia.[4]

By the second year, his anxiousness came to a boil after Milton Friedman, the big kahuna of the Chicago economics department, excoriated one of his papers. Frustrated, Booth stormed into Fama's office to announce he was leaving. "I'm outta here, I can't take it anymore," he said. After two years he had enough coursework to qualify for an MBA, but he wouldn't be completing his PhD.

Fama was disappointed, but understanding. Booth was his best student, but not everyone completes a PhD at Chicago, and his heart was clearly not in pure academic research. So the professor picked up the phone to John "Mac" McQuown at Wells Fargo—whom he had gotten to know well over the past few years, and who had always nagged Fama about sending him one of his students—and got Booth a job at his Management Sciences unit.

It proved a happy, stimulating two-year stint, despite the ongoing battles between the division and the Wells Fargo trust department and Booth primarily working on the ultimately aborted Stagecoach Fund. Aside from firmly establishing him on the practical path of business rather than academia, the experience of working on Stagecoach—which was killed by a combination of onerous regulations and tepid investor interest—taught Booth the importance of sales and actually listening to clients. It was a lesson that he would soon turn into practice.

▲

IN 1975, BOOTH LEFT WELLS FARGO to work in New York for AG Becker, a consultancy for the pension industry known for its "Green Book" tables, which compared the results of fund managers to the overall market. For an acolyte of Fama, with practical experience of the hot new subject of indexing, it was the perfect job, even though he grew increasingly cynical of the skills of traditional stock-pickers.

One day, one of the firm's clients—First National Bank of

Chicago—called up and wanted the software to run an index fund. AG Becker naturally handed the job to Booth, as the only person with at least some practical experience in the field. He had six months to complete it, and two IT people to help him. Their backgrounds were from chemical processing plants and they knew zilch about finance, but they got the job done. Thrilled, AG Becker then tasked Booth with selling their newfangled product to other investors. The first to sign up was AT&T, which was in the process of consolidating some of its Baby Bell pension plans and wanted to run an internal index fund to avoid having to pay fees for something it could probably do itself.

Booth would regularly amble over to AT&T's New York office to check up on how things were going with his client. Over time, he spotted an obvious blind spot in its mix of fund managers and financial securities—the pension plan had plenty of managers still trying to pick the best stocks in the S&P 500, as well as an internal index fund, but had no exposure to smaller stocks.

This was common among big institutional investors at the time. The stocks of smaller companies tend to be far more volatile, and trading conditions vastly trickier than for the big blue-chip members of the S&P 500. At the time, there weren't even any dedicated indices just for smaller companies. Frank Russell—a consultancy where Vanguard's Jan Twardowski went after working for Jack Bogle—launched its flagship "small capitalization" index, the Russell 2000, only in 1984. It would be years before "small caps" entered into the lexicon of finance.

But Booth thought it made sense for AT&T's pension managers to have at least some exposure to the area. Harking back to his schooling at Chicago and the theories of Markowitz, Sharpe, and Fama, he pointed out that AT&T might in the longer term generate higher returns from the greater risks they posed. At the very least, the telephone company would gain some valuable diversification by adding smaller stocks to its giant pool of IBM, General Electric, Chevron, Ford, or Boeing, he argued.

AT&T was receptive to the idea, so Booth presented it to AG Becker's executives. Larry Klotz, one of the top salesmen at the company, was intrigued. One of his clients—the chief executive of a small, listed tire company—had recently been lamenting the lack of investor interest in his stock, and mentioned that many of his peers and rivals in business suffered from the same fate. Klotz mused whether one could create an equity fund that would invest only in smaller stocks. "That would even the playing field for smaller companies," he thought. "It's the most dynamic part of the US economy, but they're being starved of capital."

After Booth's presentation, Klotz wandered over to Booth to discuss it in more detail. They reckoned there might be a business there, but Booth, mindful of the lessons of Wells Fargo's Stagecoach Fund, resolved to visit some of Klotz's pension fund clients to see if more of them might be interested. Over the summer they trekked up and down the I-75 corridor from Detroit to Cincinnati to gauge the appetite.[5] With little concrete data to point to, Booth and Klotz primarily based their pitch on how it would offer investors improved diversification—the only free lunch in finance, according to Markowitz. Talking about a "small-cap index fund" appeared to turn off pension executives, so Booth started referring to it as a "small-cap dimensional fund"—which sounded much cooler, he thought, and seemed to resonate more.

AG Becker's senior executives were less enthused, however. They had no interest in getting into the money management game. So Klotz and Booth decided to strike out on their own. But they needed money and advice. Luckily, Booth knew where to get a bit of both. He called up his old former boss McQuown, who had left Wells Fargo in 1974 and was by then consulting for various financial firms. Over the Thanksgiving weekend of 1980 at McQuown's house in Mill Valley, a scenic town in the foothills of California's Mount Tamalpais, they thrashed out the details of a new business that would sell a small-stocks index fund to pension funds.[6]

▲

SERENDIPITY THEN STRUCK. Around the same time, Booth's old Chicago compatriot Rex Sinquefield—by then running American National Bank's entire trust department and a big name in the industry, thanks to his pioneering indexing efforts and work with Professor Roger Ibbotson on *Stocks, Bonds, Bills, and Inflation*—called up Booth. The bespectacled St. Louisan was looking for someone to run his New York office, and thought Booth would be perfect. Booth revealed that he was in the process of leaving AG Becker to set up a new index fund company focused on small stocks, leading Sinquefield to come clean himself.

As it turned out, Sinquefield was feeling bored, restless, and frustrated in his job. He had just unsuccessfully pitched to American National Bank a mutual fund along the lines of what Booth was planning, and was now thinking of leaving to do it himself. Booth and Sinquefield realized that they should combine their efforts, so in June 1981, Sinquefield became a partner with Klotz and Booth in Dimensional Fund Advisors.

Given his reputation, getting Sinquefield on board was a coup. He would be the chief investment officer of the new venture, Booth its president, and Klotz head of customer relations and sales. The three founders were joined by a handful of other AG Becker salesmen, enticed by hefty commissions to make up for the lower pay, who carved up the United States into different territories.[7]

It was a good time to start a new investment firm. Interest rates were finally starting to come down, and the US stock market was about to embark on a phenomenal bull run. Pension funds, both public and private, were growing at an even quicker clip. At the end

Ted Seides, CFA
Director of Investments

protégé partners

The MoMA Office Building
25 West 53rd Street, 15th Floor
New York, NY 10019

(212) 784-6320
fax (212) 784-6349
ts@protegepartners.com

[Handwritten note at top right:] Mr. Seides — The number has to be 10 — equally weighted — + the comparator is the S+P 500, however the wager has to be substantial money with an E/c a collateral — WB

Dear Warren,

Last week, I heard about a challenge you issued at your recent Annual Meeting, and I am eager to take you up on the bet. I wholeheartedly agree with your contention that the aggregate returns to investors in hedge funds will get eaten alive by the high fees earned by managers. In fact, were Fred Schwed penning stories today, he likely would title his work "Where Are the Customers' G5s?"

However, my wager is that you are both generally correct and specifically incorrect. In fact, I am sufficiently comfortable that unusually well managed hedge fund portfolios are superior to market indexes over time that I will spot you a lead by selecting 5 fund of funds rather than 10 hedge funds. You must really be licking your chops!

To be fair, my five picks are not the ordinary fund of funds you might read about in *Barron's*. Each has been trained in the discipline of value investing with a long time horizon and has experience vastly different from the crowd of fee gatherers in the industry. You might call them "The Superinvestors of Endowmentsville."

Without diving into detail, the managers of these funds selected or helped select hedge funds at

I am flexible as to what stakes you propose. I would offer a typical "loser buys dinner at Gorat's," but I hear your going rates for a meal are higher than mine these days (though my wife and young kids might beg to differ).

Best of luck and I look forward to hearing your index selection.

Sincerely,

[signature]

Ted Seides, CFA
Director of Investments, Protégé Partners

protégé partners

When Ted Seides wrote a letter to Warren Buffett accepting his offer of a bet to pit hedge funds against an index fund, he was delighted when Berkshire Hathaway's chairman scrawled his positive response and sent it back.

The cerebral, philosophy-loving Harry Markowitz is one of the most influential economists of all time. To many admirers, his modern portfolio theory is the genesis of modern finance and underpins much of the academic groundwork behind the invention of index funds.

Harry Markowitz's protégé William Sharpe showed that the entire stock market was the optimal trade-off between risk and reward. His work earned both Sharpe and Markowitz Nobel laureates in economics, and helped pave the way for the birth of the first passive, market-tracking fund.

John "Mac" McQuown was a former farmhand and Navy engineer who entered finance with an unusual amount of drive and love for computers. The combination proved vital when he launched the inaugural index fund at Wells Fargo.

Onetime jock Gene Fama and his revolutionary efficient-markets hypothesis became synonymous with the University of Chicago and gave the intellectual cover that a bunch of finance industry heretics needed to engineer the first index funds.

Dean LeBaron, the gregarious founder of Batterymarch, was not necessarily an efficient-markets believer, but he did think an index fund was a product that would suit a lot of investors, and the idea of engineering something brand new appealed to him.

Initially, the merger of Wellington and the Boston-based firm TDP&L looked like the perfect marriage of "whiz kid" money managers with a pedigreed investment house in need of new blood—as this *Institutional Investor* cover from 1968 showed. But the marriage quickly soured.

The Bogle Boys. Vanguard's founder Jack Bogle always had a young assistant to mentor, and every year all past and present assistants would have a boozy Christmas dinner with their boss. From top left to right: Jeremy Duffield, Jim Riepe, Daniel Butler, Jan Twardowski, Duncan McFarland. From bottom left to right: Jack Brennan, Tim Buckley, Jack Bogle, Jim Norris.

When David Booth, Rex Sinquefield, and Larry Klotz teamed up to start Dimensional Fund Advisors and run the next-generation of index funds, they enlisted their mentors John McQuown and Gene Fama to sit on their board. From left to right: McQuown, Klotz, Fama, Booth, Sinquefield.

The accelerating index investing phenomenon represented a marriage of academic endeavor and the efforts of finance industry outsiders that were open to new ideas—here exemplified by John McQuown, David Booth, and Wells Fargo advisor and future Nobel laureate Myron Scholes.

Fred Grauer (left) groomed Patricia Dunn as his successor but was incensed when she appeared to undercut him in pay negotiations with Barclays, BGI's parent, and then took over the sole leadership of the company when he left. In the middle is Eric Clothier, a senior BGI executive, who fit the firm's culture of "nice, bright, and fire in the belly."

Larry Fink was a proverbial "master of the universe" bond trader at First Boston, until he was forced out after his team lost $100 million. He then founded what became BlackRock and built it into the world's biggest investment group, culminating in its audacious purchase of Barclays Global Investors, the powerhouse of passive investing.

In the early days, the investment industry mostly mocked the nascent index investing phenomenon. But once it started to gain traction, mockery turned into attacks—both vitriolic and lighthearted. This tongue-in-cheek poster produced by The Leuthold Group, an investment manager specializing in active management, adorned the offices of some of the early pioneers.

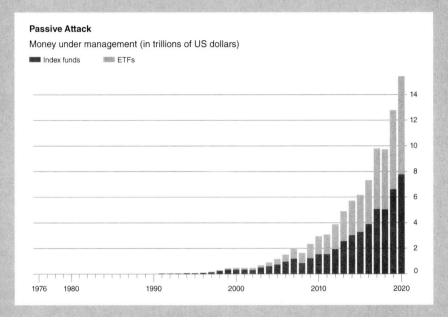

Passive Attack

Money under management (in trillions of US dollars)

■ Index funds   ▨ ETFs

Index funds may have been first invented in the early 1970s but only really started gaining in prominence in the 1990s. The last decade has seen rampant growth, with index funds—whether passive mutual funds or exchange-traded funds—gobbling up more and more of the investment industry's market share.

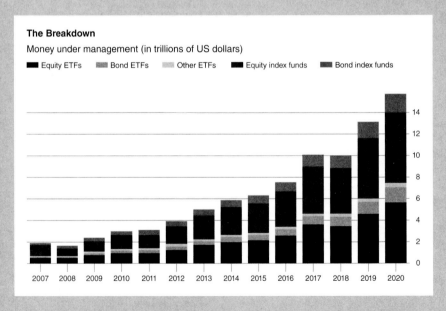

The Breakdown

Money under management (in trillions of US dollars)

■ Equity ETFs   ▨ Bond ETFs   ▨ Other ETFs   ■ Equity index funds   ▨ Bond index funds

Index funds come in many flavors, from exchange-traded notes that track the price of oil to passive money market funds. Equity index funds are by far the biggest, but bond index funds have been growing quickly in recent years and are expected to take off further in the coming decade.

of 1980, US pension plans held about $990 billion. By the end of the next decade, that had more than trebled to $3.6 trillion. When the millennium was drawing to an end, the total assets of individual retirement accounts, defined contribution plans like the 401(k), annuities, and state, municipal, and federal defined benefit plans had vaulted to nearly $12 trillion. Today, the total is north of $30 trillion.[8] The main beneficiaries were the investment firms in Boston, New York, and Los Angeles that managed the money, making it a fertile environment for aspiring financiers.

DFA still needed clients, and luckily Klotz scored some early wins. In February 1981—just two months before the still-unnamed company would open for business—he secured big commitments from State Farm, a midwestern insurance company, and the pension fund of Owens-Illinois, a big glass bottle producer.[9] This helped DFA secure an investment in the firm itself from Schroders, a big British money manager, which bought a $350,000 bond in the company that would convert into a 15 percent ownership stake after fifteen years. McQuown also invested, and personally guaranteed some loans for DFA. Sinquefield suspected that McQuown didn't know what he was signing, but McQuown insists he was well aware of the liability he was potentially taking on.

Once again, strides in the evolution of computers played a pivotal role. In August 1981, IBM launched its first-ever personal computer, initially priced at just $1,565.[10] Although puny by modern standards—an iPhone boasts about 250 times its 16K processing memory—the IBM PC quickly conquered the world. For companies like DFA, it meant that they didn't need to buy or rent time on the expensive mainframe computers that had been necessary to crunch stock market data up until then.[11] Once an oddity, computers would over the next decade start mushrooming on the trading desks of Wall Street, and help haul the financial industry into the digital era.

There was still plenty of wood to chop before DFA could launch its fund, so Booth reached out to one of the investment industry's most experienced executives for advice—Vanguard's Jack Bogle. Booth had first met him at Jim Lorie's CRSP seminars, but had gotten to know him well while covering Vanguard as a client at AG Becker. Vanguard was by then in the index fund industry itself, but Bogle kindly agreed to do all the administrative heavy lifting for DFA for a modest fee—a godsend for a small start-up.

The day-to-day back-office work involved in running a mutual fund—making sure dividends are collected, ensuring that prices are correct at the end of the day, handling stock splits, and all the necessary paperwork—can be arduous and expensive, but Vanguard naturally enjoyed abundant experience in the area. Vanguard continued to service DFA for the first three years of its existence, until it could handle the work itself.

That was not all. At the end of their meeting in Valley Forge, Bogle leaned back and advised Booth that his company would still need a good lawyer. He dug out the business card of Vanguard's own representation, handed it to Booth, and said he would telephone himself to tell the lawyer to expect Booth's call. "It turned out to be incredibly important, because no hotshot, big-time law firm wants to work with a start-up that has no track record and is operating out of my apartment," Booth says.

▲

THE NEXT STEP WAS TO assemble a board of directors. McQuown naturally signed up, but the coup was enticing Booth and Sinquefield's mentor Fama to sign on as director of research at the nascent company, in return for a small equity stake in the company. The mutual fund needed a separate board, which they rounded up largely by roaming the hallways of Chicago's business school. It ended up being a glittering array of economic superstars, such as Merton Miller, Myron Scholes, Richard Roll (one of Fama's protégés), Roger Ibbotson, and Jack Gould. Booth and Sinquefield told them they couldn't pay any compensation to begin with, but promised director fees if their new company ever made it.[12] Intrigued at the prospect of a research-led investment company, founded by two of Chicago's brightest students, that promised to translate their theories into practice, they all agreed. Their presence added some vital luster to the unknown start-up.

Another important cog fell into place soon afterward. Sinquefield's sociologist wife, Jeanne, had quickly grown sick of academia and returned to her husband's alma mater to get an MBA. A formidable woman, she then parlayed her expertise in statistics and programming—honed through long stints in the computer center at the business school—into a job at the Chicago Board of Trade, one of the oldest trading pits in the world. CBOT has since the 1930s been based in a majestic skyscraper in the heart of Chicago's financial district, and gradually emerged as a powerhouse of the financial derivatives industry that had exploded after Myron Scholes and Fischer Black published their groundbreaking model to price options—one of the most popular forms of derivatives—in 1973. At CBOT, Jeanne Sinquefield worked on designing derivatives, which is a high-octane, complex field.

Klotz and Booth quickly realized that DFA needed someone to beef up their trading systems, especially vital since smaller stocks were vastly more arduous to trade than the likes of Coca-Cola or General Motors. If they did a bad job, the fund would at best struggle to accurately mimic its underlying market, and at worst slowly bleed out through the constant churn of transaction costs. Rex Sinquefield told his colleagues he was "staying the hell out of it," but encouraged the idea, knowing how useful she could be to DFA.

Initially she spent long nights overhauling their trading system free of charge, but after a long period of incessant nagging, Jeanne Sinquefield joined DFA as its head of trading.

She played a pivotal role in its success, according to Klotz. "Jeannie was the brains behind the operations," he says. Since there was no actual index to track, DFA could be a bit more opportunistic on how and when it would trade, and Jeanne Sinquefield took full advantage of this. Later, she would be the one to interrogate all prospective traders and portfolio managers on all aspects of DFA, efficient markets, and mutual fund regulation. The multi-day oral exam was dubbed the "Jeanne Test," and those who passed had to buy everyone on the trading desk milkshakes.[13] "She was a taskmaster," says Dave Butler, today DFA's co–chief executive. "Anybody that worked with her knew that she expected perfection from everybody." Rex Sinquefield himself managed to avoid having to take the "Jeanne Test," though.

DFA's first fund was initially dubbed the 9-10 Fund, as it invested in stocks with market capitalizations in the ninth and tenth deciles of the New York Stock Exchange. This was a pool of about three hundred companies at the time, with a weighted average value of about $100 million—what would today be termed "micro caps." The most prominent examples were Smuckers, a jam producer, and crayon maker Binney & Smith. The fund would be entirely passive and try to replicate the performance of the entire universe.

In December 1981, DFA finally unveiled its maiden fund to the world. Like its index fund predecessors, it would experience a bumpy childhood. One newspaper cruelly termed it a "scrap heap fund."[14] And one of Dimensional Fund Advisors' trio of founders would be ejected in a shocking coup before it truly broke through.

Chapter 10

BIONIC BETAS

ANYONE TAKING A MIDDAY STROLL along the tree-lined, tranquil streets of Brooklyn Heights in the spring of 1981 might have heard some bizarre, otherworldly sounds emanating from the brownstone on 48 Remsen Street.

The mysterious hum came from the whirring fans of a Quotron, a refrigerator-sized machine that spat out real-time stock prices for brokers and investment managers around the world. Booth had bought a two-bedroom apartment on the top floor of the house for $75,000 in 1979. In DFA's first few months, its headquarters was Booth's spare bedroom—which meant ejecting his brother in the process. The dining room became DFA's first conference room, and the kitchen its inaugural staff canteen.

The Quotron—the financial industry's dominant workhouse until the emergence of Michael Bloomberg's eponymous data empire a few years later—was vital. But the machine was so noisy that Booth eventually had to rip out his sauna and build a soundproofed room for it. For breaks away from the "office," Booth would take midday jogs across the nearby Brooklyn Bridge that connects the borough with lower Manhattan.[1]

Things were little better in Chicago, but at least the Sinque-fields had a tiny office at 8 South Michigan Avenue, right next to Grant Park. But the first year was spent mostly on the road, with cheap flights and cheaper hotels. During one winter visit to Honey-well, the industrial conglomerate based outside Minneapolis, Sin-quefield and a colleague had to climb through a huge snowdrift to get to the hotel office of the Red Roof Inn and slip their credit card through a narrow opening in the bulletproof glass window. "You know, if we ever make any money, we are never, ever staying at a place like this again," Sinquefield told his colleague that night.*

Luckily, the US stock market rebounded in 1982, and small caps enjoyed a particularly strong year. The inaugural DFA fund re-turned nearly 29 percent, compared to the S&P 500's 14.7 percent gain. That was a boon to DFA's sales pitch, and by early 1983 its assets under management were approaching the $1 billion mark.[2] "David Booth makes it look easy . . . Business seemed to fall in his lap," the *New York Times* gushed in September that year.[3] Klotz de-scribes the atmosphere in those heady days of DFA as palpably ex-citing: "You could taste the success."

By then, DFA had a potent weapon in its sales armory. Rolf Banz, a Swiss protégé of Myron Scholes, had been using the CRSP data compiled in Chicago to calculate the average returns of smaller stocks, and found that while they were far more volatile than the

---

* The colleague, Lawrence Spieth, nearly quit at one point. Living purely on commissions was tough when sales were slow, and he had a family to support. In early 1982, Spieth had to sell one of his cars to make his mortgage payment. Later that year, with few indications that things were getting better, he walked into Sinquefield's office to quit. At that very moment, his phone rang. It was the pension fund of the Timken Company, a ball-bearings manufacturer, which told him that it would invest $10 million in DFA's fund. The commis-sion was enough to tide him over for the rest of the year, averting his resignation. (David Booth and Eduardo Repetto, "Dimensional Fund Advisors at Thirty," Dimensional Fund Advisors, 2011, 30.)

better-known blue-chip stocks, they offered far better returns in the long run. In the 1926–75 period, Banz studied, the average annual rate of return from large stocks was 8.8 percent, while smaller ones boasted an 11.6 percent rate of return.[4]

This was startling. Not only did smaller stocks offer theoretical diversification—the only free lunch in finance, as Markowitz had shown decades earlier, and DFA's main marketing pitch to pension funds—but they also did better than bigger stocks in the long run. "Giant payoffs from midget stocks," *Fortune* trumpeted in a June 1980 article that highlighted Banz's provisional findings. His PhD dissertation on the topic was formally published in the *Journal of Financial Economics* in March 1981, and showed that even adjusting for their greater volatility, small-cap stocks trounced bigger ones.[5] Sinquefield was already aware of the study, but Fama brought the thesis to the attention of Booth, who now had firm evidence that DFA's small-cap fund could give investors not only the ability to spread their eggs in more baskets, but greater long-term returns as well.[6]

This was a seminal moment, setting the stage for the development of a new approach to managing money. Mindful of marketing opportunities, DFA initially dubbed them "dimensions," but today other proponents mostly call it "smart beta" or "factor investing."

▲

THE HISTORY OF INVESTING IS ESSENTIALLY a chronicle of code-breaking. Throughout the centuries that equity markets have existed, dilettantes, theorists, and practitioners alike have conjured up stock-picking systems of varying complexity and gimmickry, all promising to unlock the riches contained by financial markets.

Many have been supposedly foolproof but zany formulae that have made no one rich but the hucksters who sold them to the gullible. But over the years there have been some approaches that have enjoyed at least a modicum of success. These range from the Dow

Theory first espoused by *Wall Street Journal* founder Charles Dow—essentially using technical indicators to try to identify and profit from different market phases—and David Butler's CANSLIM system, to the value investing school articulated by Benjamin Graham.

The earth-shattering suggestion of the research conducted in the 1960s and 1970s was that the code might actually be unbreakable, and efforts to decipher it were expensive and futile. Harry Markowitz's modern portfolio theory and William Sharpe's CAPM indicated that the market itself was the optimal balance between risks and return, while Gene Fama presented a cohesive, compelling argument for why that was: The net effect of the efforts of thousands upon thousands of investors continually trying to outsmart each other was that the stock market was efficient, and in practice hard to beat. Most investors should therefore just sit on their hands and buy the entire market.

But in the 1980s and 1990s, a new round of groundbreaking research—some of it from the same efficient-markets disciples who had rattled the investing world in the 1960s and 1970s—started revealing some fault lines in the academic edifice built up in the previous decades. Perhaps the stock market wasn't entirely efficient, and maybe there were indeed ways to beat it in the long run?

Some gremlins in the system were always known, but often glossed over. Already in the early 1970s, Black and Scholes had noted that there were some odd issues with the theory, such as how less volatile stocks actually produced better long-term returns than choppier ones. That contradicted the belief that return and risk (using volatility as a proxy for risk) were correlated. In other words, loopier roller coasters produce greater thrills. Though the theory made intuitive sense, in practice it didn't seem to hold up to rigorous scrutiny.

This is why Scholes and Black initially proposed that Wells Fargo should set up a fund that would buy lower-volatility stocks (that is, low-beta) and use leverage to bring the portfolio's overall volatility up to the broader stock market.[7] Hey, presto, a roller coaster with the same number of loops as everyone else, but with even greater thrills. Nonetheless, the efficient-markets hypothesis quickly became dogma at business schools around the United States.

The first inkling of change came in the late 1970s, from Stephen Ross, a former physicist turned economist at the University of Pennsylvania, and Barr Rosenberg, an outrageously cerebral, yoga-loving analyst who became a rock star in financial circles.

For simplicity's sake, Sharpe's original CAPM stipulated a single "market factor"—the beta—which described how much securities moved compared to the whole stock market. Its beauty was its elegant minimalism, even though it struggled to depict how markets actually worked, was relevant for only single snapshots of time, and relied on some heroic assumptions. CAPM suggested that beyond the market factor, other explanations of a stock's returns were idiosyncratic, such as company-specific issues like weak earnings, new products being launched, or a well-regarded CEO retiring.

Ross's "arbitrage pricing theory" and Rosenberg's "bionic betas" posited that the returns of any financial security are the result of several systematic factors. Although seemingly stating the obvious, this was a seminal moment in the move toward a more vibrant understanding of markets. The eclectic Rosenberg was even put on the cover of *Institutional Investor* in May 1978, the bald, mustachioed man depicted as a giant meditating guru with flowers in his hair, worshipped by a gathering of besuited portfolio managers. The headline was "Who Is Barr Rosenberg? And What the Hell Is He Talking About?"[8]

What he was talking about was how academics were beginning to classify stocks according to not just their industry or their geography, but their financial characteristics. And some of these characteristics might actually prove to deliver better long-term returns than the broader stock market.

In 1973, Sanjoy Basu, a finance professor at McMaster University in Ontario, published a paper that indicated that companies with low stock prices relative to their earnings did better than the efficient-markets hypothesis would suggest. Essentially, he showed that the value investing principles espoused by Benjamin Graham in the 1930s—which revolved around buying cheap, out-of-favor stocks trading below their intrinsic worth—was a durable investment factor. By systematically buying all cheap stocks, investors could in theory beat the broader market over time.

Then Banz showed the same for small caps, another big moment in the evolution of factor investing. Follow-up studies on smaller stocks in Japan and the UK showed similar results, so in 1986 DFA launched dedicated small-cap funds for those two markets as well. In the early 1990s, finance professors Narasimhan Jegadeesh and Sheridan Titman published a paper indicating that simply surfing market momentum—in practice buying stocks that were already bouncing and selling those that were sliding—could also produce market-beating returns.[9]

The reasons for these apparent anomalies divide academics. Efficient-markets disciples stipulate that they are the compensation investors receive for taking extra risks. Value stocks, for example, are often found in beaten-up, unpopular, and shunned companies, such as boring industrial conglomerates in the middle of the dotcom bubble. While they can underperform for long stretches, eventually their underlying worth shines through and rewards investors who kept the faith. Small stocks do well largely because small companies are more likely to fail than bigger ones.

Behavioral economists, on the other hand, argue that factors tend to be the product of our irrational human biases. For example, just like how we buy pricey lottery tickets for the infinitesimal chance of big wins, investors tend to overpay for fast-growing, glamorous stocks, and unfairly shun duller, steadier ones. Smaller stocks do well because we are illogically drawn to names we know well. The momentum factor, on the other hand, works because investors initially underreact to news but overreact in the long run, or often sell winners too quickly and hang on to bad bets for far longer than is advisable.

Whatever the reason, the existence of some persistent investment factors is today accepted by almost every (if not all) financial economist and investor. In an ingenious bit of marketing, factors are often called "smart beta." Sharpe himself grew to hate the term, as it implies that all other forms of beta are dumb.[10] Most financial academics prefer the term "risk premia," to more accurately reflect the fact that they think these factors primarily yield an investment premium from taking some kind of risk—even if they cannot always agree what the precise risk is.

An important milestone was when Fama and his frequent collaborator Ken French—another Chicago finance professor who would later also join DFA—in 1992 published a paper with the oblique title "The Cross-Section of Expected Stock Returns."[11] It was a bombshell. In what would become known as the three-factor model, Fama and French used data on companies listed on the NYSE, the American Stock Exchange, and the Nasdaq from 1963 to 1990 and showed that both value (the tendency of cheap stocks to outperform expensive ones) and size (the tendency of smaller stocks to outperform bigger ones) were distinct factors from the broader market factor—the beta.

Although Fama and French's paper termed these factors as rewards for taking extra risks, coming from the father of the efficient-markets hypothesis, it was a signal event in the history of financial economics.[12] Since then academics have identified a panoply of factors, with varying degrees of durability, strength, and acceptance.

Of course, factors do not always work. They can go through long fallow stretches where they underperform the market. Value stocks, for example, suffered a miserable bout of performance in the dotcom bubble, when investors wanted to buy only trendy technology stocks. And to DFA's chagrin, after small caps enjoyed a robust year in DFA's first year of existence, they would then undergo a long, painful seven-year period of trailing dramatically behind the S&P 500.[13]

DFA managed to keep growing, losing very few clients, partly because it had always stressed to them that stretches like this could happen. But it was an uncomfortable period that led to many awkward conversations with clients.

At one point Booth was cornered by the assistant treasurer of one big customer, who angrily grabbed his arm and snarled, "I want you to know you're the worst performing manager we have in any asset class. Do you still believe that small-cap stocks have higher expected returns?" Booth stuck to the DFA script and replied, "We believe small-cap stocks are riskier than big-cap stocks and risk and return are related. Which part of the argument are you no longer comfortable with?"[14] DFA eventually did make it through the lean years, but not without casualties.

▲

KLOTZ GREW IMMEDIATELY SUSPICIOUS WHEN both Booth and Sinquefield offered to help carry his suitcase. Although they got on well, the libertarian St. Louisan especially was not the kind of guy to carry your luggage, he thought.

When they made it up to the hotel room in Chicago, Booth wasted no time telling him, "We're taking over the company, you're out." Klotz was shocked and outraged. DFA had finally begun to turn a modest profit a year earlier, in April 1983, and he had helped bring in many of its first clients. He owned about a third of the company, and thought his agreement with the company was ironclad.

Moreover, aside from an argument with Booth over the big commissions DFA paid to its salespeople, Klotz thought their relationship was fine. Indeed, he had been more worried about Booth's desire to eject Sinquefield, which Klotz says he had discreetly expressed just months before, and had to be talked out of. That the two other founders had now suddenly ganged up on him came out of the blue, he insists.

Shocked, Klotz called his lawyer. But with the combined majority ownership of Booth, Sinquefield, and Fama, he couldn't do anything. The Chicago mob had ousted him. While Booth had wielded the knife, Klotz later saw the calculated moves of Sinquefield—a fanatical chess player—as a prime factor. "They threw me in front of a garbage truck," Klotz says. "I've had a distrust for anyone from the University of Chicago ever since."

Klotz left quietly—he didn't want to do anything to imperil the value of his stake in the company—but the result was a protracted and nasty battle. Klotz says he sued Booth for the $25,000 he says he lent him for his share in DFA's initial capital (Booth disputes this), and felt Booth and Sinquefield were trying to sabotage the sale of his shares in the company. It wasn't until 1989 that Klotz was able to find a realistic price and buyer for his stake. The DFA bylaws stipulated that the company had the right to first refusal on any shares sold by its founders, so Booth and Sinquefield eventually grudgingly matched the $8.5 million offer that Klotz had finagled.

More than two decades later, Klotz says that he has made his peace with the sudden rupture—even forgiven it. "I'm smart enough to realize that holding grudges against people that don't give a wit about you only hurts yourself and those around you," he says. But the pain and bitterness of the sudden sacking, and its long-lasting consequences—both Booth and Sinquefield are now billionaires—still clearly lingers. While the University of Chicago's business school is now named the Booth School of Business, after a record-breaking $300 million gift from the DFA founder, and Sinquefield is a political kingmaker in his native St. Louis, Klotz works as a financial advisor in Ohio.

Sinquefield declines to discuss the details of Klotz's departure. Booth remains guarded, but attributes Klotz's departure to a struggle to find the right role for him in the company. In Booth's telling, they sat down with him and said, "Larry, you're the best salesman we have, but that's the one thing you don't seem to want to do. We think that's what you ought to do." Instead, Klotz left in a huff, according to Booth. He notes that Klotz was a "fantastic salesman and a nice guy," and acknowledges that DFA's first clients were all his, and integral to getting the company up and running.

Yet underscoring the bad blood that continues to linger, in the company's official history book, published in 2011 as a gift to clients, the departure of one of its founders is given just three sentences: "Klotz's contributions to the firm's successful launch also cannot be overlooked. An outstanding salesman, he helped bring in important clients in Dimensional's early years. In 1984, Klotz moved on to other pursuits, leaving the management of the firm in the hands of Booth and Sinquefield."

The two men carved up and clarified the firm's management so that Booth focused primarily on business development, while Sinquefield focused on investment management. Around this time, they met for an informal evening chat about the future of DFA at the coffee shop at the bottom of their Chicago headquarters, and started discussing how big the company might eventually become. "I think we're going to be pretty big!" Booth insisted. Sinquefield was skeptical, and thought it would remain small. After a back-and-forth, they decided to both write down how many people they thought might be working at DFA in three or four years. They both jotted down forty, and guffawed at their different interpretations of what constituted a big firm.

At the time, DFA was still a divided organization. Booth was based in New York and reluctant to move to Chicago, and Sinque-field was in Chicago and unwilling to move to New York. It also remained a small, narrow company, virtually solely focused on sell-ing small-cap index funds to pension funds. This would change dramatically over the next decade, supercharging DFA's growth.

▲

IN JUNE 1985, DFA OPENED UP its new headquarters on Santa Monica's scenic waterfront boulevard. The temperate, steady cli-mate was a pleasant change after the severity of Chicago's and New York's seasons. DFA's business prospects also started brightening.

That year, DFA launched another US equity fund that it ini-tially called the 6-10 strategy, as it bought all the NYSE-listed stocks in the sixth to tenth decile by market capitalization. This was more of the classical definition of small caps, which was in the pro-cess of being formalized. The fund was later renamed the US Small Cap Portfolio, and its predecessor rechristened the US Micro Cap Portfolio to clarify the difference between the two.

Small-cap funds focused on Japan and the UK were unveiled in 1986. A European fund followed in 1988. The performance of smaller stocks luckily rebounded by the late 1980s, but DFA re-mained a one-trick pony (aside from a small fund that invested in short-term bonds as an inflation hedge, a pet project of Fama's).

That began to radically change with the advent of factor invest-ing. Given Fama's role at DFA, Booth and Sinquefield were well aware of the research he and French were conducting on value and size as durable risk premia from the late 1980s. Within months of their groundbreaking paper finally being published in the *Journal of Finance* in 1992, DFA had launched two value funds focused on both small- and large-cap stocks.[15]

The publication of the three-factor model was the beginning of a "big big breakthrough" for DFA, according to Sinquefield. While the company and its founders remained devotionally dedicated to the tenets of the efficient-markets hypothesis, it could now transcend its roots and become a full-fledged investment company with a panoply of different strategies—in the United States and internationally—all informed by the research of Fama, French, and others who would follow in their footsteps.

Strictly speaking, DFA didn't call its products index funds, as in many cases there weren't yet any formal stock market indices for these funds to track. The company therefore had a little more lee-way to try to squeeze a few extra returns out of the markets it at-tempted to mirror. But it did so through more opportunistic trading strategies, rather than using human discretion to try to pick stocks. That meant it generally priced its funds at about a third of a per-centage point—roughly halfway between what an index fund and a traditionally actively managed mutual fund would charge. Van-guard's Bogle would sometimes needle Booth about what he saw as high fees, but given the results, many clients were willing to pay them.

One of those clients was even willing to invest in the company itself. Schroders' fifteen-year bond came due to conversion into a 15 percent stake in 1996, and DFA wanted to buy it out. For tax rea-sons, it would be advantageous to get a few individual investors in as shareholders, so Booth asked his friend Paul Wachter—a financial advisor with a glamorous client list including U2's Bono, Billie Ei-lish, and LeBron James—for help. Wachter introduced Booth to Arnold Schwarzenegger, and the movie star snapped up an undis-closed stake. "I love that [Mr. Booth and DFA] have been true to their economic roots and have grown the company in a gigantic way without ever veering from their beliefs and theories of investing," Schwarzenegger once told the *Wall Street Journal*.[16] The actor may be DFA's most glamorous client, but he proved far from the most pivotal.

▲

DAN WHEELER'S LIFE WAS LONG a nomadic one, ricocheting from one extreme to the other like a pinball being flipped around by the paddles of fate. But eventually he would emerge as an efficient-markets zealot who would help lift DFA from the relative obscurity of managing money solely for institutions and help spread its gospel to thousands of people across the United States—and farther afield.

He grew up in a working-class neighborhood in East St. Louis, but ended up studying history at a small liberal arts college, before enrolling in the Marine Corps and volunteering to fight in Vietnam. But the rigidity of the military quickly chafed, so he turned to the private sector for something more rewarding. After a peripatetic career, ranging from accountant at Arthur Andersen, financial controller in the empire of notorious billionaire arms dealer Adnan Kashoggi, and a quickly aborted attempt to get a PhD at Berkeley, Wheeler settled down with his family in Boise, Idaho, and started teaching at the local university. A stockbroker neighbor talked him into joining his firm, Merrill Lynch, but this proved another seemingly glamorous job that quickly soured.

Merrill's brokers didn't know what they were selling their clients, caring only about churning their money to generate trading commissions. Moreover, despite the Wall Street firm's army of analysts, its stock tips seemed dismal. "I just felt people were getting ripped off day after day," Wheeler says. Frustrated, he started studying the work of Fama and his colleagues. It proved an epiphany. Wheeler quickly became convinced that markets were efficient, and people were terrible at navigating them.

So as a present to himself on his fortieth birthday, Wheeler quit Merrill to work as an independent financial advisor and set up shop in Sacramento. Resolved to avoid the core problem that dogged the industry, he joined the burgeoning movement of "fee-only" financial advisors, who instead of being paid through commissions, charged either a flat hourly rate or a flat percentage of the wealth of their clients. This meant he wouldn't need to pump high-priced financial products or constantly tout stock picks to generate commissions. Instead, he mostly put his clients' money in the Vanguard 500 fund— at the time the only passive fund available to ordinary investors.

But in 1988, he made a discovery in the pages of *USA Today*: an article about Dimensional Fund Advisors and its novel, passive small-cap fund, run by two Fama protégés who had played pivotal roles in the first generation of index funds, like the one Wheeler largely put his clients into. Excited, he reached out to the Santa Monica–based company to see if he could finagle his clients into their fund.

However, DFA's fund was available only to big institutional investors, not financial advisors like Wheeler. Both Sinquefield and Booth were skeptical of accepting any "retail money." After all, pension funds are slow to make investment decisions but committed once they finally do so, while the money of ordinary savers tends to be more fickle, making it a nightmare to manage.* Anyway, Booth and Sinquefield doubted that passive funds would ever attract a following among ordinary investors. But Wheeler insistently countered, "How do you know if you haven't tried?" In the end, DFA's founders relented—a decision none of them ever regretted.

The experiment proved so successful that Wheeler within a year proposed to Booth and Sinquefield that he set up a new DFA unit dedicated to selling its funds to fee-only financial advisors. Once again, DFA's duo were skeptical, but agreed on the proviso that Wheeler personally vet every financial advisor they worked with, to ensure that they were sufficiently committed to the company's

---

* The emergence of a "mutual fund marketplace" at Charles Schwab, the giant brokerage firm, helped Wheeler's case. This allowed independent advisors to consolidate many clients and many funds into single "omnibus" accounts, which would make it much easier for both Wheeler and DFA to handle the logistics involved in smaller retail accounts.

efficient-markets religion and that they wouldn't bail out of its funds at the first sign of a poor period of performance.

To do so, Wheeler began organizing conferences mandatory for financial advisors who wanted to gain access to DFA's funds, featuring presentations on the efficient-markets gospel and factor investing from the likes of Sinquefield, Fama, French, Scholes, and Miller, and outside speakers like Burton Malkiel.

The focus was on education, not selling DFA's funds. Attendees were fed, but had to pay for their own travel to Santa Monica. The first one attracted only seven people, but through word of mouth their popularity boomed in the 1990s. Even the company itself describes these conferences as "part investing seminar, part revival meeting,"[17] while outsiders often call them propaganda sessions. "It was beyond A.A. It was Leni Riefenstahl, but the right way," one converted financial advisor told the author Michael Lewis.[18]

Wheeler described the DFA Way to prospective partners as the "never having to say you're sorry approach." Dimensional bombarded them with data on what a terrible job most fund managers do for their clients, presented digestible versions of Chicago's academic theories, and found that people queued to sign up. Not everyone did, of course, but Wheeler knew that was inevitable. In his opening remarks at the DFA conference, he joked that the attendees "can learn this from us or you can let the market teach you. But the market charges a big tuition!"

Plenty seem to have gotten it. In his first year, Wheeler brought $70 million into the firm, $150 million in the second, and $325 million in the third. More disillusioned financial advisors and stockbrokers hungry for something more rigorous—such as Merrill's Dave Butler—were hired to further build up DFA's Financial Advisor Services. Its success helped Dimensional's assets under management grow to $34 billion by the end of the 1990s.

Today, money from financial advisors accounts for about two-thirds of Dimensional's over $600 billion of assets under management. In a testament to the strength of its indoctrination of clients, DFA even enjoyed investor inflows in 2008, the asset management industry's annus horribilis, despite the poor performance of many of its funds in the financial crisis.

▲

THE IMPORTANCE OF DFA'S "propaganda sessions" went far beyond growing the company's assets under management. By the 1980s, most investment officers at pension funds, endowments, and bank trust departments were at least aware of the academic theories and data on the underperformance of active managers that underpin index investing—even if they didn't always like or fully accept the implications. The DFA seminars and workshops have over the years played a vital role in disseminating the academic theories among America's army of financial advisors as well.

It is hard to be definitive on just how much this helped the accelerating growth of index investing in the 1990s and 2000s. But at the very least, Dimensional helped bring the concepts into the sprawling world of financial advisors, which is often Main Street's main interface with Wall Street.

Wells Fargo's Bill Fouse had years earlier jokingly recalled Joseph Goebbels's quote that "big secrets are protected by the public's incredulity" to explain why index investing wasn't catching on with the general public. DFA's zealous efficient-markets boot camps likely played a major role in eroding that incredulity. In time, the success of the factor investing approach pioneered by Dimensional would also gain wider acceptance, and is today the lens through which most of the investment world views markets—even if it remains somewhat controversial.

Nonetheless, the origin story of index investing is still incomplete. If Wells Fargo's Management Sciences unit was the original

Manhattan Project of index funds, most of the subsequent iterations were important but arguably incremental. They mostly consisted of proliferation, of spreading the approach to new corners of the investment world. Vanguard brought it to the masses, and DFA showed that index investing could be done with a twist. But these were still mostly natural evolutionary steps, building on the initial foundations established by Wells Fargo, American National Bank of Chicago, and Batterymarch.

The next stage would be the development of the equivalent of the hydrogen bomb to Wells Fargo's atomic bomb, a sea change in the history of financial markets and investing with ramifications that we are still grappling to understand today. Ironically, while Wells Fargo's crew of economic rock stars had helped develop the first index fund, its next major mutation was engineered by a group of finance industry nobodies.

Chapter 11

THE SPIDER'S BIRTH

AS USUAL, JACK BOGLE ARRIVED at his office at 7 a.m. sharp and started preparing for another long day at Vanguard's spartan headquarters in Valley Forge. As he went through his itinerary for the day, he spied one intriguing entry, a visit from Nate Most, the head of product development at the American Stock Exchange.

Bogle and Most, a bespectacled, avuncular former submariner, hit it off. They were roughly of the same generation, and both eschewed the sharp suits and polished patter of most Wall Street types. Although the gentle Most was more softly spoken than Vanguard's forceful founder, Bogle appreciated his forthright manner, his character, and his obvious intellect. He was also intrigued by what Most wanted to discuss, the outline of which Most had sketched out by letter the previous week. Yet Vanguard's chief still sent him packing.

"Nate Most was a fine gentleman, but it was the antithesis to what I like," Bogle later remarked.[1] The decision to reject Most's idea was a sliding-door moment for Vanguard and the broader money management industry, a decision that Vanguard would scramble to undo soon after the founder was forced to retire.

Most had an audacious idea for how to resurrect the fortunes of the American Stock Exchange, his venerable yet struggling employer. To do so, he wanted to make Vanguard's index funds themselves tradable throughout the day, just like any stock. These tradable fund shares would offer investors more flexibility, and bring a far broader universe of potential users to Vanguard, Most argued.

Bogle listened intently. He outlined a few practical flaws that would need to be addressed, but bluntly told Most that he wasn't interested in a partnership even if they were.[2] He feared that such a product would turn Vanguard's index funds from a long-term savings vehicle for investors into a tool for mere speculation by hedge funds and other hyperactive market participants. "You want people to be able to trade the S&P but I just want them to buy and never sell it," he told Most.[3]

What Most was describing would later morph into exchange-traded funds, or ETFs, one of the most impactful inventions in the history of investing, and the next stage in the index investing revolution.

Even more than the initial generation of index funds, ETFs are now in the process of reshaping finance thanks to their Lego-like characteristics, which allow everyone from sophisticated hedge funds to ordinary savers to better craft more tactical bets or build complex investment portfolios. Their dramatic growth is retooling trading floors, rewiring markets, rattling the investment industry, and even slowly but surely starting to impact the governance of companies in ways we are only beginning to fathom.

At the time, neither Bogle nor Most likely appreciated the import of their meeting. They parted ways amicably, and Bogle scrupulously reported the conversation to Vanguard's board at its next meeting, and why he had summarily rejected it. "Why would anybody want to buy the market at 10:30 in the morning and then sell it at one o'clock in the afternoon," he argued, according to the recollection of Burton Malkiel, one of Vanguard's directors at the time. "This is absolutely crazy," he continued griping to the board, "simply an instrument that is going to lead people astray and they're going to get killed with them."

As it happened, Malkiel also chaired the American Stock Exchange's new products committee, and was enamored with the possibilities of Most's idea. Although he had suspected that Bogle would shun the opportunity, he long regretted his decision and thought it was the biggest mistake Vanguard's founder made at the helm. "Jack had strong views, and seldom changed his initial opinion," he says. "He was an intrepid foe [of ETFs] then, and remained an intrepid foe throughout his life."

In truth, Bogle did in his later years grudgingly soften his criticism somewhat. He grew to see ETFs as an efficient way of bringing more people into the index fund revolution, even as he remained implacably opposed to the hyperactivity he feared their ease of trading might engender. But the rapidity and extent of their success still gnawed at him, as he revealed in an autobiography published shortly before his death.

"I had no idea that, within a decade, the ETF idea [proposed by Most at their meeting] would ignite a flame that would change not only the nature of indexing, but also the entire field of investing," Bogle admitted.[4] "I can unhesitatingly describe Nathan Most's visionary creation of the ETF as the most successful financial *marketing* idea so far during the twenty-first century. Whether it proves to be the most successful *investment* idea of the century remains to be seen."

▲

LIKE MANY OF HIS PREDECESSORS in the history of index funds, Most was an unlikely revolutionary. A cerebral, almost painfully modest former physicist, he stumbled into the finance industry late in life, after a peripatetic career.

Most was born on March 22, 1914,[5] to Jewish parents who had fled pogroms in Eastern Europe.[6] He grew up in California, got good grades, and excelled at UCLA. But a PhD in physics was interrupted by the Great Depression, which forced him to start working for Getz Bros., an import-export business run by the Lazarus family. His job mostly consisted of selling acoustics equipment to movie theaters that were starting to pop up in East Asia.

Then war came and once again interrupted Most's career. He was one of the last civilians to leave Shanghai before it fell into Japanese hands, and once the Pearl Harbor attack embroiled the United States, he worked on developing and testing out sonar on submarines in the Pacific.

After the war he returned to Getz, married May Rose Lazarus, and rose through the ranks of the family business.[7] He eventually oversaw all its business in Hong Kong and the Philippines, once again traveling across the Pacific to visit its factories and warehouses. He developed a fine understanding of the entire supply chain, from the extraction and refinement of the raw commodities to the financial side of things through local merchant bankers.

Unfortunately, he eventually fell out with the Lazarus family, who ran Getz, which resulted in his ejection and divorce from May Rose in the late 1950s.[8] After this, his career became nomadic and often frustrating. Between 1965 and 1970, he was executive vice president of Pacific Vegetable Oil, but the firm then folded. He then became executive vice president of the American Import Company, and then president of the Pacific Commodities Exchange from 1974 to 1976, until it too closed down.[9] The exchange's main business had been coconut oil futures, and many of its traders were wiped out when a global drought in the mid-1970s ended, sending prices plummeting.[10]

Most then accepted a relatively lowly position as a technical assistant to the Commodity Futures Trading Commission, a regulatory agency that monitors the US futures market. He worked there for a year, before the American Stock Exchange hired him in 1977 as director of commodity options development for a new trading venue it was setting up. This also quickly fizzled, but Most was kept on as head of the Amex's derivatives development unit.[11]

The Amex was nearly as old as the New York Stock Exchange, having been started in 1908 by curbstone brokers who conducted their business outdoors on Broad Street in lower Manhattan. In 1920, *Munsey's Magazine* described the mayhem vividly, as "the ululations of a madhouse—shrieks, exultant yells, heavy mutterings of anger; deep-throated growlings such as proceed from the cages of a menagerie just before feeding-time."[12]

The spectacle moved indoors in 1921, but was still formally known as the Curb Exchange long after a formal name change in 1953. By the 1970s, the Amex was the second-biggest US stock exchange, a natural home for companies not yet ready or unwilling to list on the NYSE's "Big Board." But it had fallen on hard times, plagued by scandals and trading migrating to its rival on Wall Street and the Nasdaq, an upstart all-electronic exchange.

In the 1980s, the Amex successfully seized on derivatives as a way to resurrect its fortunes, yet remained in dire straits. It desperately needed something—anything—to resuscitate its flagging fortunes.

As luck would have it, the worst day of wealth destruction Wall Street has ever witnessed provided Most and the Amex with exactly the break they needed.

▲

THE BLACK MONDAY CRASH ON October 19, 1987, ended careers, bankrupted thousands, and rippled through the global economy. A market swoon of this severity and abruptness demanded investigation, and the following February the Securities and Exchange Commission published its autopsy. The financial watchdog's report mostly blamed a nascent automated, algorithmic trading strategy called "portfolio insurance" for the severity of the tumble.

Portfolio insurance involved investors like pension funds and insurers selling stock index futures once the market had declined by a certain level, in theory insuring their market positions against downturns. But on Black Monday, the accelerating rush of futures sellers overwhelmed the market's capacity to absorb them, bled into the main stock exchange, and led to more automated futures selling, a feedback loop that turned a nasty crash into a financial heart attack.

Intriguingly, buried inside the exhaustive portmortem was a tantalizing hint from the SEC. Chapter 3 speculated that "an alternative approach be examined" and suggested that if traders could have turned to a single product for trading entire baskets of stocks, it might have ameliorated the turmoil by providing a kind of shock absorber between the futures market and individual stocks. Steven Bloom, a young colleague of Most, strode into his office and said, "Here's an opening we could drive a truck through."[13]

Most and Bloom were an unlikely duo. Bloom had a fairly orthodox entry into finance, having recently graduated from Harvard with a PhD in economics. Most was seventy-three when the SEC report was published, while Bloom was just in his late twenties.[14] Yet their collaboration proved phenomenally fertile, with Bloom's systematic brain complementing Most's brilliance and creativity perfectly. "Talking with him, one can almost hear the synapses clicking behind his glasses, gray matter powering away at high rev," one magazine observed about Bloom.[15] For Most, the sheer act of creation seemed to give him a thrill. "When you see your babies trading down on the floor, you feel a real attachment to your work that most people in this world of money never get to experience," he said.

Luckily their bosses were of a similar bent. Most and Bloom's immediate supervisor was Ivers Riley, a former Navy pilot whom the Amex had poached from the NYSE in 1987 to oversee its overall derivatives business. He was on the hunt for a "destiny-changing product" that would reinvigorate the exchange. Riley quickly saw the potential in an instrument that would "look, taste, smell, and feel like a share of stock representing the whole market, an entirely new instrument that could be the basis for many offshoots and iterations over time,"[16] and gave Most and Bloom his full backing.

"The survival of the organization depended upon innovation," Malkiel says. "And the one good thing that we had was that the New York Stock Exchange was not an innovative organization."

However, their first attempts to reverse-engineer something akin to what the SEC was obliquely asking for quickly ran aground. Moreover, the Amex was not the only struggling exchange desperate for a commercial boost and aware of the immense potential of a tradable index fund.

▲

THE PHILADELPHIA STOCK EXCHANGE WAS America's oldest, founded in 1790 and instrumental in raising money for the nineteenth-century railroad boom. But New York's emergence as the country's dominant financial center put it in the shade, and it suffered a hammer blow with the 1970 bankruptcy of railway operator Penn Central—at the time the biggest corporate failure in US history, and the PSE's biggest stock. A downward spiral was averted by an aggressive move into the burgeoning derivatives market,[17] but, like the Amex, the PSE needed a Hail Mary innovation to avoid being subsumed by one of its biggest rivals.

The SEC autopsy on Black Monday provided the break it needed. Just months after the report was published, the PSE filed a prospectus with the SEC for what it termed "cash index participation shares," or CIPs, which were a kind of hybrid mix between a stock and a derivative, designed to synthetically mimic the performance of the S&P 500.

With the details of its plans now public, rivals scrambled to follow suit. Most and Bloom, as well as the Chicago Board Options Exchange, quickly filed prospectuses for similar products, with subtly different acronyms but known as a group as "index participation shares," or IPSs. By 1989, they had started trading, and enjoyed quick success. Then rivals and regulators kiboshed them.

Unlike most countries, the US regulatory landscape is awkwardly carved up between the SEC, which is in charge of stocks and most exchanges, and the Commodity Futures Trading Commission, which was created in 1974 to regulate the US derivatives markets, such as futures, swaps, and options, which were overwhelmingly used in commodities. Some options fall under the SEC's aegis, but the CFTC has always zealously defended its turf and insisted on its preeminence over all futures, even those that are linked to stocks.

The CFTC argued that the IPSs were de facto futures contracts—not unreasonably so, given their hybrid structure[18]—and were therefore allowed to trade only on futures exchanges it regulated. Eventually, a federal judge in Chicago ruled in the CFTC's favor, and the early batch of proto-ETFs died.

Undeterred, the Amex team pressed ahead with something that might overcome the regulatory hurdles. Despite Most's age— he was seventy-five when the CFTC killed off the IPS—colleagues marveled at his energy, ability to come in every morning at 6 a.m., and irrepressible can-do bonhomie. One colleague recalls how he arrived at their office one Monday to see Most's arm in a sling, which he cheerfully revealed was due to falling out of a tree after an overambitious attempt at branch-trimming over the weekend—not something that most septuagenarians would try.

Most's eclectic background also provided the spark behind the invention of what would become known as the ETF. During his travels around the Pacific, he had appreciated the efficiency of how traders would buy and sell warehouse receipts of commodities, rather than the more cumbersome physical vats of coconut oil, barrels of crude, or ingots of gold. This opened up a panoply of opportunities for creative financial engineers.

"You store a commodity and you get a warehouse receipt and you can finance on that warehouse receipt. You can sell it, do a lot of things with it. Because you don't want to be moving the merchandise back and forth all the time, so you keep it in place and you simply transfer the warehouse receipt," he later recalled.[19]

Most's ingenious idea was to, after a fashion, mimic this basic structure. The Amex could create a kind of legal warehouse where it could place the S&P 500 stocks, and then create and list shares in the warehouse itself for people to trade. The new warehouse-cum-fund would take advantage of the growth and electronic evolution in portfolio trading—the simultaneous buying and selling of big baskets of stocks first pioneered by Wells Fargo two decades earlier—and a little-known aspect of mutual funds: They can do "in kind" transactions, exchanging shares in a fund for a proportional amount of the stocks it contains, rather than cash. Or an investor can gather the correct proportion of the underlying stocks and exchange them for shares in the fund.

Stock exchange "specialists"—the trading firms on the floor of the exchange that match buyers and sellers—would be authorized to be able to create or redeem these shares according to demand. They could take advantage of any differences that might open up between the price of the "warehouse" and the stock it contained, an arbitrage opportunity that should help keep it trading in line with its assets.

This elegant creation/redemption process would also get around the logistical challenges of money coming in and out continuously throughout the day—one of Bogle's main practical concerns. In basic terms, investors can either trade shares of the warehouse between themselves, or go to the warehouse and exchange their shares in it for a slice of the stocks it holds. Or they can turn up at the warehouse with a suitable bundle of stocks and exchange them for shares in the warehouse. Moreover, because no money changes hands when shares in the warehouse are created or redeemed, capital gains tax can be delayed until the investor actually sells their shares—a side effect that has proven vital to the growth of ETFs in the United States. Only when an ETF is actually sold will investors have to pay any capital gains taxes due.

As an exchange, the Amex might struggle to manage such a product itself. Anyway, it was interested only in the trading activity it would generate. So the Amex set about finding a partner. Most's visit to Bogle proved frustrating, and Wells Fargo—a natural partner given its position in index funds aimed at institutional investors—was simply too far away for the Amex's miniscule travel budget.[20]

Most therefore started visiting some investment firms in its own neighborhood. He first went to Bank of New York, simply because it was the closest. At the time the Amex and BNY headquarters faced each other, both overlooking the Trinity Church cemetery at Wall Street's outspring. Yet its bureaucracy meant that the job of running the first-ever ETF instead eventually fell to State Street.[21] Although Boston-based, State Street had a major Wall Street outpost not far from the Amex headquarters, and had become a major force in index investing itself, through its asset management arm State Street Global Advisors (SSGA). It was an outcome BNY would eventually rue.

Glenn Francis, who worked in fund administration at State Street, Kathy Cuocolo, head of US investment fund services, and Douglas Holmes, an index fund manager at SSGA, became particularly enamored with the idea. But not everyone at the bank was thrilled at the cost of the development, leading people involved in the project to fear for their professional futures if it proved a dud. "There were a lot of people hoping it would work, as there was career risk if it didn't," recalls Jim Ross, then a junior State Street executive who was later roped into the project.

What to call the new invention proved thorny. The State Street and Amex teams wanted something descriptive that would still easily roll off the tongue of traders. Inspired by the Amex's role in introducing American Depositary Receipts—in essence US-listed versions of stocks trading on overseas exchanges—they eventually went for Standard & Poor's Depositary Receipts, or SPDRs. They quickly became dubbed Spiders.*

There were also immense legal and operational hoops to jump through. Despite the SEC's indirect call for an instrument along these lines, anything that is open to Main Street investors will always face many questions. The Spider team also had to work out the mechanics of the creation and redemption process and ensure that it would be seamless—and be approved by the SEC. "It didn't really fit neatly into any regulatory bucket," says Clifford Weber, a former biochemist who had joined the Amex new products group in 1990. "A lot of the time was spent working with the lawyers to figure out

---

*Initially they thought of calling it Standard and Poor's Index Receipts, or SPIRs, but the team was concerned about the martial imagery of "spears" being chucked around a trading floor.

the appropriate responses to concerns from the SEC. That stuff just takes time, there's no way around it."

The person tasked with navigating this legal morass was Kathleen Moriarty, a lawyer at Orrick, Herrington & Sutcliffe. The Amex had decided to make the new product a "unit investment trust" as opposed to a fund, as it then wouldn't require a portfolio manager or a board, which Most thought added costs and little else to his brainchild.[22] Yet Moriarty still had to request a series of exemptions from the Investment Company Act of 1940—a herculean task that earned her the nickname "Spider Woman." Meanwhile, the development costs were heaping up.

The SPDR application was finally filed with the SEC in 1990, but given its novelty it faced a long and arduous approval process— despite the backing of some of the watchdog's own staff. Howard Kramer, a lawyer in the agency's markets division, was a particularly eager champion. He had been one of the authors of the Black Monday report that had inspired Most and Bloom, and as soon as he had read and digested the Amex filing he rushed into the office of his boss to explain how groundbreaking the product might prove and argue for a quick approval. "If Nate and Steve were the parents of this product, I was one of the midwives," he later joked.[23]

Yet the novelty of the structure meant that several SEC departments were involved, many of which were not set up to deal with innovative products. For example, one struggle was how SPDR's constant creating and redeeming of shares constituted a de facto perpetual initial public offering—the process through which companies go public—which normally requires a club of banks to do due diligence. The end result of all the SEC tire-kicking of the process was "paralysis by analysis," according to Kramer.

Unfortunately, the Amex and State Street weren't the only ones attempting to construct a tradable index fund, and the delay allowed others to steal in ahead of them.

▲

THE CONCEPT OF PORTFOLIO INSURANCE may have received a shellacking over its role in the severity of the Black Monday crash, but its inventors were a bunch of unusually creative, driven academics who remained uncowed by the opprobrium. Hayne Leland, John O'Brien, and Mark Rubinstein—the founders of the eponymous investment advisory firm LOR—were determined to find another big idea to restore their luster.

The trio set about devising something they dubbed "Super-Shares." The essence was an ingenious but fiendishly complex investment product that would slice and dice the entire S&P 500 into return segments for investors to choose from according to their risk appetite, and trade on an exchange. At its core was something called the Index Trust SuperUnit, which in some respects resembled what would later be known as an exchange-traded fund.[24]

After jumping through extensive regulatory hoops, the fund launched in November 1992, and initially raised almost $2 billion. But its complexity turned off many investors and brokers. "You're going to explain that? Good luck," one financier who declined to join the underwriting told a *New York Times* journalist who was attempting to write an article about the SuperTrust.[25] Although it went live before SPDR—and some of its innovative legal processes helped pave the way for what came next—the SuperTrust traded listlessly, and was eventually liquidated in 1995.

The not-so-super performance of the overly complicated structure was of little consolation to Most and Bloom, who had already had to witness a bunch of plucky Canadians stealing ahead of Team America to launch the first-ever ETF. They managed to do so mainly because of the smaller, less aggressively competitive Canadian finance industry—which led to more cross-company collaboration—and the more amenable local regulator.

The attempt was sponsored by the Toronto Stock Exchange, and leaned heavily on the Amex's warehouse receipts concept. Indeed, given that they weren't direct competitors, the US exchange was happy to advise the TSE team on the details.[26] Although it tracked only the thirty-five biggest stocks in Canada—a far easier task than the entire S&P 500—it closely mirrored the performance of the wider Toronto Stock Exchange 400 Composite Index, the country's flagship equity benchmark.

On March 9, 1990, the TSE unveiled what would be the world's first successful exchange-traded fund, the Toronto 35 Index Participation Fund, or TIPS. Although the Canadians might have crossed the line first due to a more relaxed regulator, the design of the first-ever ETF was still inspired by the Amex and State Street Spider team's frustrating but pioneering work.* Moreover, the Canadian ETF was only a modest success. Although it raised $150 million from a variety of Canadian financial institutions from the get-go, it failed to gain the hoped-for traction among ordinary investors. The ETF revolution had its first whiff of gunfire, but to really take off it still needed a successful birth in the United States, home of the world's biggest financial markets.

▲

SEEING CANADA COPYING A US invention and bringing it to life so quickly was grating to SPDR's supporters. Luckily, they also had a supporter in the SEC's chairman, Richard Breeden. After two years of back-and-forth on various aspects of SPDR—from mind-numbing minutiae to make-or-break challenges to the

---

* Peter Haynes, today head of index funds at Toronto-Dominion Bank but then a fresh-faced recent graduate on the TSE's experimental ETF team, admits they in practice copied the design of State Street and Amex, but simply got to the finish line first thanks to the more collaborative Canadian regulators: "The SEC took a long time, so we realized a product like that would work here. So when we approached the Toronto Securities Commission, it was fairly quick."

create/redeem process—he finally intervened and called a grand meeting to break the logjam.

When the assembled SPDR team from the Amex, State Street, and their lawyer Moriarty arrived at the SEC's headquarters, they were directed into a cavernous room normally used for big public events, rather than one of the usual drab conference rooms. There they confronted not only a series of tables with representatives of each relevant SEC department, but bleachers erected for all the relevant SEC lawyers to attend. "I fully expected to see lions released before we left the room," Riley later joked.[27] It worked, and in December 1992 the SEC finally gave its blessing.

The next step was to prepare SPDR for listing and trading on the Amex.* The brokerage firm Spear, Leeds & Kellogg played an important role as midwife to SPDR's launch, putting up the initial $6.5 million capital for SPDR[28] and becoming its first specialist, the firm that would ensure that it traded correctly and tracked the S&P 500. Gary Eisenreich, one of its floor traders, also caught a crucial flaw in the legal design at the last moment—the SEC's "uptick" rule that limited when people can short a security—which could have imperiled the ability of specialists to ensure that SPDR traded correctly. At the last minute, Eisenreich and Moriarty worked with the SEC to get an exemption to the uptick rule.[29]

On January 29, 1993, SPDR finally began trading, to great fanfare. Desperate for its costly experiment to be a success, the Amex ran a full-page ad in the *Wall Street Journal* touting its invention, hung a giant inflatable black spider over its trading floor, and gave away oodles of spider-themed swag to traders and investors. It charged

---

* The first step was coming up with one of the truncated stock market tickers that all listed securities require to identify themselves on Wall Street's trading screens. The S&P 500 index itself had the ticker SPX, so the marketing people attached to the SPDR project suggested that the fund could use SXY. The proposal was shot down on grounds of being too rude—to the lament of financial headline writers for years to come—so they settled on SPY as a nod to the spider nickname.

investors a fee of 0.2 percent a year—the same as Bogle's Vanguard 500 fund—and on its first day over a million shares traded, thrilling its backers.

But SPDR's toddler period proved tougher than its birth. Although it started gathering money, it did so at a sluggish pace. Trading volumes—its raison d'être, as far as the Amex was concerned—sank steadily after the first day's brouhaha, to a nadir of just 17,900 shares changing hands on June 10.[30] The problem was that it didn't have a natural constituency of supporters in the wider finance industry. Like Vanguard, SPDR didn't pay sales fees to financial advisors and brokers. That meant they had no incentive to push their clients into the new product. Although it traded like a stock, it didn't earn banks underwriting fees either. The situation was so dire that the Amex at one point even considered scrapping it,[31] given that it needed about $300 million of assets and healthy trading volumes to break even.[32]

However, they were assisted by outside supporters, such as Eisenreich. He proselytized through what he termed "cocktail investing." At every social occasion he attended, he would wax lyrical about how amazing SPDR was, and encourage people to ask their stockbroker about it so they would seem cool and cutting-edge. "I'm a horrible salesman. I really am. But I'm very good when it comes to a cause. And I looked at SPDRs as a thing I could sell my grandmother," Eisenreich later said.[33]

Slowly but surely, their efforts paid off. By the summer of 1993, SPDR finally broke the $300 million of assets mark it needed to break even on the cost of running it, and by the end of its first year it held $461 million.[34] It actually shrank in 1994, but from 1995 onward SPDR started taking off. It never looked back.

▲

ON JANUARY 29, 2013, the spiderwomen and spidermen who had launched SPDR two decades earlier gathered to ring the New York

Stock Exchange's opening bell. Though the participants were older, grayer, more wrinkled, and with some notable absences—Most had passed away in 2004—it was still a festive celebration of a staggering achievement.

Not only was SPDR by then a $125 billion behemoth, but it was also comfortably the most heavily traded stock in the world—a source of immense pride to the people who had slogged their way through its creation and troubled early years. SPDR was a product that launched an entire vibrant and still-growing industry.

For the early pioneers, it had even been woven into their personal lives, through a quirk of the trust structure they used to set up SPDR. Trusts have a finite life span, which was initially supposed to be twenty-five years for SPDR. But they can also be tied to the longevity of individual people, so it was later amended and pegged to eleven children born around 1990–93, such as Weber's daughter Emily, who was born on the same day that SPDR was established.[35] As a result, SPDR will expire either on January 22, 2118, or twenty years after the death of the last survivor of the eleven people mentioned in the trust, whichever occurs first.

After a hefty internal debate, the Amex team decided against trying to patent their invention—with seismic consequences. Given SPDR's public filings, it was easy for rivals to copy the design. Virtually anything can be put inside an ETF "warehouse," and over the years Wall Street's financial engineers have used the variants of the structure to create vehicles for investors to bet on everything from the US bond market to risky bank loans, African stocks, the robotics industry, and even financial volatility itself. Today, ETFs are a $9 trillion industry, and they account for about a third of all trading on US exchanges.

But it wasn't enough to save the Amex. In 2008, the NYSE acquired its smaller brother for $260 million. Nor did State Street emerge as the biggest winner from its pioneering role in the invention of ETFs. Due to a mix of initial indifference and inability to grasp the potential of the upheaval it started, the Boston bank eventually saw its SPDR business eclipsed by an old West Coast rival.

"Looking back, would we have liked to have done things differently? Sure," says Ross, who eventually became the chairman of State Street's ETF business. "It wasn't like we didn't invest money, we just didn't invest enough at the start. It is what it is."

Chapter 12

WFIA 2.0

BY THE SUMMER OF 1983, Wells Fargo Investment Advisors was sliding into turmoil. The argumentative pioneers who overcame their differences to launch the first-ever index fund back in 1971 had all left, and after a decade of growth money was now seeping out at an alarming rate. Despite the inventiveness of WFIA, its low fees and a huge research budget meant it had never actually managed to turn a profit. A terminal decline looked possible—perhaps even probable.

McQuown was long gone, having resigned in 1974. The sharp-shooting Vertin later retired, leaving Fouse as the keeper of the flame. But never-ending budget battles with Wells Fargo spurred Fouse to quit in 1983. He returned to his old home at Mellon Bank, where he founded Mellon Capital Management with Thomas Loeb, who had managed Wells Fargo's first S&P 500 fund. William Jahnke, another top executive, left in April along with nearly a dozen colleagues to found a financial software company.[1]

Making matters worse, it was a turbulent time for markets.

Federal Reserve chair Paul Volcker was determined to break the back of inflation, and lifted interest rates to unprecedented levels, causing a recession that rippled through the stock market. By August 1982, the S&P 500 was pretty much back at levels last seen in the late 1960s.

Although the stock market had by 1983 started to bounce back, there was little faith in the rally. Instead, investors were taking advantage of declining inflation and still sky-high interest rates to shift money out of equities and into bonds. The result was an alarming pace of outflows from WFIA. "People wondered whether the business could survive," recalls Blake Grossman, a student of Bill Sharpe's at Stanford who interned at WFIA that stormy summer.

With various other defections, the unit was so short-staffed that Patricia Dunn, a young former journalist student who had first joined Wells Fargo as a temporary secretary, was forced to pick up the reins of its $25 billion of index funds. Dunn was brilliant, charismatic, and a star in the making, beloved by WFIA's pension fund clients for helping translate the often obtuse, jargon-laden academics that populated WFIA into intelligible English.

But she was just thirty years old at the time, and married to Jahnke, one of the defectors. She feared that once the crisis passed she would inevitably be demoted, or even fired. So she took advantage of the panic at Wells Fargo over WFIA's turmoil and negotiated an extra $25,000 a month until a new head was hired, to top up her $18,000-a-year salary. It was a bold, aggressive move that led even her husband to joke that her portrait should be hung in Wells Fargo's history room next to that of Black Bart, an infamous robber of the bank's stagecoaches in the late 1800s.[2]

The relationship between WFIA and Wells Fargo was in tatters. The bankers had long been resentful that many of their asset management colleagues made more money than them, despite never having turned a profit. Meanwhile, WFIA staffers viewed Wells

Fargo bankers as simpletons who were unappreciative of their unit's groundbreaking work. Amid this turmoil, Dunn made a left-field suggestion to her superiors. Maybe they should hire back a former WFIA executive named Frederick Grauer, who had been unceremoniously sacked after a mere eight-month stint in 1980?

Although the idea might have seemed outlandish, her bosses grudgingly agreed. Wells Fargo simply didn't have the time to conduct an exhaustive search, nor were many candidates likely to be willing to dive into the maelstrom that WFIA found itself in at the time. In 1983, WFIA was even leapfrogged by Bankers Trust as the biggest manager of index funds for pension funds, a humiliating blow to the institution that had pioneered the strategy.

"WFIA was in chaos. It was viewed as a potential imminent implosion due to the defection of people and clients," Grauer recalls. "The group that remained was basically the Dutch boy with his finger in the dike, and if they left, all the money would come gushing out. And the insiders trusted me." It helped that Grauer had an academic background that made him a good fit for the office culture, and was a big believer in indexing, having bought into the concept when reading Charles Ellis's "The Loser's Game" back in 1975.

Grauer would prove more than a caretaker at the top. Not only did he steady the ship, but he laid the groundwork for a remarkable transformation that would turn WFIA from a troubled investment group housed inside a regional bank into a global asset management empire. "Fred Grauer really changed the game," says Bruce Goddard, a former executive at the company. "It was his strength of personality and drive to win that created WFIA 2.0."

▲

GRAUER SEEMED DESTINED FOR AN intellectually rewarding but anodyne career in academia. After an economics degree at the University of British Columbia, graduate studies at the University of

Chicago, and a PhD at Stanford, he gained a prestigious assistant professorship at MIT, before becoming associate professor at Columbia's business school.

However, Grauer's wife worked in San Francisco, a bicoastal arrangement that couldn't survive indefinitely. So he resolved to move westward. Berkeley offered him a job, but Grauer had become keen to try his hand at something more practical, and he called up his Stanford mentor Bill Sharpe for advice. "If you're coming out here, there's only one place that is going to be a match for you," Sharpe told Grauer. With a prestigious recommendation from Sharpe, Grauer started working at a WFIA division that advised pension funds on their portfolios and modern academic research.

The job proved short-lived. At a meeting between the top brass of WFIA and Wells Fargo, Grauer—oblivious to the simmering tensions between the two—started critiquing one of the unit's investment strategies. In the grand scheme of things, it was a minor disagreement, but airing it in front of Wells Fargo's representatives was incendiary, giving them ammunition in their corporate battle with WFIA. "I was not on the alert for stepping in a cow pie. And I did," Grauer recalls ruefully. The next day he was summoned to Vertin's office, where Fouse gravely informed him that he was fired. It was a crushing blow, especially since Grauer and his wife had just had a baby boy.

Luckily, he didn't stay unemployed long. Sharpe introduced him to some contacts at Merrill Lynch, who hired him in a hybrid role. He would be one of the Wall Street firm's West Coast equity salesmen, and on the side advise Merrill's research department. The job would pay the bills, but pushing stock trades was hardly what a onetime high-flying academic dreamt of when he left Columbia.

Some career setbacks can prove a blessing in disguise, however. Becoming a salesman forced Grauer to cut back on his academic jargon and taught him how to tell a story. Moreover, by the 1980s many traditional investment groups were grudgingly becoming more curious about the academic research coming out of Stanford, Chicago, and MIT. Grauer became a master at explaining it to them. In turn, his clients rewarded his patience with fat trading commissions. By 1983, he was Merrill's top salesman on the West Coast, making over $500,000 a year. One of his biggest clients was Wells Fargo, helping him rebuild relationships with his old colleagues at WFIA, and the respect he enjoyed internally ultimately helped him make an unlikely return in September 1983 as its head.

Stabilizing the situation required quick action. Grauer managed to talk Wells Fargo into a new arrangement for WFIA. Rather than simply be a unit of the bank's trust department, WFIA would be spun out as a separate company, owned by Wells Fargo but with its own board and with more autonomy. To stem the defections he secured an agreement that WFIA's employees would get a percentage of any profits they might eventually generate, and a slice of the proceeds if it was ever sold. Clients were successfully assuaged—the fact that index funds are largely managed on autopilot anyway helped—and WFIA gradually regained at least a semblance of stability. "It was a profoundly team effort. And we got lucky," Grauer admits.

No one knew it at the time, but the stock market's nadir proved to be August 1982. Pension funds were still skeptical of the 1983 recovery, but by 1984–85 many started feeling that their stock market portfolios were perhaps a little light. Most of them still put the majority of their money into traditional active funds, but selecting one usually entailed months of interviews and due diligence. In the meantime, stocks just kept on climbing. WFIA's canny pitch was that their index funds were a cheap, easy way for pension funds to gain exposure to the equity market while they decided where to allocate their money. Many eventually just kept it there.

By 1985, WFIA enjoyed its first-ever profitable year. By the second half of the 1980s, it was growing rapidly, transforming the fortunes of the company. What was once a lame dog began looking like a sleek greyhound. Because index fund fees are so low, they need a certain scale to cover their costs. But once that hurdle is overcome, the costs do not increase significantly with size, and extra revenues become clean profits.

Even the Black Monday crash of 1987 didn't slow WFIA's growth, despite its being a big player in the "portfolio insurance" strategy pioneered by LOR.* In 1988, WFIA made a profit of $13.5 million[3]—a far cry from its long streak of seemingly unending losses. Grauer had managed to turn an organization of wayward academics who loved Socratic debate and often impractical ideas into something at least slightly more commercially oriented.

Lawrence Tint, a senior WFIA executive close to Grauer who left in 1980 but returned in 1990, recalls how the culture had subtly shifted in the intervening years. Although the air of academia had not wafted completely out of the corridors, the work ethic had hardened, and there was a firmer focus on profits. "It was much more like Goldman Sachs than a university," Tint recalls.

Nonetheless, the culture remained gentler than is the norm in finance. At job interviews, Grauer would stress that he wanted people who were "nice, bright, and have fire in the belly." He would take colleagues out to eat at Tommy Toy's, a famous Chinese restaurant frequented by the likes of Clint Eastwood and Francis Ford Coppola. Its signature lobster dish was often washed down with grappa, a drink Grauer had grown fond of. "Fred was the man," recalled Donald Luskin, who joined WFIA in 1987.[4] "Even for a

---

* In fact, the success of WFIA's "Tactical Asset Allocation" fund—a strategy started by Fouse that flitted between stocks, bonds, and cash according to preset rules, and had just 10 percent of its money in equities when Black Monday struck—burnished its reputation.

rugged individualist like me, it was really quite easy to fall in step behind and follow him."

▲

GRAUER HAD A GRANDER VISION than just the United States. The investment industry had historically been parochial, with few firms ever succeeding abroad. American asset managers were particularly uninterested in business outside the country, given the size of their domestic market. Presciently, Grauer was convinced that the industry would eventually become more global, especially for index funds.

After all, while fund managers might need a fine understanding of each company and the environment they operate within, index funds just need a decent measure of the broader market and the technological infrastructure to track it. Grauer therefore started looking around the world for other big pots of pension fund money that WFIA might try to snag before rivals like State Street and Bankers Trust realized the international opportunities.

Japan was the obvious candidate, but it was an insular country where foreign firms often struggled. Merely setting up a local office held little chance of success. In 1989, Grauer therefore convinced Wells Fargo to sell 50 percent of WFIA to Nikko Securities, a Japanese brokerage, for $125 million. The new combined company was given the unwieldy name Wells Fargo Nikko Investment Advisors, or WFNIA, and managed $70 billion at the time. "Indexing was a scale game, and we wanted to jump ahead of our competitors and seize more assets around the world," says Grauer.

Indexing did take off in Japan, but the timing was unfortunate—Japan's bubble burst in 1990—and the marriage between high-minded American financiers and Japanese stockbrokers proved culturally messy. Nonetheless, the deal helped attract Japanese pension fund money, and brought more independence from Wells Fargo's banker overlords. Six years later, in 1994, WFNIA managed about $171 billion, and made $45 million of pretax profits.[5]

The bulk of the assets were in index funds, but it also had an increasingly successful active fund business, albeit one that was driven by data, computers, and models—"quantitative investing," in the industry's argot—rather than the hunches of human fund managers. This was similar to the factor investing approach adopted by the likes of Dimensional Fund Advisors in nearby Santa Monica, but often with several extra layers of complexity.

Index investing also started to take off into new frontiers. Passive strategies that aimed to replicate more complex markets—such as bonds, or equities in the developing world—had mostly been developed in the 1980s, but really started gaining traction in the 1990s. "It was definitely a very formative period," says Grossman, the onetime Sharpe protégé who had joined WFIA full time in 1985 and by 1992 led the company's quantitative investing team. "By the end of that decade, there was much more acceptance of indexing as a core strategy."

But Grauer was far from done. The marriage with Nikko might have been uneasy, but he still wanted to grow internationally and separate entirely from Wells Fargo, which remained a modestly sized, fairly insular Californian bank. "We were a heat-seeking missile in search of scale, given the economics of indexing," Grauer says.

Three suitors emerged: Merrill Lynch, which appealed to Grauer given his time there; State Street, which did not, given their rivalry; and Barclays Bank in the UK. In the end, Barclays' deeper pockets prevailed, and after a long courtship it bought WFNIA for $440 million in 1995. The deal ultimately proved a tremendous success, helping WFNIA break into the big UK market, but it was initially a messy process. "A lot of toes were stepped on pretty hard," Grauer recalls.

WFNIA was smashed together with the asset management arm

of Barclays de Zoete Wedd, the bank's securities division, and together they would manage $256 billion at the time.[6] Although the
combined firm was eventually renamed Barclays Global Investors,
it became a reverse takeover. Grauer soon led the combined company, its headquarters stayed in San Francisco, and the academic
culture of WFIA eventually permeated the whole organization.
"BZW was the traditional 'have a hunch, buy a bunch, go to lunch'
type of asset management. And we were all quants," recalls Ken
Kroner, a former BGI executive. BZW people who couldn't adapt
to that more data-driven culture soon left.

▲

HOWEVER, GRAUER WOULD himself soon leave. He had taken a big
pay cut to get the deal done, but his three-year contract was coming
up for renewal, and he was now in command of a vast, successful,
and international investment empire. He wanted the new contract
to include a substantial raise. In the summer of 1998, he attended a
weekend getaway for senior Barclays executives at Glyndebourne,[7]
an elegant six-hundred-year-old country house in southern England
that hosts a famous outdoor opera festival every summer. Afterward, he visited Martin Taylor, Barclays' CEO, and had tea in his
office to discuss the new contract. When it became clear his demand would not be met, he promptly resigned.

To Grauer's fury, his protégé Dunn—who he had recently promoted to be BGI's co–chief executive and co-chairman alongside
him—didn't follow suit, and picked up the reins of the organization
herself. Grauer saw it as a rank betrayal, believing that Dunn had
reassured Taylor she would stay on and emboldened Barclays in
the pay negotiations. Although Grauer said nothing publicly at the
time, wary of doing anything that would destabilize BGI, it permanently wrecked his relationship with Dunn. "I think she knew exactly what she wanted to do," he says. On the nature of their rift and

estrangement, Dunn later told her biographer, "Believe it or not, I have very few sources of heartbreak in my life. That's one of them."[8]

The abrupt departure came as a shock to the troops back in San Francisco, and the wider investment industry. "The king is dead. Long live the queen," declared one industry magazine.[9] Grauer had restored an innovative yet troubled investment unit, transformed it into one of the world's biggest money managers, and then suddenly left. "We were stunned," recalls Goddard. "But we had two parents, and we still had her. She was an incredible lady." Grauer might have disagreed, but in Dunn, BGI had an executive who would take it on its grandest and most consequential adventure.

▲

DUNN'S RISE FROM TEMPORARY SECRETARY to CEO is a remarkable tale, especially for happening at a time when the corporate ladder could be treacherous for women, and in an industry infamous for the dominance of men. While a later scandal under her watch as chairwoman of Hewlett-Packard tarnished her legacy as one of America's great corporate leaders, those who worked with her at BGI are virtually without exception glowing in their assessment of her capabilities. "She was just a phenomenally gifted leader," recalls Kroner.

Dunn grew up in Las Vegas, where her father was a talent booker at the Dunes and Tropicana hotels, and her mother a showgirl. When her father died when she was just eleven, Ruth Dunn and her three young children moved to San Francisco.[10] Pattie Dunn's good grades earned her a scholarship to study journalism in Oregon, but when her mother fell into alcoholism and homelessness, she interrupted her studies to help out. She eventually finished her journalism studies at Berkeley, but to earn some money for the family she took a job as a part-time secretary at WFIA.[11] Initially her job was mostly to fill out trade tickets for its S&P 500 fund, but her aptitude and eagerness to learn meant that she was quickly given more responsibilities. This culminated in picking up the reins of its $25 billion of index funds when Fouse, Loeb, and her then-husband Jahnke all abruptly left in 1983.[12]

Instead of that being the beginning of the end of her career at WFIA, as she had initially feared, Grauer promoted her quickly through the ranks. She started jetting around the world to visit the various BGI sites and clients, despite being petrified of flying and often violently grabbing onto next-seat colleagues whenever the jitters started. "I still have scars on my forearm from when we hit some turbulence," says Luskin.

Dunn was especially known for God-level people skills, beloved by employees and clients alike. One company legend was that she once managed to talk American Airlines into diverting one of its commercial flights so that she could make a last-minute meeting in Orlando—in midair. She later revealed to Kroner that the story was true, but left out that she was the only passenger on the flight.*

Her persuasiveness also succeeded where Grauer's forcefulness had failed, with Dunn eventually convincing Barclays to give BGI executives a more generous stock option program—something that would eventually make many of them wealthy. "A lot of people have second or third homes and nice cars thanks to Pattie," says Goddard.

However, by the late 1990s, BGI was coming under increasing commercial pressures. Index funds had become commoditized, and fees came under ferocious competition. For plain-vanilla products like an S&P-500-tracking strategy, the fees were almost zero—a

---

* She was equally adept at managing up and down. David Burkart, a young fund manager at BGI, recalls a 2000 party at a pool hall to celebrate a big investment mandate win, with Dunn in attendance. On a whim Burkart handed Dunn his cue, and she proceeded to clean the table and coolly handed it back. Other BGI executives reminisce how she always seemed to remember the name of every partner and child.

tremendous boon to people's retirement accounts, but problematic for companies like BGI. They could generate extra revenue through a process called "securities lending," in practice renting out their stocks to other fund managers who wanted to bet on them falling. But this money had to be shared with clients. And with interest rates falling, these revenues were also under pressure.

Many rivals were developing quantitative strategies similar to those pioneered by WFIA, and everyone in the finance industry was by then snapping up mathematically inclined "quants" for which WFIA had once been one of the only homes, driving up salaries.

The impact was becoming clear on the bottom line. In 1998, the year Grauer left, its assets under management grew 20 percent to over $600 billion, yet its operating profit rose only a modest 2 percent to $86 million.[13] Dunn desperately needed to find a new engine to reinvigorate its growth. Presciently, she realized that the answer might already lie in a small internal business set up as favor to Morgan Stanley some years earlier.

▲

IN THE EARLY 1990S, a Morgan Stanley executive named Robert Tull had assiduously studied the prospectuses of LOR's Super-Shares, Canada's TIPS, and the Amex/State Street's SPDR, and became enamored with the idea of listed index funds. He used them to design something the investment bank dubbed "Optimized Portfolios as Listed Securities," or OPALS.

In concept, they were similar to ETFs, but in practice they were debt securities, structured by Morgan Stanley to mimic the returns of several international stock markets, such as Germany, France, or Japan. Morgan Stanley controlled the leading indices for many of these markets, thanks to a joint venture with Capital Group, a giant investment group based in Los Angeles that had been a pioneer of investing in international markets. This collaboration was called MS-CI, which was later spun out as a separate business. Today, MSCI is one of the world's biggest index providers.

For a variety of legal and regulatory reasons, OPALS were available only to Morgan Stanley's international clients. In practice, they are the precursors to what are today known as "exchange-traded notes," synthetic securities engineered to replicate a benchmark, rather than an actual fund that warehouses securities.

Tull was an eclectic executive for the historically straightlaced investment bank. He never graduated from college, and first entered the finance industry as a commodities trader after a scrappy stint as a silver trucker. But getting shot and knifed and breaking strikes was great preparation for Wall Street, he jokes. OPALS quickly became a money-spinner for Morgan Stanley, and he was determined to do something similar for US investors. But to do so he needed an investment group to manage it—just like the American Stock Exchange had needed State Street to launch SPDR.

Tull therefore invited Dunn, Grossman, and Luskin over to lunch at Morgan Stanley's opulent dining room to explain how they wanted to launch a series of exchange-traded index funds that tracked international stock markets. SPDR was hardly a roaring success, but Luskin seemed particularly keen on the idea.

Luskin, a college dropout turned options trader, was unusually abrasive for BGI, a company that was dominated mostly by clean-cut, soft-spoken former academics like Grossman, who would debate and analyze everything to death. But even Luskin's detractors admit that he was brilliant, that he brought a lot of drive and trading expertise to the organization, and that his bluntness could be useful at a place in love with never-ending Socratic debate.

Luskin handed the practical task of building the suite of ETFs to Amy Schioldager, a fund manager responsible for BGI's international index funds. "Make it happen," he tersely instructed her, with little instruction on how to do it. Schioldager could read SPDR's public regulatory filings, but vast amounts of practical details had to be worked out, and she couldn't just call up State Street—at the time BGI's biggest competitor—and ask for help. So she and her team set about reverse engineering the whole process.

Given that Schioldager still had her regular job, it took months of intense fifteen-hour days to get it done. The payoff seemed ephemeral. She thought ETFs seemed like an interesting product, but at the time her managers mainly seemed to see it as a favor they were doing for Morgan Stanley.

The product was named World Equity Benchmark Shares, or WEBS, as a kind of homage to SPDR's spider imagery. Its prospectus was the first to use the now-ubiquitous "exchange-traded funds" term. But unlike SPDR's trust structure, they were legally structured as a series of tradable mutual funds that tracked seventeen MSCI indices, managed by BGI. Nate Most, who had retired from the American Stock Exchange after pioneering the ETF, was brought in to be chairman of WEBS.

They went live in 1996, and expectations were fairly muted given SPDR's initial challenges. At first WEBS did indeed prove a dud. Even three years after their launch, there was still less than $2 billion in BGI's suite of ETFs.[14]

At the end of the millennium, there were still just thirty-six ETFs in existence. Despite the swift success of QQQ—Bank of New York's Nasdaq-tracking ETF launched at the peak of the dot-com bubble—they managed just $39 billion at the end of 1999.[15] Underscoring the prevailing gloomy view of their potential, Morgan Stanley soon sold its interest in the business to BGI for a purely nominal sum, according to Tull, purely so that its thriving equity business could seize back some of the internal resources it consumed.

Many BGI executives were also skeptical. The company was like a financial factory designed to produce index funds, but it was focused on big institutional investors, like pension plans, endowments, and foreign central banks. ETFs, on the other hand, were primarily seen as a product for retail investors, such as everyday households managing their own retirement savings. Many at BGI therefore considered ETFs as a distraction from its core focus, and potentially even a danger to its brand. Culturally, moving into the retail space was akin to Gucci suddenly trying to sell its clothes through Walmart. Launching or acquiring mutual funds aimed at regular investors had been periodically discussed, but always nixed for these reasons.

Nonetheless, Dunn was a believer. After Grauer's exit in 1998 and her elevation, she tasked Lee Kranefuss, the energetic head of BGI's strategy group, with mapping out an ambitious course for the ETF business, involving the development of a panoply of new ETFs and a dedicated marketing and sales force. This would require serious resources, and therefore Barclays' blessing.

When Kranefuss and Dunn presented their plan to the Barclays board in London, there were a lot of blank faces. The board had just finished a discussion about the closure of high street branches in the UK, and the intricacies of ETFs might as well have been Latin (or Greek, given the popularity of its letters to denote concepts in finance). But Dunn was a persuasive advocate, and Bob Diamond, the forceful American head of Barclays Capital, its investment bank, quickly grasped the potential and helped talk the board into backing it.

The bank committed about $40 million a year for three years to the project—a huge sum that many skeptics at BGI thought was foolish. At the time, ETFs were slow to gain traction, while BGI's quantitative strategies were red-hot, leading to a nerdy, BGI-specific microcosm of the wider industry debate about active versus passive investing.

At a company retreat for BGI's managing directors at the Loews

Hotel, just off the Santa Monica Pier, Dunn tried to convince the company's more skeptical executives to back the efforts, despite the impact the cost might have on their own compensation. Some supporters were taken aback at the resistance. "That's when I became aware of people's opinions that we were eating their bonus pool," says James Parsons, who came over from BGI to be one of Kranefuss's deputies in the new venture.

Dunn pressed ahead. In May 2000, the WEBS unit was rebranded iShares. The origin of the name has been lost in the mists of time, with some executives attributing it to Apple's launch of the iMac some years earlier, while others recall that it was a placeholder reference to "index shares" that simply stuck. The relaunch was accompanied by a blizzard of new ETFs, which tracked everything from the S&P 500 to smaller stocks, value stocks, and growth stocks, and in 2002 even the bond market—a formidable feat of financial engineering at the time. This was supported by big expensive advertising campaigns to raise awareness of iShares among retail investors, from TV commercials to online ads. Eventually, iShares would sponsor everything from Cirque du Soleil to cycling and extreme sailing.

The intense, entrepreneurial Kranefuss ruffled some feathers at BGI. Some saw him as a bit of a "crazy professor" who would constantly think up kooky ideas and leave the details and implementation to others, and then take all the credit. Others simply continued to resent the cost of building up the ETF business, as it directly affected BGI's profits and therefore their year-end bonuses.

But his zeal proved instrumental in building up iShares as a separate brand inside BGI, with a distinctive, cultish culture of its own. This was essential, as Kranefuss believed the deliberative, academic milieu of BGI was antithetical to quickly building a new business and being successful in a retail market. "BGI had the sharpest people in every area of the business, but it was a college campus," recalls

Parsons. "Lee created a culture that moved quickly and without ego." Kranefuss even moved iShares into a different building at 388 Market Street in San Francisco, a block away from BGI's main skyscraper headquarters at 45 Fremont, to help inculcate a different team spirit.

One of Kranefuss's ingenious strategies was to get index providers in many cases to sign fixed-term exclusivity agreements—with the duration ranging up to ten years—preventing other aspiring ETF manufacturers from using them for their own products. For example, BGI secured through a generous licensing fee the sole use of Russell Indices' well-known small-stocks benchmark for its iShares Russell 2000 ETF, which it launched in May 2000.

Given how investors preferred the use of brand-name indices, and how investor inflows and tradability is a virtuous circle for ETFs, it essentially allowed BGI to seize and fortify important tracts of the investment landscape undisturbed. The iShares Russell ETF alone manages about $70 billion today, more than its three biggest competitors combined. It was in effect what Silicon Valley today terms a "blitzscaling"—a well-funded, rapid, and aggressive move to build an unassailable market share as quickly as possible.

BGI was braced for an aggressive response from State Street and especially Vanguard. Given the latter's commanding position as a pioneer of low-cost index funds for the masses, many executives assumed that it would seize much of the nascent ETF industry as well. Instead, they faced surprisingly little competition. "Frankly, it was quite a relief when Jack Bogle went on the offense against ETFs," Grossman recalls. "He was quite a visionary in so many ways, but as a result that really held Vanguard back for a number of years."

Vanguard belatedly launched its first ETF in 2001, and State Street steadily built up its own suite of ETFs. But BGI became the runaway leader by aggressively building an entire ETF platform, a kind of menu from which investors could select whatever financial slice they might fancy. Financial advisors took almost instantly to iShares, but to BGI's delight, many institutional investors and hedge funds also quickly embraced its ETFs as an easy way to manage their portfolios or make quick tactical bets. That helped make iShares a crossover hit. By 2007, BGI reported pretax profits of $1.4 billion, thanks in large part to iShares growing dramatically to $408 billion on the eve of the financial crisis.[16]

▲

GRAUER HAD RESURRECTED A WILTING business and turned it into a global investment giant, while Kranefuss was the driving force behind the growth of iShares. But the success of BGI's ETF business would not have happened without Dunn. She championed the unit when even many of her senior executives were profoundly skeptical, and coaxed Barclays into supporting the expensive relaunch of its ETF unit. "iShares would not exist without her, full stop," says Parsons. "She was a steadfast believer."

Yet Dunn didn't stay long enough at BGI to see the fruit of her labor, and her final days as its head were troubled. In September 2001, she was diagnosed with breast cancer, requiring intensive treatment. She also began to grow increasingly frustrated by Barclays, and quietly started exploring a management-led buyout of BGI—a secretive project code-named Project Amethyst.[17]

Together with Hellman & Friedman, a big private equity firm, Dunn in early 2002 plotted to buy BGI from Barclays for $1.4 billion and run it as an independent asset management company partly owned by its own executives. But some of the practicalities of the buyout proved insurmountable. In the end, Barclays decided it didn't want to sell its investment arm, period.[18] Dunn's relationship with London was permanently impaired in the process, with some at the bank considering her machinations akin to high treason.

Worse, in May 2002, Dunn was diagnosed with melanoma,

another type of cancer that required more extensive chemotherapy. Seeing no other options, she resigned from BGI in June. Diamond, the imperious American head of Barclays Capital, its freewheeling investment bank, was named chairman of BGI to keep a closer eye on it. As a result, a period of ownership characterized by some BGI executives as "benign neglect" started becoming far more hands-on. However, under Diamond's control the company finally started churning out the hefty profits it had always promised.

Dunn eventually recovered, and became chairwoman of Hewlett-Packard in 2005. But her stewardship of the technology giant ended in scandal. Under her watch the company hired private investigators to spy on some of its board members, and Dunn resigned in 2006 after the extent became public, even though she herself had not authorized the snooping. She was then also diagnosed with advanced ovarian cancer, which eventually led to her passing away in 2011, at just fifty-eight years of age.

Yet her importance in the history of index funds is clear. Not only was she an exceptionally rare female head of a major financial firm—alone notable, given that even two decades later it remains a rarity—but she was instrumental in seeing the potential of ETFs, ensuring that BGI leapfrogged their pioneer State Street, reestablished its reputation as the "temple of beta," and built a finance-altering industry.

It was a startling success story that attracted envy across Wall Street—nowhere more so than at an ambitious, gung-ho New York investment group called BlackRock.

Chapter 13

LARRY'S GAMBIT

ON APRIL 16, 2009, ROB KAPITO went to the newly built Yankee Stadium, where the pride of New York was taking on the Cleveland Indians. The economy was in shambles, after the US subprime mortgage crisis triggered a near-fatal heart attack for the global financial system, and many Wall Streeters were desperate for any fleeting distractions. But the balding former bond trader was not there to watch a game of baseball.

Kapito was on a secret mission that would not only transform the fortunes of his employer, BlackRock, but change the face of the financial industry. Bob Diamond, the chief executive of Barclays, was watching the game from his corporate box at Yankee Stadium, and Kapito needed an urgent, discreet chat with his old friend. So he scalped a ticket and made his way to the Bronx.

Barclays had taken a plunge by acquiring the US parts of Lehman Brothers when the investment bank imploded in 2008, but the deal quickly became a dead weight dragging Barclays down as well. By early 2009, Barclays itself was scrambling to raise money and avoid having to take a UK government bailout. That meant it was open to selling the family silver, including its well-regarded asset management arm Barclays Global Investors. It would even be willing to sell it off piecemeal. In early April, Barclays accepted a $4.2 billion offer from CVC, a big London-based private equity firm, for BGI's rapidly growing iShares ETF unit.

Crucially, the agreement included a forty-five-day "go-shop" provision, which permitted Barclays to talk with other people who might be interested in topping CVC's offer. This gave BlackRock an opening—but one it had to seize quickly.

It had been quietly on the prowl for an acquisition to get a foothold in the fast-growing ETF industry since at least 2007, when BlackRock's CEO, Larry Fink, had tasked his strategy supremo, Sue Wagner, with investigating how they could jump into the fray. Her conclusion was that the best way to do so was through an acquisition, and now all of a sudden the leading player was on the auction block. The well-connected Fink had heard through the grapevine that CVC was deep in talks with Barclays well before the deal was announced and had been plotting to intervene ever since.* So Fink sent Kapito, BlackRock's president, with an urgent message to Yankee Stadium.

The Yankees beat Cleveland that night, setting themselves up for ultimately winning the 2009 World Series, their first championship in nearly a decade. But Kapito missed the entire game, and to this day cannot even remember who played. He rushed up to Barclays' corporate box, knocked on the door, and asked Diamond to come out for a chat. Diamond agreed, and went for a walk with Kapito. "Do you want to play checkers, or do you want to play chess?"

---

* As is often the case, various reports over the years have differing timelines and details of how the deal came through, and the main people involved also all have slightly different accounts. This account attempts to reconcile the versions into one narrative.

BlackRock's president asked Diamond, and proceeded to present his proposal.

Instead of selling just iShares to CVC, Barclays should sell all of BGI to BlackRock, in return for a big slug of money and stock in the combined company. This way, Barclays would both get the capital it needed to avoid a bailout—which would come with onerous government strings—and still enjoy an interest in its money management arm through a big block of ownership in BlackRock, which would be transformed into a giant of the investing world.

"That's a very intriguing idea," Diamond replied, who as it happened had already gotten board approval to explore the sale of the entire business, and thought of BlackRock as a natural buyer. They paced around the corridor outside Barclays' box for thirty minutes to sketch it out further, culminating in an agreement that Diamond and his chairman, John Varley, would come to visit Larry Fink the next day.

The stakes were enormous. If it proved successful, a combined BlackRock-BGI would be the undisputed titan of asset management—controlling over $2.7 trillion at the time—and help reshape the industry's landscape. It could catapult Fink from a highly regarded Wall Street leader into the rarefied ranks of corporate executives referred to by only their first name, and decisively move passive investing from the investment industry's hinterland to center stage.

But the proposed deal was fraught with dangers. The financial industry was still reeling from its biggest crisis in a century, and paying the billions of dollars BGI would cost would be a daunting task for BlackRock. Moreover, smashing together a traditional, famously aggressive Wall Street investment group with the index-oriented strategies and laid-back academics of BGI would be a cultural and practical nightmare, at a time when markets and the global economy were still recovering from the convulsions of 2008.

It was an outrageously ambitious gambit from a former bond trader ousted from his first job on Wall Street after losing a cool $100 million.

▲

"TITAN OF FINANCE" WAS HARDLY written in Fink's stars. He was born on November 2, 1952, and grew up in Van Nuys, a nondescript neighborhood in Los Angeles' San Fernando Valley, mostly notable for being where the original *Terminator* movie was largely filmed. Yet there was little that was cinematic about his early life. His father owned a shoe store in Van Nuys, while his mother was an English professor at California State University's Northridge campus. The transplanted midwesterners encouraged structure but independence for their kids, letting the young Larry go on holidays alone when he turned fifteen years old. He didn't do as well academically as his older brother, though, so he had to help out at his father's shop from ten onward—a chore his more gifted sibling was exempted from.

Fink met his future wife—the petite, dark-haired Lori—at high school, and both went to study at UCLA, with Fink majoring in political theory. The Cold War had stirred an interest in the battle between capitalism and communism, but it was hardly the culmination of a lifelong dream. It was just a fascinating subject, and he had no clear career plan mapped out.

Aside from some basic economics, Fink took no business studies until his senior year, when on a whim he took some graduate classes in real estate. He got to know the professor who taught them, who invited Fink to be his research assistant. Thus the budding real estate developer moved straight to UCLA's business school. However, the plan of entering the property industry gradually faded. His father-in-law was in real estate, and Fink wanted to do something different, maybe something more international. But he had no clear idea of what that might mean. So, like many bright young men without a firm idea of what they wanted to do, except make some good money, Fink strutted off to Wall Street, long-haired and sporting a turquoise bracelet given to him by Lori.[1]

He had several offers from top investment banks, but to his chagrin flubbed the final interview with Goldman Sachs. "I was devastated, but it ended up being the blessing of blessings," Fink recalls. Instead, he went to First Boston, another pedigreed firm, where he started working in 1976. He was placed in its bond trading department, and, given his real estate background, was mainly trading mortgage-backed bonds. He proved a rare talent, and was by 1978 running the department. There he built a close-knit, hardworking, and ferociously loyal unit around him.

Many were Jewish—in the 1970s and 1980s, Italians and Jews were still often held at arm's length at Waspier Wall Street firms like First Boston—leading some there to dub Fink's desk "Little Israel." His manager told him to hire a "wop" to work on the desk when everyone else was off for the Jewish holidays, a working-class Wharton graduate from Monticello named Robert Kapito. But when Rosh Hashanah arrived, it turned out that Kapito was as Jewish as the rest of the desk. Despite the casual xenophobia of the era, Fink loved it at First Boston, which was at its core scrappy and meritocratic. The reality was that no one cared who you were, as long as you made money. And Fink made money, and reaped the rewards.

Brilliant, aggressive, and inventive, Fink became instrumental in creating and developing the vast US mortgage-backed bond market, together with his great rival at Salomon Brothers, Lewis Ranieri. Mortgage bonds bundle together the payments of many individual mortgages, and are then sliced and diced and bought by investors according to their risk appetite. Although they led to disaster in 2008, when structured conservatively they can help lower borrowing costs for mortgages, and give pension funds and insurers a valuable investment opportunity.

Although he was more cerebral than many bond traders, Fink's ego grew in tandem with his success, and his cockiness grated with some colleagues. "I was a jerk," he once admitted.[2] Nonetheless, Wall Street loves success more than modesty. Fink became the youngest managing director in First Boston's history. When he was just thirty-one, he became the youngest member of its management committee, after having made the firm an estimated $1 billion. The sky seemed the limit.

But then the sky came crashing down. "My team and I felt like rock stars. Management loved us. I was on track to become CEO of the firm," Fink later recalled in a speech.[3] "And then . . . well, I screwed up. And it was bad."

In the ferocious competition with Salomon to be top dog of the mortgage-backed securities market, Fink's desk loaded up on huge positions in 1986.[4] But disastrously, the hedges his team had put in place to protect themselves fizzled when interest rates unexpectedly fell, losing the desk an estimated $100 million. Despite the money Fink had made First Boston in the preceding decade, he went from CEO-in-waiting to outcast. Still, he continued to work for First Boston for nearly two years, until he eventually quit in early 1988.

His once-ebullient self-confidence gradually ebbed away during the awkward exit. "I became a leper at the firm," Fink recalls. "I'd walk down the hallways and people would look at me differently. I felt that the rest of the firm was angry at me . . . I felt abandoned. It didn't feel like a team anymore." Nonetheless, the lessons of that humiliation proved invaluable, and Fink was not ready to pack it in.

Some years earlier, he had become phone pals with Ralph Schlosstein, an investment banker focused on the mortgage industry at Shearson Lehman Hutton. Both Fink and Schlosstein were early risers, and would call each other frequently around 6:30 a.m. to chat about financial markets before the morning hubbub started.

"There weren't many other people to talk to at that time," Schlos-stein observes. In March 1987, they happened to be in Washington at the same time, and on the same flight back to New York that evening, so they had dinner together. It proved a pivotal meeting.

Both were Democrats—Schlosstein had even been a Treasury official in the Carter administration before heading to Wall Street—but mostly they talked about work, with both expressing dissatisfaction with their jobs and a desire to start something new.[5] That initial conversation steadily grew into something firmer, especially after the Black Monday crash, which hammered home how quickly markets were evolving. They started sketching out plans for a company that would model every single security, aggregate them into a portfolio, and better analyze all the risks they contained. "It became clear that many investors that were buying a lot of these new financial products didn't really understand them," Schlosstein recalls. "That was really the genesis of BlackRock."

On a chilly day in February 1988, Fink and Schlosstein went for a walk up Park Avenue to discuss the particulars of their new venture over lunch. Before they even reached the restaurant they had come to an agreement. "You know, we haven't talked about the economics between the two of us. What were you thinking?" Fink asked Schlosstein. The Lehman banker suggested a 60–40 split, with 60 percent ownership going to Fink. "I was thinking two-thirds, one-third," Fink countered. Schlosstein then suggested five-eighths and three-eighths, to which Fink agreed. It took minutes, and was the last time the two founders ever discussed the subject.

Four days after he formally resigned from First Boston, Fink invited a select group of people to his house to discuss the new venture. From First Boston came Kapito, Fink's right-hand man on the mortgage trading desk; Barbara Novick, head of portfolio products; Ben Golub, a cerebral math wizard who had designed many of the bank's risk management tools; and Keith Anderson, one of First Boston's top bond analysts. From Shearson Lehman, Schlosstein brought Susan Wagner and later Hugh Frater, two of its top mortgage bond specialists. But their specialties were less important than their personal competence. "We were predominantly picking high-quality athletes," Schlosstein says. Together, they resolved to start a new bond investment firm built on modern technology and sounder risk management.

The six other founders insisted that they should have an equal stake with each other for the first three years. "You can put ten brilliant people in a room, and if they're not rowing the same direction, you will get nowhere," Wagner argued in Fink's house. "If we want to get everyone rowing the same direction, then really, you should give all the partners the same equity and the same compensation." Fink and Schlosstein were initially skeptical, wondering how they could manage the business like a kibbutz. But they quickly relented, and never regretted it. "They were absolutely right, it was one of the best things we did," Schlosstein says. "For the first three years, all they did was focus on the size of the pie, rather than the size of their slice."

They still needed money to launch, so Fink got out his Rolodex. He got in touch with Steve Schwarzman and Pete Peterson, two former Lehman bankers whose firm, Blackstone, was on its way to becoming a rising star of the private equity industry. Fink had even helped it raise its first $560 million buyout fund in 1987. Schwarzman in turn reached out to Bruce Wasserstein—First Boston's flamboyant mergers and acquisitions head and a Wall Street legend—who told him that Fink was "by far the most gifted person at First Boston."[6]

Reassured, Blackstone agreed to house the new venture in its offices and bankroll it with a $5 million loan, in return for a 50 percent stake.* Fink himself received a 2.5 percent slice of Blackstone.[7] Given Blackstone's emerging brand, Fink and Schlosstein decided to hitch their ride to it, naming their new company Blackstone Financial Management.

Up and running, they made their first hire—Charlie Hallac, one of Golub's former colleagues at First Boston—and set about trying to win clients, for both a new bond fund and the supporting technology service that Golub and Hallac were building. This was envisaged as a cutting-edge solution for bond traders and investors so that they could avoid the debacle that had befallen Fink at First Boston, and was dubbed the "Asset, Liability, Debt and Derivative Investment Network," or Aladdin. The first version was coded on a $20,000 Sun workstation wedged between their office fridge and coffee machine.[8] More First Boston people followed, leading the firm to leak that Fink had actually been fired—a common "scorched earth" Wall Street tactic against former employees.

Fortunately, Blackstone Financial Management enjoyed a strong start. American Savings and Loan became the first advisory client, even though Aladdin wouldn't become a formal division of its own for another dozen years. By the end of 1988, the company had $8 billion under management in several closed-end funds focused on mortgage bonds. This despite having virtually zero actual asset management experience between them. Gold-plated connections helped. Blackstone's Peterson, a former commerce secretary for Richard Nixon, got former Federal Reserve vice chair Andrew Rimmer to serve as a board member of BFM's new funds, while Schlosstein milked his ties to the Carter administration to land former vice president Walter Mondale. Their luster proved invaluable.

"We started our business with what I would call 'trust me'

---

* BlackRock's internal history pins Blackstone's ownership stake at 40 percent.

money, people that believe that you are going to do well even though you've never done this before," says Schlosstein. He recalls how Chrysler's treasurer called after its pension fund had waived its normal requirement for a five-year track record and invested $35 million[9] in a BFM account, and said clearly, "Don't fuck it up. My neck is on the line."

Anderson became its first chief investment officer, purely because he was the only one with concrete, albeit brief, experience from the money management industry. The other roles were gradually formalized, although long remained fuzzy. Anderson was supported by Kapito, who became head of portfolio management. Wagner, Novick, and Frater spent most of their time on winning clients and strategy, while Golub and Hallac worked on Aladdin.

Although there were the occasional intra-founder squabbles, it remained an extraordinarily tight-knit group, both professionally and personally. Fink, Kapito, and Schlosstein would go to competitive wine-tasting events together, with groups of roughly a dozen high-powered people from finance, industry, and medicine. Everyone would bring a bottle of wine, and whoever brought the lowest-rated one in the blind tasting would have to pick up the dinner tab—unless someone ranked their own wine the worst, in which case they would have to pay.

Business also grew briskly. Of the $5 million credit line from Blackstone, it had drawn down only $150,000, and that was quickly repaid.[10] Within its first six years, BFM managed about $23 billion, and the eight founding partners had been joined by about 150 employees.[11] "It really was magical the first few years," Fink recalls with fondness.

But the company was heading toward a rupture with Blackstone that would lead to a dramatic recasting of the company once known as BFM.

▲

BLACKSTONE'S SCHWARZMAN HAS himself become one of the finance industry's most powerful and wealthiest players, with a fortune now estimated at over $26 billion. But he didn't amass this through a relaxed attitude to money. That eventually led to an acrimonious divorce between Blackstone and its burgeoning bond investment arm.

Schlosstein and Fink wanted to build a big business, and enticed many new partners by offering slices of equity—something that gradually diluted Blackstone's ownership. When it fell to about 32 percent in 1992, Schwarzman told them that he would tolerate no further drops—an intransigence that some colleagues thought was related to a costly divorce Schwarzman was going through at the time.[12] Schwarzman denies this, and felt they had an agreement that further dilutions would have to come from Fink and Schlosstein, and he was simply sticking to it.[13] He did, however, later admit that it was "a heroic mistake" to precipitate a rupture with Schlosstein and Fink.[14]

Initially, Fink and Schlosstein explored the idea of going public to get out from under Blackstone's thumb, but by 1994 they insisted on an outright sale. "What Steve was doing was an anathema to us," says Schlosstein. They also resolved that the company should have its own name and distinct identity.

All its funds had tickers starting with the letter B, but an agreement with Blackstone stipulated that the new name could not include the words "black" or "stone," limiting their options. "We were moving toward calling ourselves Bedrock," Fink later recalled.[15] "But too many people related that to the Flintstones." On the other hand, the founders loved the name "BlackRock," with Fink especially taken with the capitalized R. So they appealed to Schwarzman and Peterson, pointing out that Morgan Stanley's split from JP-Morgan in the wake of the Great Depression burnished both firms. Peterson and Schwarzman were both[16] tickled by the idea of Black-Rock as an homage to Blackstone, and blessed the new name.

In June 1994, they finally got their wish, when BlackRock Financial Management sold for $240 million to PNC Bank in Pittsburgh. By 1998, PNC had folded all its money management operations into BlackRock, bringing it its first mutual funds. Fink and Schlosstein then convinced PNC that the best solution for both the bank and BlackRock was to sell 20 percent of it back to its management, and list a chunk of the remaining business on the stock market. "Had that not happened, BlackRock would not be anywhere near where it is today," Schlosstein argues. "We would have been a subsidiary of a regional bank, and none of us would be there."

The long-mooted initial public offering finally arrived on October 1, 1999. BlackRock's assets under management had by then vaulted to $165 billion. But the IPO bombed. The stock was priced at just $14, right at the bottom of the $14–$17 range that its bankers at Merrill Lynch had touted to investors, and down from the earlier $16–$20 range Merrill had initially hoped for.

That price valued BlackRock at just under $900 million, a bitter disappointment to Fink. But it was the peak of the dotcom boom, and investors had eyes for only hot tech stocks. They certainly didn't give a hoot about a low-profile investment group that managed bond portfolios for pension funds. Fink was tempted to cancel the listing, but Merrill Lynch's chief executive, David Komansky, called and didn't mince his words. "What the fuck are you doing?" he yelled at Fink. "Just do the IPO. If you do your job well over the next four to five years, it will be a distant memory. Just do the fucking IPO now. Don't be a fucking asshole."

Moreover, despite the modest price, it failed to get the big first-day pop that all stock market debutantes hope for, while two other listings that same day soared. The ultimate indignity was that Fink didn't even get to ring the New York Stock Exchange's ceremonial bell that day. The NYSE instead handed Fink the booby prize of ringing the closing bell at 4 p.m. the following Friday—a time when no one is watching. "It was the ultimate slap in the face for how crappy we were," Fink says.

Nonetheless, the stability of BlackRock's business started shining brighter once the dotcom bubble burst, leading its shares to trade at a premium to the rest of the investment industry. That meant it could now use its own shares as currency with which to buy rivals, growing through acquisitions rather than by just banging on the doors of clients or starting new teams from scratch. The history of the investment industry is riddled with acquisitions gone awry, but BlackRock used its listing to transform itself from a narrow bond investment house into the world's biggest money manager.

BlackRock first started sniffing around potential deals in 2002. One target was Merrill Lynch Investment Managers, the investment bank's sprawling asset management arm. But talks with Merrill Lynch's new chief executive, Stan O'Neal, went nowhere. Another candidate was Barclays Global Investors, after Pattie Dunn's private equity buyout had collapsed and she had once again been diagnosed with cancer. In 2004, Barclays quietly offered to sell BGI to Black-Rock for about $2 billion. But—perhaps fortunately—it never progressed.

At the time, BlackRock's founders saw the millions of dollars that BGI was spending on advertising its new iShares unit as an easy cost to cut. "We were licking our chops," Schlosstein recalls. "We thought this would be a home run acquisition." But BlackRock didn't want to pay the tentative asking price, and eventually Barclays decided it didn't want to sell its asset management unit anyway. It is possible that BlackRock would have realized the potential of the nascent iShares unit had it swooped then. Nonetheless, it turned its eyes elsewhere, letting iShares continue its meteoric rise.

The first deal came in the summer of 2004, when BlackRock bought State Street Research, a money manager owned by insurer MetLife (unrelated to the larger State Street in Boston). Most of SSR's assets were in equity and real estate funds, giving the bond-focused BlackRock a foothold in these markets for the first time. The deal cost $375 million in BlackRock stock and cash, and the combined company would manage about $366 billion.

The diplomatic and affable Schlosstein was handed the job of leading the integration. Wary of the litany of failed investment industry acquisitions, he resolved to act decisively but as fairly as possible. "We made difficult decisions, but to the best of my knowledge there's no one walking the world of finance that will say Ralph Schlosstein misled me or treated me disrespectfully," Schlosstein says. "Often these things get off track because people don't do that. So even when there's bad news I've tried to deliver it clearly and respectfully."

The SSR acquisition also taught BlackRock the importance of moving swiftly and forcefully when it acquired a business, imposing one single culture and leaning heavily on Aladdin as a unifying technological backbone. These were lessons it would soon apply to a far bigger, more complex deal. One that very nearly didn't happen.

In June 2005, months of acrimony at Morgan Stanley—one of Wall Street's biggest and most pedigreed investment banks—finally resulted in the ouster of its chief executive, Philip Purcell. The board then quietly reached out to Fink to see if he might be interested in the job. The prestige appealed to Fink, but he wanted Morgan Stanley to also buy BlackRock, something the board refused. Instead, they turned to John Mack, a charismatic if aggressive former Morgan Stanley executive who had been defenestrated by Purcell years earlier.

Mack—nicknamed "Mack the Knife" for his ruthlessness—was

a close friend of Fink's. Once he took over he called BlackRock's founder to suggest that they actually pursue the acquisition that Fink had suggested. Fink would become president of Morgan Stanley, and presumably Mack's heir apparent. However, when they got down to the nitty-gritty of the details, a multitude of differences became clear. Primarily, it boiled down to Mack wanting control of BlackRock, while Fink thought some independence was essential for BlackRock to continue to thrive. The talks dragged on for months without getting anywhere.

Then, out of the blue, Fink learned that O'Neal was now open to the idea of selling Merrill Lynch Investment Managers, but hadn't told Fink because he knew BlackRock was deep in talks with Morgan Stanley. So Fink reached out through back channels and engineered a breakfast meeting with O'Neal at Three Guys, a restaurant on the Upper East Side. Within fifteen minutes they had the major contours of a deal, signing the food menu to commemorate a provisional agreement, and the rest of the details were worked out in just two weeks. On Valentine's Day 2006, the deal was announced. But if State Street Research had been a hearty appetizer to digest, MLIM's size and complexity amounted to a five-course meal.

On paper, the deal looked perfect. MLIM had a strong presence among ordinary retail investors with its mutual funds, as well as an extensive institutional business in Europe and Asia—areas where BlackRock had a negligible presence. Meanwhile, its presence in fixed income was miniscule, aside from a few municipal bond funds. Together, it would constitute an industry colossus with almost $1 trillion under management. Moreover, the deal would be paid for in stock: Merrill Lynch would receive a 49.8 percent stake in the combined business, while PNC's share would go down to 34 percent. BlackRock's senior executives were confident that they could run the combined group, given that MLIM had been somewhat neglected by the investment bankers of Merrill Lynch.

Schlosstein was once again tasked with the integration, and, mindful of the dangers of a drawn-out, distracting consolidation, he moved with alacrity. By the time the deal was finalized at the end of September 2006, the work was all but done, even if there were still plenty of subsequent headaches. Once again, Aladdin was the secret sauce behind the deal's success, according to BlackRock executives. "With most big financial mergers, you're doing systems integration four-five years afterwards, or sometimes never. The scalability of Aladdin is an enormous, enormous benefit," says Schlosstein.

MLIM executives were divided on the acquisition. Some were relieved to be part of a more dynamic, standalone asset management company after Merrill's long neglect. Others chafed at what they perceived as BlackRock's arrogance. The gravel-voiced Kapito in particular rubbed many people the wrong way—something that would later repeat itself in the BGI deal. Several former MLIM and BGI executives compare him to Mike "Wags" Wagner, the aggressive but ferociously loyal hatchet man of fictional hedge fund manager Robert Axelrod in the Showtime series *Billions*. In contrast, Schlosstein and Sue Wagner generally acted as the silk to Kapito's steel. "Sue was a brilliant organizer," observes one former BlackRock executive who joined through the MLIM acquisition. "Larry would have ideas, and she would get it done. She was absolutely essential to Larry."

Despite the practical details of the MLIM integration falling to Schlosstein, many executives stress that the success of the deal was thanks to Fink, a workaholic with a prodigious grasp of both corporate minutiae and overarching strategy. "Larry was astonishing on the level of details he knew. I don't like him, but he's a phenomenal businessman, and he lives for BlackRock," observes one former senior executive. "When he leaves it will be like when Alex Ferguson left Manchester United . . . It is impossible to overstate how Black-Rock's journey is the journey of a single man."

Amid all this corporate tumult, the monolithic unity of Black-

Rock's founders started to erode. Frater was the first one to leave, pushed out to lead PNC's real estate business in early 2004. Schlosstein was next, announcing his departure to set up an investment firm toward the end of 2007. He was soon followed by Anderson, who left to set up a hedge fund.

All went on to enjoy prestigious post-BlackRock careers. Frater became the chief executive of Fannie Mae, Schlosstein the head of boutique investment bank Evercore, and Anderson for a period ran George Soros's legendary hedge fund. Hallac, an exacting taskmaster who played an instrumental role in the success of BlackRock, passed away in 2015, after a long battle with colon cancer. His understated but pivotal importance to BlackRock made him a revered and much-missed colleague. "Hallac was the piece of sand in the oyster," observes one former BlackRock executive. "He was critical to the organization . . . A sloppy answer was never allowed." Hallac worked up until the moment he passed away, dying with a BlackBerry in his hand, according to company legend. To this day, the mention of his name brings a mournful mien to the face of other senior executives, especially Fink.

However, losing Schlosstein was probably the biggest blow for Fink, who was initially resentful over his friend's decision to leave. But eventually he made his peace with it. At his leaving dinner, Schlosstein toasted his relationship with Fink, and said, "I don't think anyone else in my position has ever said this, but I've been the number two to the same person for twenty years. And there was never a moment in those twenty years where I thought, 'I wish he weren't here and I had the job.'"

▲

THE METTLE OF THE REMAINING founders was tested like never before in the financial inferno that started spreading soon after the MLIM acquisition was complete. The global financial crisis came as a shock, with Fink initially downplaying the wider dangers of the subprime housing mess when it started to creak in early 2007,[17] and a BlackRock investment in New York's Peter Cooper Village ending up a disaster.[18] But BlackRock was still able to navigate the resulting mayhem better than many other investment groups.

Underscoring Fink's resurrection as a major Wall Street player, in early 2008 he was the top contender to become the new CEO of Merrill Lynch, losing out only after he insisted the board authorize a thorough analysis of the investment bank's subprime exposure[19]—something that might ultimately have saved the company, which was later subsumed by Bank of America. "I didn't want to go into a snake trap," Fink later recalled.[20] "I said for me to even consider it I needed to have my team go in and look at the balance sheet. And I was never allowed to do that. The whole process was infuriating."

Despite this personal setback, BlackRock emerged as one of the winners from the crisis, thanks partly to the growth of its "Solutions" business, which had expanded far beyond just offering Aladdin to outside clients.* Its expertise in analyzing complex structured bonds had first been established in 1994, when General Electric asked it to value the assets on the balance sheet of Kidder Peabody, the venerable but struggling brokerage firm it owned. By the time the financial crisis erupted, the Solutions unit was a fully fledged, high-wattage financial advisory group with deep expertise in the plumbing of markets.

Everyone from Wall Street rivals to foreign central banks and the US government itself was clamoring for its help in analyzing the toxic securities that nearly brought the system crashing down. "When we did Kidder Peabody, it was an X-ray machine," according to Rob Goldstein, a senior BlackRock executive.[21] "When we

---

* As it happened, BGI was the first investment group to sign up as a client, for its bond business, according to Schlosstein.

had the opportunity to work on the most recent crisis, it was an MRI machine."

BlackRock's prestigious mandates to help the US Treasury and the Federal Reserve sort out the detritus of the financial crisis first started the envious mutterings about Fink's influence. But it was the deal to acquire BGI—and the painful yet ultimately successful integration of it into BlackRock—that would make him the informal king of Wall Street.

Chapter 14

DEAL OF THE CENTURY

IN EARLY 2009, MARK WIEDMAN was invited to lunch by Fink. Over an overflowing table of sushi at a swanky midtown Manhattan restaurant, they discussed Wiedman's mounting frustrations at BlackRock. The tall, wavy-haired, gregarious executive worked in the company's advisory group, and as a former senior Treasury executive had been intimately involved in its crisis cleanup operations. But he had fallen out with his immediate superior, and was desperate to switch lanes.

"I love working here. I just want to be happy coming in on Monday mornings," Wiedman complained. "I will do anything, even janitor." BlackRock's bespectacled chief seemed understanding, and as they picked at the sashimi and tempura, Fink revealed that he might have something new in the works. "I've got an assignment for you," he said. "We're about to buy this company called BGI . . . Why don't you run the integration?"

Wiedman was aware of the company but knew little about it, having never actually worked in the asset management industry himself. "Sounds great!" he nonetheless replied, desperate for a new job, whatever it might be. But for Fink, the reasoning was simple. Ralph Schlosstein, whose diplomatic touch had ensured the successful integration of State Street Research and Merrill Lynch Investment Management, was no longer at BlackRock. The Yale- and Harvard-educated Wiedman might not have been steeped in financial theorems, but had the intellectual chops to stand up to BGI's academics, as well as the social graces needed for the tricky job, and was seen internally as a Young Turk destined for great things. This job would allow him to prove it.

But then things went silent. Behind the scenes, completing the acquisition was proving fraught with difficulties. In fact, the investment industry's deal of the century nearly collapsed at the last minute.

Fink's initial conversations with Barclays Bank had gone well enough for BlackRock to send a delegation to visit BGI's senior executives in San Francisco for another round of discreet talks. Unfortunately, they didn't stay secret for long. Some eagle-eyed BGI employees spotted a black car waiting outside their headquarters with the name "Larry Fink" on a note in the window,[1] even as CVC's executives were in the same building examining iShares' books.

Luckily, the mishap didn't leak out into the press and scupper the talks, but then Bank of New York Mellon emerged as another potential buyer of BGI. Vanguard and Fidelity were also sniffing around iShares. Moreover, just as BlackRock was preparing to unveil the deal, its financing suddenly looked dicey.

Part of the acquisition would be paid for in BlackRock shares. But Barclays needed a big chunk of cash as well to avert a government bailout, so Fink had stitched together a multibillion-dollar financing package by calling on many of BlackRock's clients. The Qatari sovereign wealth fund was supposed to stump up $3 billion, but at the last minute—after Fink had already secured the approval of his board—the Qataris prevaricated. It appeared that a local potentate was keen to get in on the deal personally. But Fink wanted a bunch of strong institutional investors to support the deal, not individuals, no matter how rich or royal they were. He felt jerked around by the Qataris, and he was willing to walk away from the deal rather than compromise. So on June 10, Fink suddenly found himself with just twenty-four hours to raise the $3 billion—a massive task at a time when many were still reeling from the financial crisis—to save the acquisition.

That Wednesday, Fink ensconced himself at BlackRock's headquarters and called in the favors of a lifetime. A call to the China Investment Corporation, the country's sovereign wealth fund, led to a $1 billion commitment within an hour.[2] But he had to hit up a panoply of other potential investors until 4 a.m. that night, before returning to the office at 7:30 a.m. to continue working the phones up until when the deal was supposed to be made public.

It worked. At 8:20 p.m. in New York on June 11, 2009, Black-Rock announced that it had struck an agreement to buy BGI from Barclays in a deal valued at the time at $13.5 billion, through a combination of cash and the UK bank acquiring a 20 percent stake in BlackRock. CVC received $175 million as compensation for Barclays breaking its deal to sell iShares.

Wiedman remained oblivious to all this drama until Sue Wagner—BlackRock's petite, bang-haired chief operating officer and cofounder—abruptly called him out of a training session to help draft the press release announcing the deal. Soon afterward, Wagner hosted a call for BlackRock's top executives to lay out its rationale, and the assumptions underpinning it. Not everyone was thrilled, with some querying the growth assumptions for iShares, BGI's crown jewel. But at that stage it was a done deal. All that counted was making it a success, come hell or high water. For a period, it was mostly hell.

"It made us a truly global firm, but it also crossed a Rubicon in the industry. We suddenly became both an alpha and index house," says Wiedman. "This ignited deep, intense theological debates paralleled only by the wars of religion in the sixteenth century," he jokes.

▲

OVER IN SAN FRANCISCO, the initial response was a mix of relief and dismay. Many were at least reassured that the CVC deal for iShares was dead. After all, private equity ownership is never appealing, and disentangling the ETF unit from the broader company would have been a logistical nightmare at best, and fatal for iShares at worst. The iShares division was a brand and a sales force, and while its culture had become increasingly distinct from BGI, it was not really a standalone business. The actual product engineering was done by the mothership.

Senior managers had therefore secretly begun working on finding alternative suitors for the entire company, such as Bank of New York, Vanguard, Fidelity, and Goldman Sachs. Blake Grossman, by then BGI's chief executive, was also quietly exploring whether he could entice another private equity firm to bid for the entire group, so that BGI could finally become an independent asset manager. But the global economy was a mess, and there weren't many potential bidders who had the available firepower needed to acquire the entire company. At least BGI had long been an Aladdin client, there was a cordial relationship between the two organizations, and Grossman knew Fink personally and respected him greatly.

"There was a great deal of relief that things were resolved," Grossman recalls. "We had a new owner, which was highly regarded and stable. After all, there were a lot of other things going on in markets at the time. And BlackRock had a well-developed playbook for acquisitions and integration."

To get people on board, Fink hosted a bunch of top BGI executives for dinner in a private room at Fifth Floor, a Michelin-starred restaurant in San Francisco's Hotel Palomar. Together with Kapito, Golub, and a select number of top BlackRock executives and their BGI counterparties, they went around the table talking about their philosophies and values, to help get a sense of how the cultural mix would work. Many of BGI's top brass left that dinner feeling reassured.

Others could sense trouble brewing. The rank-and-file BGI view was largely that BlackRock consisted of a bunch of knuckle-dragging former bond traders who had built their business through acquisitions, not the innovation and brilliance that they thought was their hallmark. Although there was some grudging respect for BlackRock's commercial accomplishments, many at BGI saw its Wall Street culture as the antithesis of the cerebral, collegiate milieu of BGI.

Many therefore thought the two organizations were fundamentally incompatible. "There were senior people at the firm who said that they would never work for BlackRock," recalls Ken Kroner, the head of BGI's quantitative strategies at the time. "And it was not a small number."

The haughty superiority of BGI executives could also rub Black-Rock employees the wrong way. They argued they brought rigor and commercial sense to an organization still more college campus than global money manager. "They didn't think we were as clever as them, that we cut corners," recalls one former BlackRock executive involved in the integration. "BGI thought they should get mandates simply because they were the smartest people in the room, but that doesn't work."

Moreover, BGI was not in the greatest of positions to be snooty at the time. It had become increasingly aggressive in sweating the "securities lending" revenues it made from renting out shares in its index funds. When the financial crisis blew a hole in some of the assets BGI had invested in, Barclays had to step in and backstop its clients. BGI's quantitative active money management arm had also

suffered a nightmarish spell, and was hit by a wave of investor outflows as a result.

▲

THIS WAS THE CULTURAL AND logistical maelstrom that Wiedman
stepped into. While the size of BlackRock doubled, its complexity
quadrupled. Ensuring that the biggest deal in asset management
history didn't end up a monument to hubris was going to be a daunting task.

Wiedman was paired with Manish Mehta, Grossman's right-hand
man, who flew over to New York with BGI's head of human resources
for a meeting with their counterparties at BlackRock. Mehta, a consummate details man with a Wharton MBA and a background in
consulting, walked into BlackRock's dimly lit conference room with
an exhaustive project plan he had quickly put together, and started
going through the minutiae of what would undoubtedly be a herculean project. Wiedman swiftly pushed it aside, and instead started
asking a series of personal questions of Mehta and his team, such as
where they came from and what they were like.

"It was like a culture shock for them. But born out of that was a
close personal working relationship," Wiedman argues. "Fundamentally, integrations are about people and how they work with
each other, not project plans." He was particularly delighted to learn
that Mehta had gone to the high school where John Hughes's *The
Breakfast Club* was set.

Their close relationship proved vital in the subsequent integration. Especially so because many BGI people quickly clashed with
other senior BlackRock people. Once again Kapito proved a lightning rod for criticism. One former BGI executive recalls a party
designed to bring the two senior executive teams together, where
Kapito began discussing his passion for wine collecting with a few
fellow oenophiles from BGI. When one of them asked BlackRock's

president how big his wine cellar was, Kapito turned crimson and angrily barked, "What, you want to know how big my dick is too?" The BGI executives were shocked into silence.

Even among BlackRock veterans, Kapito's aggressiveness was infamous and often grated. "People don't mind blunt, but they don't like disrespectful," observes one former top executive. "He's arrogant, and has a mean streak," says another. Nonetheless, Fink has remained resolutely loyal to Kapito, who he points out might be a "complex man," but is as warm as anyone once you get to know him, and "bleeds BlackRock."

Fink's support is well founded, according to Kapito's defenders—and even some who have personally clashed with him. They attribute some of the hostility to Kapito to the fact that unpopular decisions always fall to BlackRock's president, allowing Fink to rise above the fray. But when it boils down to it, they are the inseparable yin and yang at the heart of BlackRock.

"The biggest mistake you can make at BlackRock is believing you can ever play one off against the other. There's not a photon of daylight between them," observes a former senior BlackRock executive. "Rob would be wholly unsuccessful without Larry, but what people don't realize is that Larry would probably be wholly unsuccessful without Rob. The two of them are like salt and pepper shakers. They are very different, but they go together."

Fred Grauer, BGI's godfather, experienced this himself. To send a calming message to BGI's management ranks, Fink had hired Grauer back as a "special advisor" to help on the transition. But Grauer grew concerned about Kapito's influence and mistakes he thought he was making, and he told Fink. When Kapito learned about this, Grauer was quickly sidelined. Fink doesn't recall the episode, but it made a strong impression on some former BGI people.

"Larry is the leader, but Kapito is his Svengali, and a very dangerous man. You do not cross Kapito, period," says a person familiar with the conflict. "The litmus test at BlackRock is personal loyalty, above all. It overrides almost every other value." Other BlackRock employees confirm that fealty is an important aspect of the firm: "There is one word I associate with the culture at BlackRock," says one, "and it's loyalty."

In contrast, former BGI and BlackRock people laud the job that Wiedman did. Although he occasionally came off as zany and chaotic, many credit his brilliance, voluble character, and empathy with making a success of the deal—ably assisted by Mehta and Hallac. "Mark is fantastic. Boy did he ever do a good job," says Kroner. "He and Charlie Hallac were two of the senior BlackRock people who actually spent time in San Francisco, got to understand our culture, and recognized that there were some things they did differently that they shouldn't impose on us. If it wasn't for Mark and Charlie, we'd still be struggling to integrate the two organizations."

▲

WIEDMAN DOES HAVE SOME REGRETS, among them not being clearer from the outset that this was an acquisition, not a merger. Although the word "acquisition" seems more aggressive, he feels that more clarity would have made the process cleaner and less awkward—something that Wiedman feels Kapito realized quicker than most.

Moreover, BlackRock was prepared for cultural clashes, having seen much the same with MLIM, where even old internal rivalries faded when BlackRock came in. "I think I could take two identical cultures, identical with groups of different people who never met each other, put them in a room, and they would hate each other," Wiedman observes. "And it would have nothing to do with culture. It would happen because nothing unifies people more than a new enemy."

There were two aspects that did catch BlackRock unaware. The first was practical. The size of BlackRock and BGI meant that there was far more overlap among clients than they had appreciated. Not only was sorting out the new sales teams and divvying up the relationships akin to trench warfare, but many investors have a hard cap on how much business they can have with a single asset manager, so BlackRock lost many mandates in the coming months. The second one was simply the distance—both culturally and physically—between New York and San Francisco. While everyone could move into one building in London, Hong Kong, or Tokyo, and regional outposts can keep their own regional identity and local reporting lines, that was impractical with San Francisco and New York, which after all are in the same country. But BGI's West Coast headquarters was too big to shift wholesale to New York.

Sometimes this regional issue could be manifested in seemingly trivial ways. BlackRock had a corporate account with American Airlines, which has a hub in New York but not in San Francisco. BGI had an account with United Airlines, which allowed them to fly around the world without connecting flights. When BlackRock took over, it wanted to save $2 million a year by forcing former BGI people in San Francisco to join its American account, but it faced a rebellion. Ultimately, the former BGI managers promised to find $2 million of savings elsewhere in the business to keep their account with United.

In the end, BlackRock in practice decapitated the leadership of the San Francisco office and moved most of the reporting lines to New York. That got rid of the awkward parallel organization charts, but meant San Francisco for a period "lost its mojo," Wiedman admits. Kroner attributes the ultimate success of the acquisition to a belated recognition that while the combined company's vision and values had to be in sync, exactly how they were expressed could be different in different offices. San Francisco could be more laid-back and cerebral, New York pushier and more commercial, as long as they were all pulling in the same direction. "BlackRock allowed San Francisco to keep its culture, and then things started to work relatively smoothly," Kroner says.

Yet all told, Wiedman estimates that the full integration took three long, difficult years. The iShares unit was particularly slow to fold fully into BlackRock, with the job completed only when Wiedman was rewarded for his diligence by being given the job of running all of BlackRock's indexing and ETF businesses in 2011. Today, the hyperactive, garrulous former lawyer leads BlackRock's international business and corporate strategy, and is considered a leading contender to take over the entire company when Fink finally steps down.

▲

ON DECEMBER 1, 2009 — the very day the deal formally closed—the big blue BGI sign on its headquarters at 45 Fremont came down, and a large silver BlackRock sign went up in its place. Even the door logos, office letterhead, and pens were all branded BlackRock that day.

Although it was an important aspect of BlackRock's thesis that integrations have to happen quickly and forcefully, and that it was imperative to impose the "One BlackRock" ethos immediately, some former BGI executives saw it as a symbolic slap in the face. Fink, on the other hand, was complaining to some former BGI executives that he had overpaid for what was turning out to be a complex headache. Given that the deal was partly in BlackRock's own stock, which had climbed between the deal's announcement and its closing, the final price tag came to $15.2 billion.[3]

What followed was a round of layoffs, coupled with a steady number of defections. Estimates for how many BGI managing directors left in the years following the acquisition are in the 50–75 percent range. "It was an extraordinary exercise in the Machiavellian method," observes one former senior BGI executive. "The prince [Fink] needed all the barons to commit to total loyalty, and basically killed off all the barons that wouldn't do so."

Fink is unrepentant. He attributes the unusual success of Black-Rock acquisitions to a belief that one organization has to have one overarching corporate identity and a willingness to enforce it—something that other asset managers have been leery of given the often messy fallout. "It's so hard to execute. You lose a lot of people who quit, because they want to have their own fiefdom, their own silo," he says. "But we never allow that."

To be fair, many BGI executives had become wealthy through the acquisition, thanks to the equity ownership they had secured through Grauer and Dunn's tortuous negotiations with Barclays over the years. It was therefore natural that many would cash out and move on. Moreover, despite the exodus of BGI people, the deal proved a stunning success, vindicating Fink's audacious decision to acquire it in spite of the shell-shocked global economy at the time.

Some BlackRock executives say even Fink underestimated just how valuable BGI—and iShares especially—would turn out to be. "It's like a matryoshka doll, where you keep opening the dolls and each doll is more beautiful than the first," observes one. However, BlackRock was quick to grasp how big it could become, and proved more adept at commercializing and expanding it than even BGI.

Despite his detractors, many at BlackRock also attribute its success to Kapito's operational savvy, which has permeated the company. Perhaps more than any other area of money management, index investing requires operational brilliance. One S&P 500 index fund is like any other, but if you can build the internal processes so that you can provide it more cheaply, efficiently, and with better service than anyone else, you will win.

BlackRock has, in effect, done for investing what Henry Ford did for the car, constructing a financial assembly line that produces products for investors more efficiently than almost anyone else. "The main reason for BlackRock's success is the incredible operational excellence that has been built into the firm. That has allowed them to build massive scale that no one else has accomplished," argues one former senior executive. "Kapito, who has more of the focus on the plumbing and the wiring, therefore deserves as much of the credit as Larry does for building BlackRock. Kapito is maniacal in driving efficiency through a phalanx of great operating executives."

However, the strategic vision was Fink's. What he realized—perhaps even better than BGI—was that while its people were important, the indexing business is fundamentally an engineering product. In fact, that it takes humans out of the equation is one of the core reasons for its success. Just as BGI's clients hadn't really cared when Grauer abruptly left in 1998, they didn't mind when BlackRock took over either. "Do you care who runs Toyota? I just want to know that the car works," observes Wiedman. "Indexing isn't personalized. It's a franchise business."

In the process, BlackRock's culture has also evolved. Amy Schioldager, who had worked on BGI's first-ever suite of ETFs, elected to stay at BlackRock after the deal, and rose to lead its indexing business until she retired in early 2017. While there was a culture clash at first, Schioldager said she appreciated what Fink, Kapito, and BlackRock brought to the table, and thrived in the new environment. "Ten years later, I think the New York office is a little kinder, gentler place, and the San Francisco office is a little toughened up," she says. "The culture has come out a little between them."

Despite some strife, the daring deal has proven phenomenally successful. BlackRock is today a powerhouse that manages over $9 trillion. That is more than the annual economic output of Japan and Germany combined, and more than twice the assets under management of Fidelity, historically the biggest beast of the US investment industry jungle.

Its dominance is largely thanks to BlackRock's business acumen supercharging BGI's already industry-leading index fund franchise. In the summer of 2014, the ETF business crossed the $1 trillion mark, which Wiedman celebrated with a party in London where he wore a "trillion-dollar suit" made from dollar-bill-patterned cloth— a suit that was for a period displayed in a small, informal museum on the seventh floor of BlackRock's New York headquarters. This landmark is now a distant memory. By the end of 2020, the iShares unit managed $2.7 trillion, while BlackRock's institutional index investing business is close to $3 trillion. Together they account for well over half the company's overall assets under management.

The success is reflected in the price of BlackRock's shares. The stock market value of BlackRock itself is now well over $130 billion, more than even Goldman Sachs. In fact, it is more than the combined values of T.Rowe Price, Franklin Templeton, Invesco, Janus Henderson, Schroders, and State Street—some of its biggest competitors.

Less tangibly but no less importantly, "Larry" has emerged as the new king of Wall Street, someone who had founded a small bond investment house just two decades earlier and swiftly built it into a vast financial empire, the likes of which has never before been seen. Indeed, Fink is arguably the most powerful person in global finance today, a consigliere to presidents and prime ministers and with clout in almost every major corporate boardroom in the world. Quirkily, he even helped bring the world Maroon 5, having bankrolled the record company that gave the band its first deal.[4]

▲

THE SUCCESS OF BLACKROCK IS a monument to one of Fink's enduring lessons from his First Boston debacle. When he gave the commencement speech to UCLA's students in 2016, the former Bruin revealed how the setback scarred him: "I believed I had figured out the market, but I was wrong—because while I wasn't watching, the world had changed."[5]

Fink then recalled how UCLA's legendary basketball coach John Wooden had led the school's team to ten championships in a dozen years, by constantly adapting to how the game was changing. Wooden once said that "if I am through learning, I am through," something that has become a leitmotif for BlackRock's founder. His timely acquisition of BGI shows how Fink understood better than most how the investment game was changing, and how he adapted quicker than everyone else.

The index fund revolution had finally won. From its modest, iconoclastic roots, it had now finally established itself in the heart of Wall Street, and is now gradually taking over more and more of the investment world. The finance industry may be unpopular, but this has so far been a boon to humankind, with everyone directly or indirectly reaping the benefits through cheaper savings. Just over the past two decades, the cost of a US mutual fund has now nearly halved.[6]

Fink compares the impact of ETFs to how Amazon has transformed retail, with lower prices, convenience, and transparency. "The asset management industry was never designed for those things. It was designed with opaqueness and complexity," he says.

Nonetheless, growth of this magnitude is starting to raise some thorny questions around the dizzying pace of innovation that might not always serve the best interests of investors or the health of the financial system, the consequences of passive funds accounting for more and more of the global investment industry, and the narrowing club of titans dominating the index fund business.

Chapter 15

PURDEY SHOTGUNS

FAITH HAD ALWAYS BEEN CENTRAL to the life of Robert Netzly, sustaining him through a tough childhood and an itinerant career that veered from youth pastor to online sales at a car dealership. But he discovered his calling at Wells Fargo—the spiritual birthplace of the index fund.

Netzly had ended up at Wells Fargo's wealth management division after the Volkswagen dealership he worked at went bust in the financial crisis of 2008. While searching online for a Bible study on finance to teach at his church, the conservative Christian stumbled over an article on how the Bible's principles, rather than purely financial considerations, should inspire an investment portfolio. The slender man with thick dark glasses and stubble, who looks more like an accountant at a tech company than a smooth-talking stock-pusher, was intrigued.

Religion came early to Netzly. His parents were both drug users, who divorced when he was three, after his father fell into full addiction. His mother cleaned up, and raised Netzly and his younger, autistic brother. But the church quickly became an important pillar in Netzly's life, even if he didn't feel entirely comfortable discussing his faith until adulthood.

As a financial advisor, Netzly was familiar with "socially responsible investing," which avoids areas like polluting heavy industry, weapons manufacturers, and gambling. But he considered it in the thrall to liberal principles far removed from his conservative evangelical ones. However, the idea of "biblically responsible investing" immediately resonated. It was like the Holy Spirit itself reached out and gripped his heart.[1]

Curious, Netzly went through his own investment portfolio more thoroughly, and was aghast to discover that three big pharmaceutical stocks he owned made money from drugs used in performing abortions. To someone who was president of a pro-life pregnancy center in his spare time, it was anathema. That wasn't the only thing that troubled him in his personal portfolio. "All manner of unholiness festered in my investment lineup like some 'Hottest Stock Picks' newsletter from hell," he later recalled.[2]

The discovery shook the young financial advisor to his core. Netzly reckoned he couldn't in good conscience keep working at Wells Fargo and put clients into stocks he thought were riddled with evil. He went home to his wife that day and told her he thought God had a different plan for him. "Okay . . . you know we have two babies and a mortgage, so what's the plan?" she asked anxiously.[3] Netzly replied that he had no idea, and that they would simply have to pray on it. A few months later, he left Wells Fargo to set up Christian Wealth Management, which would advise the devout on how to invest entirely according to what they see as Christianity's guiding principles, a concept known as "biblically responsible investing." Luckily, the business took off, and CWM eventually became a big network of Christian financial advisors doing the Lord's work. By 2015, it had about $40 million under management.

But there was one big obstacle. Many financial advisors who wanted to join were by then mostly putting their clients' money in cheap index funds. That inevitably meant investing in an array of companies they found distasteful. Traditional active funds might have discretion, but were not much better at avoiding sinful areas, and their expense and uninspiring performance was off-putting.

Netzly reached out to several index fund providers about setting up a more bespoke product for his clients. This would screen out sectors and companies that directly or indirectly profited from things he found sinful, such as abortion and pornography, or those that actively supported the lesbian, gay, bisexual, or transgender "lifestyle," as they saw it. Unsurprisingly, the intolerance and likelihood of a public backlash spooked any mainstream providers from partaking in the project. So Netzly was forced to go it alone. In 2015, he founded Inspire Investing, which by 2017 started launching a series of "biblically responsible" exchange-traded funds.

The company uses a system to grade companies according to their adherence to conservative Christian values and then turn this into indices for the ETFs to track, allowing it to entirely eschew any companies it found problematic. These ranged from obvious ones, such as alcohol producers, to the more controversial, such as Apple and Starbucks, for their corporate support for LGBT rights. Naturally, it caused a furor. "We certainly don't hate anybody, and we want the best for everyone, but obviously we have differences of opinion on what that looks like," Netzly observes.

In practice, this methodology has meant an eclectic mix of energy companies, miners, some retailers, computer chip maker Nvidia, and—oddly enough—the UK's Royal Mail and Top Glove, a Malaysian rubber glove manufacturer that also produces condoms. Nor does the Lord seem to know quite what to make of Inspire's ETFs, given their mixed performance. Its inaugural product, BLES— an appropriate ticker for a Bible-inspired ETF—has underperformed the global stock market since its inception, while BIBL, which invests in bigger stocks than the more diverse, international BLES, has largely matched the S&P 500.

Nonetheless, Inspire has been a success, with its overall stable of biblical ETFs now managing just over $1.3 billion by the end of 2020. "We want to glorify God to the utmost, and want to inspire transformation for God's glory throughout the world, and we saw this ETF idea as the best way we can do that," Netzly says. "Praise God it worked out."

Despite the controversy caused by the Bible Belt–friendly ETFs, Inspire Investing is a vivid example of how ETFs have transformed the index fund industry. What was once overwhelmingly only a stock market phenomenon, and fairly plain-vanilla, is now establishing beachheads in virtually every corner of the financial system, thanks to the technology of ETFs.

But what some proponents see as a vibrant ecosystem of financial products suitable for every conceivable taste is increasingly becoming a treacherous jungle. The ETF has supercharged index funds, yet the ease with which almost any financial security can be packaged inside means that it is now allowing investors to make the same costly mistakes that first nurtured the industry in the first place. "The ETF is a little bit like the famed Purdey shotgun that you buy over in London," Jack Bogle once remarked.[4] "It's the greatest shotgun ever made. It's great for killing big game in Africa, but it's also great for suicide."

▲

BARCLAYS GLOBAL INVESTORS MIGHT HAVE been the first to realize that ETFs constituted a new financial technology with vast potential, but it was far from the last. The blitzscaling approach taken by iShares in the early 2000s has become what even some ETF fans term a "spaghetti cannon,"[5] with an array of providers churning out increasingly niche products, shooting them against the wall, and seeing what sticks.

In 2000, there were still just 88 ETFs with just $70 billion of assets, compared to over 500 index mutual funds that managed $426 billion, according to data from the Investment Company Institute. A decade later, the number of ETFs had swelled to 2,621, narrowly surpassing the number of index mutual funds, but in money terms still trailing slightly behind the $1.5 trillion that their more conventional, mainstream counterparts managed. By the end of 2020, there were nearly 7,000 ETFs globally with $7.7 trillion of assets, according to the ICI. That is over twice as many traditional index funds tracked by the ICI, in money terms as finally large as their older cousins, and approaching the number of actively managed mutual funds in the United States.

The vast majority of the money is housed inside the big, mainstream ETFs, such as State Street's pioneering SPDR, or the equivalent S&P 500 ETFs managed by rivals BlackRock and Vanguard. It is also still primarily a US-based industry. Outside of Japan, the first Asian ETF was launched in 1999, and Europe saw its first one in 2000, yet ETFs listed on North American exchanges still account for almost two-thirds of the total, according to JPMorgan.

Nonetheless, the past decade has seen accelerating growth across the world, and an almost comically exotic list of new ETFs has been launched. Even proponents have grown alarmed. Bill McNabb, who succeeded Jack Brennan as Vanguard's chief executive in 2008 and ramped up the investment group's ETF business, in 2016 attended the industry's biggest annual conference in Florida, the four-day Inside ETFs jamboree, and pleaded with the attendees to moderate the proliferation.

"The industry is [introducing a new] ETF, it feels like, every 30 seconds," McNabb complained to the audience.[6] "We have to be very careful. If we go too far as an industry, people will have doubts about the original construct. And some categories are pretty esoteric." Vanguard's chief executive noted darkly that there was an uncanny historical parallel: "This is like the 1980s and mutual funds. Things did not end well for all those funds."

It is fair to say the attendees of the carnival-like conference just outside Miami took little note of McNabb's consternation. Investors have in recent years been able to buy niche, "thematic" ETFs that purport to benefit from—deep breath—the global obesity epidemic; online gaming; the rise of millennials; the whiskey industry; robotics; artificial intelligence; clean energy; solar energy; autonomous driving; uranium mining; better female board representation; cloud computing; genomics technology; social media; marijuana farming; toll roads in the developing world; water purification; reverse-weighted US stocks; health and fitness; organic food; elderly care; lithium batteries; drones; and cybersecurity. There was even briefly an ETF that invested in the stocks of companies exposed to the ETF industry. Some of these more experimental funds gain traction, but many languish and are eventually liquidated, the money recycled into the latest hot fad.

The companies that churn out these esoteric products argue that in a free market they have every right to be experimental and see what might gain investor favor. After all, sometimes a bit of luck is all it takes. HACK, an ETF that buys the stocks of companies with cybersecurity businesses, launched shortly before Sony Pictures Entertainment suffered a catastrophic data breach in 2014, culminating in the publication of a series of embarrassing internal emails. This caused an immediate and massive upswing in HACK's fortunes, which saw its assets rocket from zero to almost $1.5 billion by mid-2015. Eventually it led to a vitriolic fight among its sponsors for the lucrative management fees it was throwing off like candy.

Others take time. The Van Eck Vectors Gold Miners ETF took two years to cross the $1 billion mark, but is now a $16 billion fund.* Successes like this are becoming rarer, but the hope that they will stumble onto a winner is what sustains many smaller ETF providers.

If almost eight thousand ETFs sounds like a lot, it pales next to the supernova explosion of financial indices. What was once an unglamorous side business is now a wildly lucrative industry thanks to the proliferation of index funds, with the biggest players like S&P Dow Jones Indices, MSCI, and FTSE Russell churning out a staggering number of benchmarks for clients. The Index Industry Association, a trade body of its biggest players, has counted nearly three million "live" indices being maintained by its members.[7]

There are thousands more being maintained by various banks, which construct them to produce bespoke investment products for their clients, and index fund companies making their own to avoid paying the chunky licensing fees to the major index providers—something dubbed "self-indexing."[†]

In contrast, there are only about forty-one thousand public companies in the world today.[8] In reality, probably only three to four thousand of those stocks are tradable. For evidence that the indexing revolution is now eating itself, this is often offered up as exhibit A.

▲

WHAT TO MAKE OF ALL THIS? Mockery of a good idea gone mad is tempting. In 2018, Inigo Fraser-Jenkins, an analyst at financial

---

* Even this is considered a fairly quick success story nowadays. An ETF that buys tiny "small-cap" silver miners got virtually zero traction for over three years after launching in 2013, bumbling along with less than $10 million in assets, and then largely stayed below $100 million for another four years, before shooting up to over $800 million in 2020.

† Qontigo, an analytics company owned by Deutsche Börse, the German stock exchange, has even launched a DIY index construction "studio," allowing anyone to create any kind of benchmark they want, and then outsourcing the duller ongoing maintenance work to Qontigo.

research firm Bernstein, poked fun at the index "singularity" through a work of fiction that envisaged a lonely, anonymous hero with a herculean task: to create all possible stock market indices. "Some said that the apparently useless indices should not be created, or if created but then subsequently regarded as superfluous then they should be ruthlessly culled," Fraser-Jenkins wrote of his hero.[9] "He fought back against this idea. Who was to say which was a useful one and which was a useless one?" The hero's ultimate goal, however, was to create one single index, an Ultimate Index to end all other indices. What would that look like, Fraser-Jenkins's protagonist mused?

> *Surely that would be a thing of beauty and hence in a sense be an art work as well? Some said that it would represent the optimal allocation to all possible assets. He was increasingly sure that it should not and could not be confined to just the stock market. Thus it would be the amalgam of all stocks, bonds, commodities and other financial assets held with weights such that they represented human societies' needs for these different types of capital, by fulfilling this need the index at once performed a social good and also guaranteed its own success. Others doubted that this could exist, was society so self-aware that it knew what its optimal allocation to all assets should be?*

The snarkiness is a tad overdone. Many of the three million indices in existence are in reality simply uncontroversial, different flavors of the same thing. For example, there might be indices for the S&P 500 denominated in scores of different currencies, or custom ones that screen out gun stocks, or Islamic ones that exclude alcohol producers, casinos, and banks. Others tweak weightings according to measures of environmental, governance, or social standards rather than their stock market value. The three million indices also include the vast global bond market, as well as commodities. Just like how the twenty-six letters of the English alphabet can produce an infinite number of spy thrillers, teenage fiction, heavy literature, and verbose books on index funds, there is no real limit to how many financial indices can or should be produced.

Nonetheless, the explosion of indices and index funds of various stripes is emblematic of a worrying trend. The genesis of index funds was the realization that most people—whether experienced professional money managers, a dentist investing for their retirement, or unemployed twentysomethings day-trading to make a quick buck—make terrible investors. The best long-term results come from buying a big, well-diversified portfolio of financial securities, and trading as little as possible. Jack Bogle built a vast financial empire around these two basic principles.

Yet there is in practice little meaningful difference between taking a bet on a hot dotcom stock and on a biotech or robotics ETF. The line between "active" and "passive" investing has always been a fuzzy one, given that choosing what index fund to invest in is unavoidably an active choice. The construction of indices is also rarely an entirely quantitative endeavor, with most index providers applying at least a degree of discretion to their decisions. Thus the securities in a benchmark also reflect "active" choices—but by a largely anonymous index committee, rather than a portfolio manager at Fidelity or T.Rowe Price, something the next chapter will explore in more depth. The recent proliferation of ETFs of indexes has completely obliterated the always blurred line between active and passive investing, with potentially harmful consequences.

Especially so considering that the construction of the underlying index may be relatively opaque. In some cases, the opacity is even deliberate. The newest trend is for "actively managed" ETFs. Essentially, they are traditional funds with the usual medley of analysts, traders, and portfolio managers who use the superior ETF structure—tradable and in the United States tax-advantaged—rather than the conventional legal vehicles that have been the norm for most of the post–World War II era.

Bear Stearns launched the first active ETF all the way back in 2008. It invested in short-term debt instruments and was given the ticker YYY—naturally leading to jokes about "why why why" would any investor want an actively managed ETF. Growth has been slow, with the assets of actively managed ETFs still about $240 billion by the end of 2020, due to some major drawbacks. The biggest is the fact that ETFs have to disclose their holdings daily. Doing so is, after all, vital for the smooth functioning of the create/redeem process pioneered by Nate Most that makes them tradable. But many active managers hate broadcasting their top trades to rivals.

However, after years of lobbying, the US Securities and Exchange Commission has now started approving workarounds that allow "semi-transparent" ETFs, which publicly disclose their holdings with a long lag. The investment world is abuzz about this, given that it holds the tantalizing possibility of helping reverse the outflows that active funds have suffered year after year. Given the finance industry's fondness for acronyms, these are often dubbed ANTs—or active nontransparent ETFs.

Nonetheless, it remains to be seen what the investor interest will be. Cathie Wood, a prominent US technology investor, has managed to build an active ETF empire thanks to her bets on hot stocks like Tesla. Yet the tax advantage exists only in the United States, and while daily transparency may not be essential to most investors, the higher fees of actively managed ETFs mean that they are unlikely to challenge the supremacy of traditional, dirt-cheap index funds.

Some see the long roll call of ETFs as a welcome sign of the industry's success. Finally, investors don't have a narrow choice of a few simple index funds, and can choose whatever strikes their fancy. Whatever your investment palate, there is now a flavor of ETF to tickle it. That may be true, but the downsides are real: The evolution and proliferation of ETFs are giving investors the ability to commit the same original sin that many of the inventors of index funds hoped to cure.

Yet even the myriad "thematic" ETFs that are being cranked out are not as potentially problematic as the suite of derivatives-based index funds that have emerged over the past decade. It is telling that the industry's "Big Three"—BlackRock, Vanguard, and State Street—and many of their smaller rivals have eschewed these, concerned that these more niche, complex products may tarnish the entire index fund universe.

▲

IN EARLY 2018, THE STOCK MARKET was basking in the afterglow of President Donald Trump's corporate tax cut, which had added at least some temporary vim to a steady if disappointingly slow economic expansion since the financial crisis. US equities were setting record high after record high, and broke the 1960s and 1990s records for the longest streak without a big drop. Unfortunately, the tranquility didn't last much longer.

After a few days of nervy trading in late January, the stock market started careening lower on February 5. By the end of the day, the S&P 500 was down 4 percent—the biggest one-day decline since the depths of Europe's crisis in 2011. By the end of the week, the US equity market had suffered one of the fastest 10 percent corrections in history. All told, global equities lost $4.2 trillion of value in just five days, in dollar terms more than the total loss suffered by the Nasdaq when the dotcom bubble burst in 2000–2002.

The proximate trigger had been a bond market selloff that

investors fretted would infect stocks as well. But this failed to explain the severity and swiftness of the decline, given that the economy was humming along at the time. Instead, it turned out that a
handful of fiendishly complicated ETFs that packaged together financial derivatives to allow ordinary investors to bet on the US
stock market's volatility remaining subdued exploded that day. Although they managed only $3 billion at the time, their collapse be-
came the proverbial snowball that started an avalanche, by triggering
a rush of automated selling orders by other investment strategies
tied slavishly to the level of volatility.

Technically, the biggest of these volatility funds—the Velocity-
Shares Daily Inverse VIX Short Term ETN, known mostly by its
equity ticker XIV—was what is called an exchange-traded note, or
ETN. These are the distant offspring of Bob Tull's OPALS, tradable funds that look and smell like a traditional ETF but are in reality synthetic debt securities structured by Wall Street's financial
engineers to mimic the performance of an index. Their greater flexibility makes it easier to construct funkier products, such as "leveraged" ones that use financial derivatives to juice up the potential
returns, or "inverse" ones that allow investors to bet on prices falling.
The umbrella term for everything in the wider family is exchange-
traded product, or ETP, but in practice everything often gets
lumped together and referred to as ETFs.

XIV was an inverse ETN linked to the Vix index. The Vix is
often dubbed Wall Street's "Fear Gauge," as it uses derivatives prices
to divine the expected short-term volatility of the US stock market.
In other words, this fund—which anyone could buy, no matter what
their financial savvy—was in practice a package of derivatives of
derivatives. It profited handsomely as long as volatility remained
quiescent, but blew up in spectacular fashion once the calm shattered. Worse, the complex dynamics of the fund meant that its collapse leaked back into the main stock market and worsened the

selloff. Many ordinary investors, unaware of the wild complexities and vulnerabilities lurking inside XIV and its cousins, were wiped out.*

XIV was quickly closed down by its sponsor, Credit Suisse. BlackRock, fearful that the debacle might harm the image of the broader ETF universe, put out an unusually bluntly worded statement: "Inverse and leveraged exchange-traded products are not ETFs, and they don't perform like ETFs under stress. That's why iShares does not offer them."[10]

Many inverse, leveraged, and otherwise derivatives-based ETPs suffered another blow in the market mayhem that followed the COVID-19 pandemic. Over forty—most of which linked to commodity indices—were quickly aborted by their sponsors, while others had their wings clipped, but not before causing some ructions.[11] For example, USO, an ETF that invests in oil derivatives, contributed to the remarkable sight of US crude prices in April 2020 briefly falling into negative territory for the first time in history. Bond ETFs also stirred concerns in March, as we shall see in chapter 17. Nonetheless, the events of February 2018 and March 2020 have done little to dent the popularity of derivatives-based ETPs.

The first leveraged ETF was launched by a small upstart investment group called ProShares in 2006, and the overall assets held by leveraged or inverse ETFs rose to over $70 billion by early 2018, according to Morningstar data. Following a spate of outflows in the wake of the XIV shenanigans, they wouldn't hit that mark again until December 2019, but by March 2021 their assets had vaulted to over $130 billion. Even that underestimates their day-to-day impact on markets, given that most are designed primarily as short-term

---

* Two day-trading amateur musicians hit by its implosion mocked their own mistake with a parody song set to Tom Petty's "Free Fallin'," and uploaded it to YouTube. "It's a long day, watching a correction / The S&P crashing through the floor / I bought the XIV, 'cause I'll make my money back / I'm a bad boy, 'cause I bought even more / Now XIV is free fallin' / Yeah, XIV is free fallin'," they sang mournfully in the video.

trading tools rather than as long-term savings vehicles, which means that they rarely amass huge assets compared to their plain-vanilla peers.

▲

AFTER A RELENTLESS DECADE, there are signs that the index fund launch bonanza is slowing down. Most major tracts of industry real estate are now utterly and likely permanently controlled by a handful of big players, chiefly BlackRock, Vanguard, and State Street. Most major and minor niches likewise.

There will undoubtedly be more product innovation in the index fund industry, of varying usefulness and value. Yet it is revealing that there has been a steady uptick in ETF closures in recent years. The shakeout caused by COVID-19 has lifted the population of the ETP graveyard to well over the thousand-casualties mark. More are undoubtedly coming. Some industry insiders are therefore more excited by what they think could be the next big iteration in the indexing revolution: direct indexing.

Netzly is not alone in wanting more customizable index funds— for example, ones that screen out coal companies or arms manufacturers. That is now relatively easy to do, with most major index providers offering different flavors of their biggest products. Direct indexing takes this to the natural next level. Rather than buy an index fund or ETF, an investor would buy all (or nearly all) the individual securities in a benchmark—allowing them total freedom to create their own flavor of investment portfolio, and, at least in the United States, more efficiently harvest any losses on individual securities. Imagine it being like having all the stocks of the S&P 500 or FTSE 100 as the default option, and then simply ticking off companies that don't appeal. Hey presto, a bespoke index fund tailored perfectly to the customer's sensibilities, which they can tweak when and in what ways they see fit.

Direct indexing is not entirely new, but three recent developments have transformed its prospects. First, technological advances mean that it is now much easier to implement in practice. What was once a computer processing sinkhole is now more straightforward. Second, trading costs have plummeted in recent years, and are in some cases free, making the cost more competitive versus buying a cheap, simple index fund. Third, the emergence of "fractional" shares—the ability to buy part of a share of a stock if it is too expensive—has helped make direct indexing possible for a broader range of investors.

It remains to be seen whether direct indexing really does represent the next stage of index investing—index investing 3.0. In truth, many big institutional investors are in practice already there, and most ordinary investors will likely continue to prefer the one-click ease of buying one or several broad index funds, rather than fiddle around with individual holdings or weightings. If taken to an extreme level, there is little meaningful difference between direct indexing and simply buying an undiversified handful of stocks.

Regardless, it is abundantly clear that for the foreseeable future, the gushing inflows into traditional index funds and ETFs are going to continue—even though the impact on markets, the investment management business, and the finance industry as a whole is also becoming more apparent.

Chapter 16

THE NEW CAPTAINS
OF CAPITAL

TESLA'S STOCK WENT ON A wild ride in 2020, powered by the devotion of the electric car company's army of ordinary investors, who were suddenly stuck at home and day-trading their stimulus checks to pass time while the coronavirus pandemic raged. But in November, the rally received another huge jolt that would help make Elon Musk's company one of the most valuable in the world.

Despite its dramatic stock market gains over the past decade, S&P Dow Jones Indices—one of the biggest providers of financial benchmarks—had long refrained from adding Tesla to its flagship index, the S&P 500, for one simple reason: To be included, a company has to be consistently profitable, a requirement that Tesla had struggled to meet.

But Tesla's notching up four consecutive quarters of profits by the summer of 2020 finally made it eligible, with the mere possibility helping fuel the rally. When S&P Dow Jones Indices' committee of benchmarking bureaucrats finally announced in late November that Tesla would indeed be included, it triggered a spasm of trading that sent its stock soaring, lifting its stock market value to north of $400 billion. By the time it was actually included in the S&P 500 on December 21, its shares had rocketed 70 percent since the announcement, valuing Tesla at over $650 billion.[1]

How could a tweak to a financial index—which is often overshadowed in the popular consciousness by the venerable Dow Jones Industrial Average—suddenly cause Tesla to become worth hundreds of billions of dollars more? In short: index funds.

Although Tesla would henceforth become an investable company for all fund managers who benchmark their performance against the S&P 500, they at least have a choice whether to buy or not. The trillions of dollars in passive index strategies that slavishly track the index have no option but to acquire stock in the proportion to the company's weight in the benchmark, whatever the price or attractiveness of Tesla's business.

The companies that provide financial market indices were long considered humdrum utilities, often started as adjunct businesses to big financial newspapers like the *Wall Street Journal*, the *Financial Times*, and Japan's *Nikkei*. No one really considered them a big revenue stream. Today, creating benchmarks is a wildly profitable industry in its own right, dominated by its own "Big Three"—MSCI, FTSE Russell, and S&P Dow Jones Indices. Together, they have a market share of about 70 percent. Collectively, they arguably constitute the most underappreciated power brokers of the financial world.

Quite simply, they have morphed from simple snapshots of markets into a force that exerts power over them—largely thanks to the growth of index funds, which in practice delegate their investment decisions to the companies that create the benchmarks.

The money that index providers now in practice steer is gargantuan. Between the publicly known and quantifiable universe of index-linked mutual funds and ETFs, as well as the more opaque number of index-oriented strategies managed internally by the likes of endowments, pension funds, and sovereign wealth funds, there is now likely over $26 trillion tied directly to a variety of financial benchmarks.* The biggest shareholders in almost every major US company are now index funds, and internationally the trend is heading the same way.

This is still considerably smaller than the broader global investment industry—ranging from high-octane hedge funds and private equity firms to traditional mutual funds—and the even bigger global pool of financial assets. But index funds are still growing at a rapid pace, seizing market share from their pricier rivals. The impact of that growing heft is therefore becoming harder to ignore, with even some proponents now admitting that there are mounting signs that the index fund tail is beginning to wag the market dog. Index companies themselves are the biggest beneficiaries, in terms of both hard dollars and soft power.

▲

THE DISCREET INFLUENCE OF INDICES often goes unnoticed, even by people inside the finance industry itself. But as Tesla showed, the fate of companies can be made by having one's stock or bonds included in one of the major indices.†

In smaller stocks with lower trading volumes, the impact can be astonishing. In 2019, a small, profitless Chinese marble producer called ArtGo climbed 3,800 percent after MSCI announced that it would be included in one of its influential benchmarks. But when MSCI changed its mind after some analysts raised concerns over the opaqueness of the company, the shares completely collapsed,

---

* See how I reached this rough, overall estimate for the size of the index strategy universe in chapter 1.
† Ejections can also be painful. Société Générale and BBVA, two of Europe's biggest banks, saw their stocks tumble on September 3, 2020, when it was announced that they would be dumped from the EURO STOXX 50 index, the European equivalent of the S&P 500.

wiping out all its gains and then some.[2] Further highlighting the rising impact of index companies, an employee of S&P Dow Jones Indices was in 2020 charged with insider trading after he netted an estimated $900,000 by trading ahead of some of his company's benchmark inclusions.[3]

This index inclusion effect is not solely because of passive investing. Traditional active managers are also constrained in how much they can invest outside their benchmarks. While they do not have to invest in a company that makes it into their index—passive funds naturally have no choice—many end up doing so. Financial derivatives such as futures are also often linked to these benchmarks. So even if the index fund had never been invented back in the 1970s, indices would still be influential, albeit to a lesser degree.

Some recent academic research also indicates that the index inclusion effect might be fading. A 2020 paper by Benjamin Bennett, René Stulz, and Zexi Wang found that the uplift from joining the S&P 500 has gradually declined and now disappeared, despite the growing heft of index funds. This may be related to investors betting on speculated index inclusions, so that the uplift is largely already baked into the stock price by the time it is announced, or simply that companies might become more complacent once they join the S&P 500, hurting their returns.[4]

Nonetheless, other studies have come up with different results, and what is inarguable is that membership in one of the big stock market indices clearly matters greatly, for both investors and the companies themselves—with Tesla a prime example. And the biggest cause is the growing pool of passive investing strategies that are irrevocably tied to indices. At the time of Tesla's inclusion, S&P Dow Jones estimated that index funds would mechanistically have to sell $51 billion worth of other shares and plow that into Tesla's stock.[5]

Why does this give power to indexing companies? Because of

the knotty, underappreciated nature of creating benchmarks. Indices are usually seen as an objective reflection of markets, or at worst a decent snapshot of them. When people talk about what the US stock market did on any given day, chances are good that they are using the S&P 500 as a proxy. The reality is somewhat messier.

While most indices are largely chosen according to hard, quantitative measures, what measures to use and how to weight them are choices in the hands of the index providers. Two legal scholars once termed the temptation to see indices as near-Platonic, purely mathematical constructs as the "myth of objectivity."[6] An element of human discretion is inevitably and unavoidably part of the process.

For example, S&P Dow Jones Indices in 2017 decided that its flagship US benchmarks would henceforth not permit the entry of companies with multiple share classes.[7] This was a big deal. Sometimes founders want to list a big chunk of their company but still retain control. One way of doing this is to sell to the investing public shares with economic rights, but little or no voting rights, and issue a separate type of share to themselves that allow them to keep control of the board of directors. Prominent examples of this include Google and Facebook. S&P Dow Jones Indices decided that these companies would be allowed to stay in the S&P 500 index, but new members would have to adhere to the "one stock, one vote" principle.

This was largely applauded at the time, as an indexing company taking a strong stance on an important cornerstone of egalitarian shareholder democracy, with every stock being worth the same. However, it is a potent example of how S&P Dow Jones and its rivals exert de facto influence over core areas of corporate governance through their setting of standards. It may have been the right choice, yet one could argue that these are areas best left to lawmakers and regulators, not private companies.

Another example is Unilever's reversal of a decision to move its headquarters from London to the Netherlands. The venerable consumer goods conglomerate believed that its dual UK-Dutch structure, an odd historical legacy of a 1929 merger between a British soap maker and a Dutch margarine producer, was an unnecessary headache. When they discovered that consolidating operations in the Netherlands would have meant dropping out of the UK's FTSE 100 index, forcing many of its biggest shareholders to dump their shares, they were forced to change course.[8]

Even mundane choices like what industry a company is in can have big implications. Without looking under the hood, many investors may be surprised to learn that State Street and Vanguard's US technology ETFs—which together manage over $80 billion—don't actually include Amazon, Facebook, and Google's parent Alphabet, simply because they are classified as a retailer and communications companies, respectively, by S&P Dow Jones Indices. In contrast, Apple, primarily a maker of physical devices, and credit card companies Mastercard and Visa are classified as technology stocks.

Such classifications are always subject to debate, and it is tempting to see it as a niche issue. Yet the indirect consequences can be huge, given the implication for the resulting money flows. As a result of the passive investing boom, index providers have gained "a position of private authority in capital markets with profound politico-economic consequences," according to a 2020 paper by Johannes Petry, Jan Fichtner, and Eelke Heemskerk, titled "Steering Capital."[9] Changes in criteria may be the result of painstaking consultation between index providers, their clients, and affected companies, but at the end of the day are defined by the indexing companies themselves.

"Hence, in this new age of passive asset management, index providers are becoming gatekeepers that exert de facto regulatory power and thus may have important effects on corporate governance and the economic policies of countries," the three academics argue.

▲

AS THE "STEERING CAPITAL" PAPER alludes to, even countries have been forced to recognize the importance of financial indices. That has occasionally led to secretive but furious lobbying campaigns to have their stocks or bonds included, upgraded, or at least not downgraded by some of the more influential benchmark providers.

In 2016, MSCI—the dominant provider of international stock market indices that helped birth BlackRock's iShares—threatened to downgrade Peru from an "emerging market" to a more lowly "frontier market," because of the small size of the local bourse. Although this is a seemingly esoteric distinction between two separate categories for developing countries, the more mainstream MSCI EM index was at the time tracked by $1.5 trillion of money—both active and passive—while the MSCI Frontier index had a mere $12 billion linked to it.[10] A downgrade could therefore have been disastrous for foreign investment in the small Latin American country. Moreover, it would have had negative spillover effects for other countries in the frontier-markets benchmark, such as Pakistan and Nigeria, which would suddenly suffer a far lower weighting in the index if Peru's stock market joined.

Eventually, intensive lobbying efforts by Lima and promises to nurture its small bourse convinced New York–based MSCI to stay its hand,[11] much to the relief of Peru's finance minister, Alonso Segura Vasi. "Investors' decisions to invest in the market are significantly guided by their decisions, whether they put you in the index or do not put you in the index," he later told Bloomberg.[12] "They do control the fates of companies' and countries' access to capital markets."

Greece, on the other hand, enjoyed no such succor when it became the first Western country to be relegated from the "developed
market" category by MSCI, FTSE Russell, and S&P Dow Jones
following the country's economic crisis. Not that this was necessarily a disaster. In some cases, it is better to be a big fish in a smaller
pond. Greek stocks arguably benefited from the relegation to
emerging-markets status, which was better than languishing as an
infinitesimal part of bigger benchmarks for investors primarily interested in the giant companies of Western Europe and the United
States. South Korea, for example, appears happy to stay classified as
an emerging market despite being wealthier than many countries
judged to be developed markets: After all, it is arguably better to
have a hefty weighting in a supposedly less prestigious index, as
long as enough money tracks it.

It is not just smaller countries that care intensely about what
indices they are in these days. Even China launched a ferocious
campaign against MSCI—reportedly including threats against its
local business[13]—to get its stock market included in its EM index.
In 2018, Beijing won, with China finally included and with the
promise of a gradual but steady increase in its heft in the index.

On one hand, the inclusion made perfect sense. After all, China
is the world's second-biggest economy, its companies are enormous
and attractive to investors, and the authorities had worked hard to
level up its regulatory and technological infrastructure and improve
the functioning of its vast financial markets. Index decisions are
taken after long-running, often exhaustive consultations with local
and international financial institutions, and according to a host
of public and transparent quantitative yardsticks and technical re-
quirements. MSCI insisted that it was not pressured into the decision, and pointed out that index decisions are taken by a department
separate from its commercial operations.

Nonetheless, not all investors were thrilled by MSCI's move, given that China's stock market remains relatively underdeveloped and unsophisticated even by emerging-markets standards. Politically, it also became contentious, especially in the United States. For example, Hangzhou Hikvision, a Chinese state-controlled maker of video surveillance cameras that had recently been put on a US government blacklist that prevents American companies from doing business with it, was added to MSCI's flagship index.[14]

Opprobrium naturally followed. Republican senator Marco Rubio blasted the decision, arguing that it would cause billions of dollars of US savings to automatically slosh into Chinese companies of dubious quality, and in some cases work directly against American interests. "We can no longer allow China's authoritarian government to reap the rewards of American and international capital markets while Chinese companies avoid financial disclosure and basic transparency, and place U.S. investors and pensioners at risk," Rubio thundered in a June 2019 public letter to Henry Fernandez, MSCI's chairman and chief executive.[15] "What MSCI is doing is allowing the Chinese Communist Party controlled market . . . to access a critical source of capital and clothe itself in a facade of legitimacy."

▲

THE POWER OF MSCI, FTSE RUSSELL, and S&P Dow Jones Indices is largely over only stock markets. Of even greater and direct importance to countries are their presence and weighting in various influential bond market indices. These may not have the cachet of the brand-name stock market benchmarks bandied about on TV bulletins, but indices like the Bloomberg Barclays Global Aggregate or JPMorgan's EMBI and GBI-EM are also powerful in their own way.

Bond indices are funny beasts. It makes perfect sense to set the relative weightings of companies in the big stock market indices according to their overall value. So Apple has a bigger weighting than Under Armour. But bond market benchmarks are weighted according to the value of debt issued. So, perversely, the more indebted a country or company, the more heft it should have in an index.

Moreover, the greater the price a bond is trading at, the greater its weighting, even if that means it in practice offers a negative interest rate—a phenomenon that has become increasingly common given the vast monetary stimulus unleashed by central banks in recent years. In other words, the peculiarities of bond indices mean that passive bond funds are compelled to buy negative-yielding debt, in practice locking in a guaranteed loss if the debt is held until it matures.

Vladyslav Sushko, an economist at the Bank for International Settlements, and Grant Turner of the Reserve Bank of Australia also found in 2018 that index funds may be encouraging greater risks in the bond market. Given the importance of getting into an index, but the irrelevance of traditional creditor protection clauses for inclusion, companies appear to be issuing larger bonds with longer maturities and less rigorous investor protection, they found.[16] The reality is that bond indices—even more so than stock indices—were never really designed to have investment products built upon them, only to be vaguely reflective of the fixed-income markets. And it shows.

Peculiarities aside, bond indices are quietly important to countries in a very direct way, even if this isn't always apparent to politicians and the wider population. Given their importance to investors—many will be wary of investing in bonds outside their benchmarks—being included can lower a country's borrowing costs. Bond benchmarks have become so important that even the International Monetary Fund has started to examine the implications for flows of global capital and potential dangers to the health of the global financial system. While inclusion in a major bond index may be a boon, it also brings with it what the IMF terms "stability risks," given that it ties the fate of countries more closely to the fickle flows of international capital.

Index funds remain small players of the vast global bond market, but their heft is growing. Investor inflows into passive bond funds have accelerated in recent years, and are gradually approaching the $2 trillion mark—up tenfold over the past decade. Vanguard's Total Bond Market Index Fund alone manages over $300 billion, making it the biggest single fixed-income investment vehicle on the planet. When it finally became the largest, Vanguard crew members teased its manager, Josh Barrickman, by adorning his desk with paper crowns from Burger King, a reference to Bill Gross, the former manager of the world's biggest bond fund at Pimco, who was often referred to as the "bond king."[17]

As the IMF noted, the impact on the bonds of emerging economies is starting to become particularly noticeable. A 2018 paper by Tomas Williams, Nathan Converse, and Eduardo Levy-Yayati found that the "growing role of ETFs as a channel for international capital flows has amplified the transmission of global financial shocks to emerging economies."[18] In other words, while ETFs are helping funnel money to the developing world, their tradability makes countries more susceptible to sudden shifts in global investor sentiment, irrespective of domestic factors.

For the most part, the big indexing companies—and the big index fund providers that have in effect ceded them so much power—do their jobs with diligence and honesty, fully aware of the importance of their decisions and the responsibility it entails. Yet their transformation from dull, utility-like data providers to the biggest gatekeepers of money in the world—with the power to not just indirectly affect the fate of big public companies but to shape the life of millions of people—means that more scrutiny is not just warranted, but necessary.

Although hardly a front-page subject—at least not yet—the rising influence of index providers has not gone unnoticed by many regulators. The European Securities and Markets Authority, the continent's main pan-regional financial watchdog, now subjects all benchmark providers to more supervision and inspections. Industry insiders admit that it is likely only a matter of time before the US Securities and Exchange Commission does something similar. In the meantime, there are an increasing number of examples of how the peculiarities of indices are now subtly altering the fabric of markets in a multitude of ways—sometimes causing some odd glitches along the way.

▲

STOCKS OFTEN MOVE IN MYSTERIOUS WAYS, with no cogent explanation for their ebbs and flows—even though that doesn't stop analysts and financial journalists from trying to thread together a narrative that fits. But even by the standards of financial markets, the sudden slump in a bunch of small US gold-mining stocks in the spring of 2017 seemed bizarre.

The price of gold was on the upswing, climbing to a five-month high that week. There were no hints of waning demand for lustrous jewelry that underpins the precious metal. Instead, the core reason could be found in the peculiarities of ETFs, and the occasional ripples they can trigger in markets. Indeed, a single fund, the VanEck Vectors Junior Gold Miners ETF—the little brother of VanEck's $16 billion main gold-mining stock ETF—was causing the unexpected movements.

At the start of 2016, the Junior Gold Miners ETF managed a mere $1.3 billion, but by February 2018 its assets under management had ballooned to a peak of almost $6 billion. That meant it had grown too big for the index of tiny "micro-cap" gold-mining stocks it tracked, in some cases hitting regulatory limits on how much it could own of each company. As a result, the ETF would struggle to match its index, potentially opening up a "tracking error," which is considered a cardinal sin in ETF-land. MVIS, Van Eck's separate but related indexing business, therefore announced in April 2017 that it would tweak its benchmark, almost doubling the market value of gold miners the ETF was allowed to invest in. That made sense, but anticipating that some companies would as a result be dumped by the index, other traders jumped ahead of the rejig, ditching stocks that were going to lose out and sending tremors through the universe of gold-mining stocks.[19]

Although this all happened in a minor, inconsequential slice of the US stock market, the ructions were a potent illustration of the impact even minor index rejigs and anticipated ETF flows can have. It is far from the only such example. In January 2020, the stocks of Tanger Factory Outlet Centers and Meredith Corporation, an Iowa-based magazine publisher, went on a roller-coaster ride due to the mechanics of ETFs.

Both companies had long struggled, sending their shares down sharply in 2018–19. However, Tanger and Meredith insisted on maintaining their dividend payments to investors. That meant that State Street's $20 billion dividends-focused ETF started acquiring huge chunks of their stock. Unlike most ETFs, which track indices weighted purely according to the stock market value of companies, the SPDR S&P Dividend ETF tracked a benchmark called the S&P High Yield Dividend Aristocrats. This is instead weighted according to a company's "dividend yield." Put simply, the higher the dividend relative to the share price, the higher the yield.

When Tanger's and Meredith's stocks swooned, even as they maintained their dividend, it meant that the State Street ETF kept on buying even as other investors fled, up to a maximum 4 percent ceiling. As a proportion of the ETF's overall assets the stocks remained modest holdings, but State Street's ownership was huge compared to the dwindling size of the companies. Moreover, other dividend-focused index funds were also snaffling up their shares. By mid-January, index funds owned over half of Tanger's stock, and nearly 40 percent of Meredith—with the SPDR S&P Dividend ETF alone accounting for roughly half of that.[20]

The problem was that the Dividend Aristocrats index includes only companies with a stock market value of at least $1.5 billion, regardless of their dividend, and both Tanger and Meredith eventually shrank below that mark. That meant that when S&P Dow Jones indices removed their shares from the index on January 24, the ETF had to dump their shares. Given the size of its holdings relative to the shrinking size of the stocks, the result could have been mayhem—except for another wrinkle.

Most index funds generate extra revenues through securities lending, loaning out the shares to traders who want to bet on them falling. The trader in practice rents the shares for a period, sells them, and hopefully buys them back after a fall, pocketing the difference, a process known as short-selling. Given their fading fortunes, short-sellers had swarmed over Meredith and Tanger. But to sell the shares the Dividend ETF had to first recall those it had rented out—forcing short-sellers to buy them back to hand them over again, causing the share prices to spike.[21] That helped soften the impact of State Street's ETF from selling, but the consequence was that the two stocks fluctuated wildly through January.

Yet small, idiosyncratic instances such as these obscure the wider distortive impact of index funds, according to some skeptics. They fret that the undoubted benefits for many investors are increasingly outweighed by the more ephemeral costs to the overall health of financial markets—as the next chapter will explore.

Chapter 17

THIS IS WATER

DAVID FOSTER WALLACE HATED public speaking. So it was with a hefty dose of trepidation that the writer walked up to the lectern at Kenyon College on a sunny day in May 2005. The combination of heat and nervousness meant he sweated through the black robe he wore for the occasion.[1]

"If anybody feels like perspiring, I'd advise you to go ahead, because I'm sure going to," the shaggy-haired writer said, fetching a handkerchief from under his gown to wipe his face. Wallace then proceeded to deliver what would become one of the most celebrated commencement speeches ever given.

The opening parable was attention-getting in its simplicity and power. Two young fish swim along in the sea. They meet an older fish who casually greets them: "Morning, boys. How's the water?" The two young fish then swim on for a bit, before one eventually turns to the other and asks, "What the hell is water?" Wallace's point was that the "most obvious, important realities are often the ones that are hardest to see and talk about."

For him, that meant learning how to tackle the struggle, loneliness, and tedium of everyday adult life by consciously nurturing a sense of awareness and empathy. But for a growing band of indexing skeptics, Wallace's tale of two young fish oblivious to a pervasive reality that surrounds, sustains, and shapes everything around them is also the best way to describe the impact of passive investing on markets.

Michael Green is one of a growing number of people sounding the alarm. An intense, cerebral man in his early fifties, with short dark hair and the weary tone of a Cassandra whose fate is to never have his prophecies believed, Green first rose to prominence in geekier corners of the finance industry after making a killing on betting against the volatility-linked exchange-traded products that blew up in February 2018.[2] At the time he worked at Thiel Macro, a hedge fund run by Peter Thiel, the Silicon Valley investor. Green is now chief strategist at Simplify Asset Management—ironically a provider of active, options-based ETFs—but has made alerting people to what he thinks are the dangerous vagaries of passive investing his mission.[3]

Green reckons that Wallace's "This Is Water" parable is the perfect metaphor to describe passive investing's now all-encompassing effect on markets and his industry. "Indices were designed as measures, but once you begin investing in them you actually distort them," Green argues. "The moment they became participants and began to grow, they affected markets." He is far from the only critic of passive investing. But few outdo his fervor and articulacy. And if even some of his thesis is correct, then passive investing has some thorny problems to confront.

▲

SOME OF THE NEGATIVE side effects are fairly uncontroversial, with only the degree and importance disputed by proponents and detractors of passive investing.

Given that most index funds are capitalization-weighted, that means that most of the money they take in goes into the biggest stocks (or the largest debtors). Critically, and contrary to popular conception, an index fund does not automatically buy more of a security simply because it has gone up in price, given that it already holds that security. But if the fund takes in *new* money, then that will go into securities according to their shifting size, and that can in theory disproportionately benefit stocks that are already on the up. For instance, over the past four decades, on average 14 cents of every new dollar put into the Vanguard 500 fund or State Street's SPDR would have gone into the five biggest companies. A decade ago it was closer to 10 cents. Today, it is over 20 cents—the highest on record.[4] Although those bigger companies are, well, bigger, those extra cents can have a disproportional market impact, according to a 2020 study.[5] In other words, size can beget size, a dynamic that could contribute to the tendency of financial markets toward bubbles, according to critics.

Moreover, the "outperformance" of index versus most traditional active managers can therefore, at least in theory, become a self-fulfilling prophecy: Their holdings benefit from inflows in perfect proportion to their holdings. Given the enormity of the flows into index funds over the past decade, that can have a marked impact. Active managers are in effect competing against a rival who controls and influences the yardstick of success. Critics like Green concede that part of the outperformance of index funds is thanks to some of their core advantages—such as reduced costs from less hyperactive trading and lower management fees—but argue that a big chunk of it is increasingly accounted for by this effect.*

Index fund skeptics argue that in the past, traditional active

---

* This might help explain why even Warren Buffett seems to have lost his touch in recent years: Shares in Berkshire Hathaway have also underperformed the Vanguard 500 fund he once championed against Ted Seides's hedge funds for most of the past decade.

fund managers would play an important role in buying what they thought were undervalued stocks or in some cases shorting overvalued ones. This would ensure that the market as a whole remained relatively "efficient"—to use Eugene Fama's formulation. But the sheer scale of index funds means that trying to tilt against their force will nowadays mean that active managers will almost inevitably underperform those same indices in the longer run, the critics argue.

Moreover, Green argues that index funds are contributing to a secular increase in average stock market valuations seen since the financial crisis of 2008—but at the same time making markets more fragile in a downturn.

One aspect of this is largely technical, if important. Active managers typically hold around 5 percent of their money in cash, in case they suffer outflows or enticing opportunities present themselves in a selloff. But index funds carry as little cash as possible to avoid diverging from their index. In other words, every dollar handed to an index fund goes straight into the market, while on average only 95 cents of a dollar given to an active manager does so. That cash component will always drag on the performance of an active manager when markets are rising. With so much money gushing from active to passive funds, that leads to a secular increase in valuations, Green argues. It is debatable how meaningful this is when stacked up against other trends that have boosted corporate profits and stock valuations in recent decades—such as the decline in antitrust enforcement, globalization, the fading power of labor unions, and sagging interest rates, which boost the value of all financial assets—but it is potentially a partial explanation. The flip side is that index funds sell quickly if they suffer outflows, as they have no cash buffer.

Yet in Green's view, the biggest effect comes from how index-tracking strategies have now vacuumed up so much of the stock market. They have been the dominant "bid"—Wall Street parlance for the buyer—for stocks over the past decade. That leaves fewer shares for everyone else, even though their holdings aren't excluded from index calculations. This is an issue because most big benchmarks like the S&P 500 are nowadays "float"-adjusted rather than purely value-weighted. In other words, how much space they have in an index is determined by the value of shares that are actually freely available to trade, rather than its total value.

Imagine a $10 million public company whose founder owns half of its 1 million shares. That means 500,000 shares still trade freely on the stock market, and their $5 million value determines its weighting in indices—not $10 million. But index funds might now own another 20 percent, which they never sell unless they suffer investor withdrawals. That means other investors are in practice buying and selling just 300,000 shares worth $3 million, even though the value used to calculate the company's index weighting is $5 million.

Incremental buying—from active managers or index funds seeing further inflows—can then push the price up more aggressively, simply because there are fewer sellers around. In extremis, a kind of black hole of passive investing sucking up more and more freely traded shares can cause prices to go parabolic, Green argues, almost as if index funds are like a hoarder sitting on a warehouse of antibacterial soap in a pandemic. As a corollary, if the indexing tide ever goes out, then the detritus left in its wake could be much greater—simply because of the weight of selling that would happen and the winnowing pool of potential buyers. The dominant bid for equities would vanish, and almost all one would be left with are sellers.

Of course, both ordinary investors and professional money managers have throughout history proven perfectly able to inflate bubbles and fuel crashes, whether in individual stocks or markets as a whole. If size really did beget size, then ExxonMobil would still be the world's most valuable company, as it was when indexing started to take off. It doesn't really make sense to exclude index fund–held shares from calculating a stock's free float. After all, passive funds do buy and sell all the time according to the ebb and flow of investor money, even if it has mostly been flow in the long run. And for the time being, passive investing vehicles still hold only one-seventh of the US stock market, for example, and far less elsewhere. They are not yet as all-pervasive as water is to fish. Nor is passive investing the homogeneous blob that critics often imagine. Trading volumes are also for the most part higher than ever, suggesting that the market's vibrancy is hardly eroding with the rise of passive investing. It is tempting to dismiss many of these the concerns as the shrill self-serving scaremongering of industry incumbents coming under intensifying pressure from a cheaper, better rival.

Nonetheless, academics are starting to find some evidence suggesting that index funds are having a potentially disruptive impact in some subtle ways. For example, some studies indicate that the growth of index funds means that financial securities now move more in lockstep, rather than according to their idiosyncratic characteristics,[6] or that stocks with higher ETF ownership are more volatile than the norm.[7]

Even the Federal Reserve has noted how the shift from active to passive investment strategies "has profoundly affected the asset management industry in the past couple of decades, and the ongoing nature of the shift suggests that its effects will continue to ripple through the financial system for years to come."[8] In a typically balanced fashion, the Fed's economists found that the tectonic shift from active to passive investing is "affecting the composition of financial stability risks by mitigating some and increasing others." Yet critics like Green insist this evenhandedness amounted to a whitewash.

"These strategies have become so large that they are quite plainly and empirically affecting the underlying markets themselves," he argues. "We're now starting to see the fragility associated with these things."

▲

MANY OF THE SKEPTICS ARGUE that the biggest fault line lies not in the big, mainstream index funds that invest in stocks, but in ETFs that track less traded, more idiosyncratic markets—such as bonds.

Carl Icahn, the famed corporate raider, once went as far as to call BlackRock "a very dangerous company" due to its being the world's biggest provider of fixed-income ETFs, while sitting next to Larry Fink on an industry conference stage.[9] With the mischievousness and nonchalance that comes with age and what Wall Street calls "fuck-you money," he predicted how the bond market would eventually "hit a black rock." The frustrated Fink, unused to such criticism coming from a fellow finance industry titan at a public event, pushed back. "Carl, you're a good investor, but you're wrong again," BlackRock's founder insisted. The audience was transfixed by the unusually testy public clash.

To many critics there is a potentially dangerous feature at the heart of bond ETFs. While ETFs trade like shares on a stock exchange, some bonds trade only rarely, and often via only investment banks like Goldman Sachs, Barclays, or Deutsche Bank, who act as crucial intermediaries. This is especially true for corporate debt, a market where ETFs are starting to become increasingly important. Of the 21,175 publicly registered US corporate bonds outstanding in 2018, only 246 of them traded at least once a day that year, according to research by Citigroup. But almost every corner of the fixed-income market is less actively traded than stocks. The worry among some skeptics is that a bond ETF struck with a spate of investor withdrawals might be unable to sell its holdings to meet them, and collapse.

That could in turn spark fears over fixed-income ETFs at large, leading to a frenzied rush for the exit that triggers a broader bond market collapse.

These fears rose like a specter at the depths of the COVID-19 crisis in March 2020, when the prices of many bond ETFs careened lower, opening up sizable discounts to the theoretical value of their holdings. Normally, specialized trading firms known as "authorized participants" that ensure ETFs trade smoothly by handling the creation and redemption of ETF shares—the process invented by Nate Most—would be able to take advantage of these dislocations. They would buy shares in the beaten-up ETF, exchange them for a slice of the underlying bonds, and then sell them, easing the dislocations. But the bond market was so dysfunctional that trading froze up and the arbitrage became almost impossible. It was only when the Federal Reserve stepped in with the full force of its monetary arsenal—including a pledge to buy bond ETFs—that the disorder faded.[10]

To their critics, that it took the might of the US central bank to stem the turmoil was evidence of the fragility represented by the "liquidity" mismatch between bond ETFs that trade continuously through the day and the less traded securities they contain. That BlackRock was selected to manage the Fed's ETF purchases also reeked of a conflict of interest to some observers.

However, March 2020 arguably proved that the ETF structure is actually more supple than the critics say. Bond ETF prices became unmoored because no one could sell the underlying bonds, whose seemingly more resilient prices were simply stale. The discounts ETFs traded at were basically an illusion, with the ETFs actually reflecting the "true" level of distress in the bond market.[11] Nor did they necessarily worsen the selloff. Because the arbitrage froze, investors were largely just trading the shares of the fixed-income ETFs—which essentially became closed-end funds that traded freely.[12]

In other words, the discounts were a symptom of the financial stress, not a cause of them. In a way, bond ETFs played the crucial role of shock absorber that initially sparked the idea in Nate Most's Amex team over three decades earlier. Yes, absorbing the shock of all that selling caused bond ETFs to drop precipitously, and perhaps one or several would somehow have broken rather than bend to the winds had the Fed not acted. But the turmoil in the broader bond market would likely have been worse had ETFs not existed to absorb the selling spree, and bond-focused mutual funds were just as at risk—if not more so—from an inability to sell their holdings to meet a flurry of investor withdrawals.

As a result, even some past skeptics now quietly admit that fixed-income ETFs held up far better than they would have expected, and fans crowed at their success. "I marvel that so many people don't understand ETFs," notes BlackRock's Larry Fink. "They're still just superficially saying they're 'bad' or they're not going to work, and then they've been proven wrong in almost every market disruption, especially in the weeks of March."

Similarly, despite frequent predictions of financial doom when the supposedly fickle inflows into index funds inevitably go into reverse, investment in them has time and again proven far "stickier" than money in traditional, active funds. "This suggests that the net flows of passive funds may be less reactive to poor returns and that these funds' growth may be beneficial for financial stability," the Federal Reserve noted in its report on the industry in 2018.[13]

The potentially distortive effect of the rising tide of passive investing—in both stock and bond markets—is a real concern. But this is nothing new. One can see parallels between the birth and growth of index funds in financial markets and the introduction of an alien animal into a natural ecosystem that then creates havoc— such as the importation of European pigs to Australia in the late eighteenth century. Yet it is important to remember that financial markets have always been a dynamic ecosystem, which eventually adapts to the emergence of new beasts in the jungle, whether it was the investment trusts of the nineteenth century, the birth of mutual funds in the twentieth century, or more recently the emergence of hedge funds. Each of these new "species" has for a period caused anguish and gloomy prognostications, but over time added to the vibrancy of the overall ecosystem.

So it will likely prove with index funds, even though the debate over their impact on financial markets will undoubtedly grow in the coming years. And the disruptive impact passive investing is having on the rest of the financial industry is already becoming abundantly clear.

▲

ELIZABETH FERNANDO SUSPECTED something was afoot when her new boss summoned her for an unscheduled meeting in his glass goldfish-bowl office in the middle of the investment floor of USS, one of the biggest private pension plans in the UK, the £75 billion Universities Superannuation Scheme.

She led its stock-investing team, and had picked up that its new head, Simon Pilcher, wanted to shake things up. Fernando feared that her job might be on the line after twenty-five years at the pension fund, but at least she hadn't been called into the more discreet conference room where such unwelcome announcements were usually made.

However, it turns out that Pilcher was planning on more than just letting Fernando go: The executive had decided to shutter the entire £14 billion internal stock-picking team for mainstream markets such as Japan, Europe, and the United States, and divert the money elsewhere, into more "thematic" strategies primarily directed by quantitative, computerized models.[14] Fernando had to sit stony-faced through the meeting—given how everyone on the floor could see them—and was only afterward able to walk across the floor and find a quiet room where she could collect her thoughts. It felt like she had failed a test she didn't even know she was taking, and the decision simply didn't make sense to her.

Fernando's team of fund managers had excelled, with USS's latest annual report bragging that the group had outperformed its benchmark to the tune of £389 million over five years after costs. Nonetheless, Fernando was told the decision was final, and she couldn't tell any of her colleagues until Pilcher was ready to make a public announcement. Rather than face being dishonest to her team in the meantime—annual performance appraisals were about to start—she started going to the gym all the time, working out her frustration on the treadmill.

On February 12, 2020, Pilcher finally sent an email announcing the "difficult decision" to "reshape" its equities team "to focus our internal investment capabilities on where we can add the most value." That meant shifting away from picking stocks to a more "thematic strategy"—without clearly saying what that meant, except that Fernando and twelve of her colleagues would likely be out of a job. This despite the fact that Pilcher stressed that "performance across the equities mandate was strong in 2019 and the team should hold their heads high."[15]

The fate of USS's band of stock-pickers is no isolated example of how violently the pendulum has swung against traditional investment styles in favor of quantitative and passive ones over the past decade.*

The index fund pioneers still vividly remember the scorn with

---

* All told, over $2 trillion has gushed out of traditional, actively managed mutual funds since the eve of the last financial crisis in 2007–8, according to estimates from EPFR, an industry data provider. That is nearly as much as the value of the entire French and German stock markets combined. Bond funds have been more resilient, yet inflows into passive fixed-income vehicles have outpaced those into traditional funds over the same period— something that not so long ago would have been unthinkable. Moreover, this data is for only publicly reported funds, and the trend is likely even more advanced among institutional investors.

which they were long held, and the reluctance of many investors to embrace passive investing, even when the performance of the portfolio managers was frequently lamentable. Today, even fund managers who manage to beat their benchmarks are no longer safe from the revolution unleashed by John McQuown, Jack Bogle, and Nate Most. Voluminous research since the initial, inspirational spate of work in the 1960s and 1970s has kept hammering the point home that active management is for the most part still a "Loser's Game," as Charles Ellis termed it back in 1975.

The seminal paper in the field was published in 1991 by William Sharpe, whose theories underpinned the original creation of the index fund, and was bluntly titled "The Arithmetic of Active Management."[16] This expanded on Sharpe's earlier work, and addressed the suggestion that the index investing trend that was starting to gain ground at the time was a mere "fad."

The paper articulated what Sharpe saw as two iron rules that must hold true over time: The return on the average actively managed dollar will equal that of a dollar managed passively before costs, and after costs the return on that actively managed dollar will be less than that of a passively managed dollar. In other words, mathematically the market represents the average returns, and for every investor who outperforms the market someone must do worse. Given that index funds charge far less than traditional funds, over time the average passive investor must do better than the average active one.

Other academics have later quibbled with aspects of Sharpe's 1991 paper, with Lasse Heje Pedersen's "Sharpening the Arithmetic of Active Management" the most prominent example. In this 2016 paper, Pedersen points out that Sharpe's assertions rest on some crucial assumptions, such as that the "market portfolio" never actually changes. But in reality, what constitutes "the market" is in constant flux. This means that active managers can at least theoretically on average outperform it, and they perform a valuable service to the health of a markets-based economy by doing so. Nonetheless, Pedersen stresses that this should not necessarily be construed as a full-throated defense of active management. "I think that low-cost index funds is one of the most investor-friendly inventions in finance and this paper should not be used as an excuse by active managers who charge high fees while adding little or no value," he wrote.[17] "My arithmetic shows that active management can add value in aggregate, but whether it actually does, and how much, are empirical questions."

Can one unearth above-average fund managers, who can consistently or over time beat the market? Once again, the academic research is gloomy for the investment industry. Using the database first started by Jim Lorie's Center for Research in Security Prices, S&P Dow Jones Indices publishes a semiannual "persistence scorecard" on how often top-performing fund managers keep excelling. The results are grim reading, with less than 3 percent of top-performing equity funds remaining in the top after five years. In fact, being a top performer is more likely to presage a slump than a sustained run.[18]

As a result, as Fernando's defenestration highlighted, the hurdle to retain the faith of investors keeps getting higher, even for fund managers who do well.* In the 1990s, the top six deciles of US equities-focused mutual funds enjoyed investor inflows, according to Morgan Stanley.[19] In the first decade of the new millennium, only the top three deciles did so, and in the 2010–20 period, only the top 10 percent of funds have managed to avoid outflows,

---

*Active managers often insist that their true worth will become apparent only in a bear market. They argue that their nimbleness will allow them to sidestep the worst of the downturn and take advantage of the recovery, even as index funds slavishly do whatever the market does. Reality is less forgiving. While there are always some fund managers who prove their worth, most actually still underperform index funds even in a downturn. That is why every single bout of major market turmoil since the 1970s has actually accelerated the shift into passive investing, rather than slowed it down.

and gathered assets at a far slower pace than they would have in the past.

In a telling example of the pendulum's swing in favor of index investing, Clarence Herbst, a big donor to and alumnus of the University of Colorado, in 2020 sued its endowment over its continued use of active managers. Despite the $2 billion endowment outperforming most other universities' over both the short and medium term, the lawsuit pointed out that it would have done even better by simply putting its money in the Vanguard 500 fund over the past decade—even though that would be a far less diversified, riskier way of investing than the typically balanced approach taken by most endowments. Although Herbst's lawsuit was dismissed by a Denver judge, these are issues that virtually every big investor now has to wrestle with.

But if the overall effort of active managers is a boon to the health and efficiency of markets—and by inference the health of an economy—what are the implications, and is there a limit to how much money can be managed passively before the individual benefits to investors are swamped by the collective cost to us all?

▲

FERNANDO IS NO APOLOGIST FOR the investment industry, arguing that despite huge strides over the past two decades there are still many mediocre money managers who spend too much time and money chasing the latest hot idea. As a result, retail investors often "get taken for a ride," she concedes. But she worries that the now-indiscriminate shift into passive investment strategies is eroding the central role that financial markets play in the economy, with money blindly shoveled into stocks according to their size, rather than their prospects.

"The stock market is supposed to be a capital allocation machine. But by investing passively you are just putting money into the past winners, rather than the future winners," she argues. In other words, beyond the impact on markets or other investors, is the growth of index investing having a deleterious impact on economic dynamism?

The most cutting, colorful illustration of this conundrum is from Inigo Fraser-Jenkins, the Bernstein analyst who penned the sarcastic homage to a fictional indexer attempting to build the Ultimate Index. In 2016, Fraser-Jenkins published an even punchier report entitled "The Silent Road to Serfdom: Why Passive Investment Is Worse Than Marxism." His argument was that at least communist countries attempted to allocate resources to the most important areas. This may be less efficient than the decentralized, markets-oriented allocation method of capitalism, but it is still better than blindly allocating money according to the vagaries of an arbitrary index.

Although the framing was deliberately provocative, it is undeniably true that index funds are free riders on the work done by active managers, which has an aggregate societal value—something even Jack Bogle admitted. If everyone merely invested passively, the outcome would be "chaos, catastrophe," Bogle noted a few years before passing away. "There would be no trading. There would be no way to turn a stream of income into a pile of capital or a pile of capital into a stream of income," Vanguard's founder observed in 2017.[20]

Bogle rightly pointed out that the likelihood of such a scenario—where everyone was merely invested in an index fund—was zero. But some investors and analysts fret that given the strength of the trend toward greater passive investing, the market's efficiency will gradually atrophy, with potentially dire consequences. "A given investment in active may or may not be the best decision for an individual particular investor but for the system overall there is a benefit in the efficient allocation of capital," Fraser-Jenkins argued.[21] "Rather than looking at the real economy and seeking to understand its future development, passive allocation self-referentially looks to the financial economy to inform its asset allocation choices."

There is a conundrum at the heart of the efficient-markets hypothesis, often called the Grossman-Stiglitz Paradox after a seminal 1980 paper written by hedge fund manager Sanford Grossman and the Nobel laureate economist Joseph Stiglitz.[22] "On the Impossibility of Informationally Efficient Markets" was a frontal assault on Eugene Fama's theory, pointing out that if market prices truly perfectly reflected all relevant information—such as corporate data, economic news, or industry trends—then no one would be incentivized to collect the information needed to trade. After all, doing so is a costly pursuit. But then markets would no longer be efficient. In other words, someone has to make markets efficient, and somehow they have to be compensated for the work involved.

This paradox has hardly held back the growth of passive investing. Many investors gradually realized that whatever academic theory one subscribes to, the cold unforgiving fact is that over time most active managers underperform their benchmarks. Even if they do beat the market, a lot of the "alpha" they produce is then often gobbled up by their fees. With his usual wit, Bogle dubbed this the "Cost Matters Hypothesis."[23] However, the truth of the Grossman-Stiglitz Paradox does raise some pertinent questions around whether markets may become less efficient as more and more investing is done through index funds.

The hope of many traditional investors is that markets will eventually reach a tipping point where they are so inefficient that it opens up a bonanza of lucrative opportunities for them to take advantage of. But so far there are no signs of that point approaching. Some analysts are skeptical that there will ever be a promised land of abundant alpha.

Michael Mauboussin, one of Wall Street's most pedigreed

analysts and an adjunct professor at Columbia Business School, has an apt metaphor to show how the hope among many active managers that index funds will eventually become so big that markets become easier to beat is likely in vain: Imagine that investing is akin to a poker game between a bunch of friends of varying skill. In all likelihood, the dimmer players will be the first to be forced out of the game and head home to nurse their losses. But that doesn't mean that the game then becomes easier for the remaining cardsharps. In fact, it becomes harder, as the players still in the game are the best ones.[24]

Although financial markets are a wildly more dynamic game, with infinitely more permutations and without the fixed rules of poker, the metaphor is a compelling explanation for why markets actually appear to be becoming harder to beat even as the tide of passive investing continues to rise. Mediocre fund managers are simply being gradually squeezed out of the industry. At the same time, the number of individual investors—the proverbial doctors and dentists getting stock tips on the golf course and taking a bet— has gradually declined, depriving Wall Street of the steady stream of "dumb money" that provided suckers for the "smart money" of professional fund managers to take advantage of.

Perhaps there may be an element of the distortionary effects fingered by the likes of Green. But most fund managers willingly admit that the average skill and training of the industry keeps getting higher, requiring constant reinvention, retraining, and brain-achingly hard work. The old days of "have a hunch, buy a bunch, go to lunch" are long gone. Once upon a time, simply having an MBA or a CFA might be considered an edge in the investment industry. Add in the effort to actually read quarterly financial reports from companies and you had at least a good shot at excelling. Nowadays, MBAs and CFAs are rife in the finance industry, and algorithms can read thousands of quarterly financial reports in the time it takes a human to switch on their computer.

In fact, the number of CFAs per listed company has risen from four to fifty-one in the past two decades, according to Citi. These days, even PhD economists aren't guaranteed jobs in asset management, unless they have married their degree with a programming language like Python, which would allow them to parse vast digital datasets that are now commonplace, such as credit card data, satellite imagery, and consumer sentiment gleaned from continuously scraping billions of social media posts.

Beating the market is not impossible. But the degree of difficulty in doing so consistently is far greater than it was in the past. Even giant, multibillion-dollar hedge funds staffed with an army of data scientists, programmers, rocket scientists, and the best financial minds in the industry can struggle to consistently outperform their benchmarks after fees. To use Mauboussin's poker metaphor, not only are the remaining players around the table the best ones, but new ones entering the game are even more cunning, calculating, and inscrutable than in the past.*

▲

THE RESULT IS THAT EVERY facet of the money management industry is being altered by the advent of index funds. Many financial advisors no longer bet on the latest trendy stock or rock-star fund manager at Fidelity; they put their clients into a mix of index funds.

---

* The data bears this out. In addition to a "persistence scorecard," S&P Dow Jones Indices publishes snapshots of how many mutual funds beat their benchmarks. Most years, a majority underperform their indices, whatever the market. Over multiple years, the data becomes progressively grimmer. As of June 2020, only 15 percent of US stock-pickers had cumulatively managed to surpass their benchmark over the last decade. In bond markets, it is a similar tale, albeit varying depending on the flavor of fixed income. The data is more favorable for fund managers in more exotic, less efficient asset classes, such as emerging markets, but on the whole the data is clear that in the longer run most fund managers still underperform their passive rivals after fees.

Private banks in Zürich or Singapore are starting to eschew hedge funds in favor of constructing diversified portfolios of ETFs. Even hedge funds themselves increasingly use ETFs to implement their trades.

The impact has been profound, compressing profit margins in an industry that once enjoyed wild profitability. Although asset management remains a lucrative business, most trends are pointing the wrong away. Fees are under relentless pressure. When Fidelity—which eventually swallowed its misgivings and belatedly jumped into the index fund game—launched the first-ever zero-fee ETF in 2018, it sent tremors through the stocks of rival money managers, as people started to realize that the end game is likely to be cost-free investing, at least for simple, plain-vanilla index funds.

In 2019, Cyrus Taraporevala, the head of State Street Global Advisors, joked at a conference that the industry was at a crossroads, with "one path leading to despair and utter hopelessness, the other to total extinction."[25] Although he was being tongue-in-cheek, his words were indicative of the widespread pessimism in large parts of the investment industry. Tellingly, the shares of publicly listed asset managers have now as a group underperformed the broader US stock market for over a decade, with BlackRock the sole, noticeable exception.

This is in turn starting to reshape the broader finance industry, which is in part set up to service the investment industry, by executing trades, churning out economic research, and providing other services. The novelist Gary Shteyngart once spent a year studying Wall Street for a book, and noted afterward that the finance industry is akin to a "helper animal" that in nature cleans the teeth of a bigger beast in return for morsels of food. "Everyone in New York who's not a portfolio manager is just this little helper animal, and their existence is tied into the health of the greater animal. If the main animal perishes, the whole ecosystem goes," he told the magazine *Barron's*.[26] This may seem like artful exaggeration of a professional writer, but there is an element of truth to it, at least when it comes to the finance industry.

With their clients evolving rapidly, investment banks, stock exchanges, corporate law firms, accountants, and brokerages have no choice but to change with them. This ranges from financial research departments setting up dedicated teams to analyze ETFs to traders retooling their desks to reflect this new force in markets. How corporate bonds move around is being reshaped by the rise of big ETFs. Bankers in mergers and acquisitions departments have to consider what Vanguard or BlackRock might make of the corporate raids they launch, while those in equity and bond departments that help take companies public or sell their debt have to think of ways to ensure that their clients' securities make it into the all-important indices.

Yet ultimately the effects of the index fund revolution will stretch far beyond the confines of the finance industry. The biggest emerging flashpoint—and one that some in the index industry will privately but grudgingly concede is valid—is what the growth of passive investing means for how *all* public companies are run. This was vividly illustrated in the aftermath of a uniquely American tragedy.

Chapter 18

OUR NEW CORPORATE OVERLORDS

IT WAS A SUNNY DAY in Florida when Nikolas Cruz was dropped off by an Uber driver at his former school in Parkland on the afternoon of February 14, 2018. The skinny nineteen-year-old walked up the stairway into Marjory Stoneman Douglas High School, loaded an AR-15 semiautomatic rifle he had hidden in his black backpack, and started mowing down students.

In just six minutes, Cruz murdered seventeen people, a massacre so senseless and brutal that it reawakened America's gun debate. It followed a predictable pattern of liberals demanding stricter controls, and conservatives insisting that the immediate aftermath was a time for "thoughts and prayers," not hasty action.

But for the first time, index funds found themselves dragged into the tragedy, after activists pointed out that they were among the biggest owners of the biggest listed gun manufacturers. David Hogg, a survivor of the massacre, even called for people to boycott BlackRock and Vanguard.[1] This was awkward for the two investment giants, as the gun stocks were in their index funds. Whatever the personal views of their executives, they could not sell as long as the companies remained in the indices their funds tracked.

Both Vanguard and BlackRock vowed to meet with the gunmakers and ask for plans on how to mitigate the risks posed by the proliferation of their firearms and prevent more tragedies like Parkland. They would also offer index funds that excluded gunmakers for any investors who wanted this. "For manufacturers and retailers of civilian firearms, we believe that responsible policies and practices are critical to their long-term prospects. Now more so than ever," BlackRock said in a statement.[2]

Across the indexing industry, imbroglio sparked a quiet debate about what should or could be done. After watching the grim news on TV, shell-shocked surviving students and their teachers being ushered out of Parkland school by police, Jack Bogle mulled sending a public letter to gun manufacturers appealing for a less recalcitrant attitude and more concrete action to prevent more such massacres. "You cannot see teachers walk out with these kids and be the same person afterwards," he said mournfully. Yet fundamentally, real tangible action must be taken by politicians, not index fund providers, Bogle concluded.

The reality is that index funds cannot sell their shares, and they cannot tell a gunmaker to stop making guns. The result was therefore little more than hand-wringing. Yet the Parkland tragedy and its aftermath highlighted how the rising size and influence of the index fund industry's "Big Three" is starting to gain attention, and how the pivotal battlefield will in the future likely be when, how, and why they exercise their mounting power over companies around the world.

"Parkland was interesting. It was such a tough question for an organization like BlackRock," notes one former senior executive at the company. "Are you going to make a moral statement and sell those gunmakers, but introduce tracking error? In the end, we just offered separate funds that excluded them. But the more BlackRock is out there talking about how companies should be run, the more the answer that 'it's in the index' is not going to fly."

This is quite the shift. In the early days, critics focused on how investors should not "accept mediocrity." That attack eventually foundered on the spiky rocks of hard data. Evidence that index funds make markets more bubbly or fragile remains inconclusive at best. The newest and arguably most potent line of criticism is what the growing heft of passive investing means for corporate governance, and the implications of a strengthening industry oligopoly.

The term "corporate governance" may seem dry and niche, something that only geeky lawyers might care about. But it is of vital importance. Companies enjoy immense clout in the modern world, and their biggest owners are often—and increasingly—the index funds provided by the likes of BlackRock, Vanguard, and State Street. This is not an issue they can duck, as even a decision not to exercise that power is a decision with consequences.

In his twilight years, Bogle himself grew increasingly perturbed by the inevitable end result of the economies of scale in indexing, pointing out that if the trend toward an increasingly entrenched oligopoly continued, then just a handful of firms would eventually enjoy voting control over every single large listed US company.

"Public policy cannot ignore this growing dominance, and consider its impact on the financial markets, corporate governance, and regulation. These will be major issues in the coming era," he wrote shortly before passing away.[3] "I do not believe that such concentration would serve the national interest."

▲

PAUL SINGER IS A TRIM, silver-haired, bearded, and bespectacled septuagenarian who resembles more the lawyer he used to be than the fearsome hedge fund raider he is today known as. His firm Elliott

Management famously successfully hounded Argentina through courts across the world after the country defaulted in 2001, eventually extracting $2.4 billion from Buenos Aires. In 2017, he wrote a letter to investors that rained brimstone onto passive investing instead.

The main thrust of his incendiary letter was that corporate accountability has been declining for decades, and that the rise of index funds was exacerbating it.[4] Whatever their investment merits, Singer argued that they constitute lazy, inattentive owners, who encourage corporate sloth and waste that in extremis might ultimately rob the broader economy of some of its dynamism.

"As more and more investable money is managed without regard to research, evaluation, corporate governance, quality of management and an actual assessment of long-term prospects, and instead is delegated to the index-constructors and the purveyors of index products, what does that trend mean for capitalism? Growth? Innovation?" he asked rhetorically.*

Historically, many investment groups have in practice outsourced much of the hard but dull, unglamorous work around corporate governance to a small club of consultancies known as "proxy advisors." The biggest by far are Glass Lewis and Institutional Shareholder Services. Between them, they utterly dominate this niche industry, and are a quietly influential duo at the heart of the crossroads between the corporate and financial worlds.

Glass Lewis attends more than 25,000 annual meetings across over 100 markets around the world every year. ISS brags that it covers about 44,000 meetings in 115 countries. Together, they advise thousands of investment groups with cumulatively tens of tril-

---

* The section of the letter on passive investing was titled "Comfortably Numb," a reference to the Pink Floyd song and the approach Singer argued that too many investors are currently taking.

lions of dollars' worth of assets, and make millions of votes every year on their behalf.

Many corporate executives resent the often formulaic approach of the proxy advisors, and see relying on them as an abdication of an investor's responsibility. This is partly self-serving, as they dislike the proxy advisors' views on compensation, for example. Yet there is an element of truth to it. Most investment groups don't want the hassle of having to deal with many mundane issues across hundreds or even thousands of companies they own shares in. ISS's and Glass Lewis's raison d'être is to relieve them of this headache.

Active managers also use proxy advisors, but point out that they always have the option of selling if they dislike a company's direction, while index funds have to stick it out. Passive ones counter that as de facto "permanent capital," they actually have more ability and willingness to encourage change than shorter-term active managers who may be gone tomorrow. "We're going to hold your stock when you hit your quarterly earnings target. And we'll hold it when you don't. We're going to hold your stock if we like you. And if we don't. We're going to hold your stock when everyone else is piling in. And when everyone else is running for the exits," Vanguard chief executive Bill McNabb said in a 2015 speech.[5] "In other words, we're big, we don't make a lot of noise, and we're focused on the long term. That is precisely why we care so much about good governance."

Nonetheless, stung by criticism that passive funds are passive owners, the big index fund companies are changing tack. Much of the humdrum work around corporate governance—routine resolutions, approving auditor reports, and so on—will remain with the proxy advisors, but State Street, BlackRock, and Vanguard have in recent years been building up big "stewardship" teams. These are dedicated to monitoring all the companies their funds invest in, engaging more frequently and thoroughly with their boards, and not necessarily voting at annual meetings on autopilot. "The growth of indexing demands that we now take this function to a new level," Larry Fink admitted in his annual letter to corporate executives in 2018.[6]

Singer feels this is little better than a fig leaf. He stresses that he does not question the professionalism of these stewardship teams, and concedes that from a ten-thousand-foot level corporate governance may have improved a little due to their efforts. Indeed, the three finance professors Ian Appel, Todd Gormley, and Donald Keim have found that rising index fund ownership leads to more independent board directors, for example.[7] But Singer argues that given the size of the index fund providers, they are still far too small to do the comprehensive, granular work needed for well-judged positions on the thousands of companies and the myriad important issues that often crop up in their governance.[8]

Nonetheless, real changes are afoot, especially in areas related to "ESG," a buzzy acronym in financial circles these days that stands for environmental, social, and governance. Incorporating ESG principles—essentially shunning companies that fail on one or more of these aspects, or cajoling them in the right direction—is one of the biggest trends sweeping across the investment landscape at the moment.

While passive investors cannot sell, there are many other weapons in their arsenal, ranging from quiet lobbying to voting against the reelection of individual board members or nixing compensation plans. Although ESG is easy to dismiss as grandstanding, or even "greenwashing," there are myriad signs that a subtle but real shift is happening.

▲

EVERY AUGUST, FINK TAKES A bunch of friends and colleagues for a three-day fly-fishing trip to a camp near Lake Iliamna in southwest Alaska. It is a near-religious getaway for BlackRock's founder, an opportunity for the consummate schmoozer to glad-hand other business titans who are often invited along, as well as catch some trout and grayling. But his 2019 fishing trip turned into a conversion with potentially wide-ranging implications for companies across the world.

Alaska had just suffered its warmest July on record, and massive, destructive wildfires had broken out across the state, blanketing swaths of the normally bucolic countryside in smoke.[9] Soon afterward, Fink took his wife, Lori, on a safari in Botswana's Okavango Delta, a lush oasis in the mostly arid Kalahari Desert. But extreme temperatures had dried the normally swampy delta that year, causing elephants and other fauna to die in droves.

Fink had long worried about the impact of human-caused climate change. Yet the trips to Alaska and Botswana hammered home the sense that this was an immediate and pressing crisis that had to be dealt with. After years of mulling it, Fink finally decided to swing the full force of BlackRock in response.

His 2020 annual letter to corporate executives of companies BlackRock is invested in was a bombshell. It promised that Black-Rock would double the number of sustainability-focused ETFs it offered to 150, dump thermal coal companies from all actively managed funds, require that companies publish rigorous, standardized reports on various sustainability metrics, and start assessing them "with the same rigor that it analyzes traditional measures such as credit and liquidity risk."

In sum, Fink was arguing that the dangers posed by climate change were so great that they constituted an investment risk, and as a fiduciary BlackRock had no choice but to act forcefully. "I believe we are on the edge of a fundamental reshaping of finance," Fink wrote.[10] "Every government, company, and shareholder must confront climate change." And in case corporate boards didn't get the message, he included an explicit warning: "We will be increasingly disposed to vote against management and board directors when companies are not making sufficient progress on sustainability-related disclosures and the business practices and plans underlying them."

Some cynics say that BlackRock's pivot was triggered more by the recent loss of a mammoth index investment mandate from Japan's giant $1.6 trillion Government Pension Investment Fund, reportedly over concerns that the asset manager wasn't taking ESG issues seriously enough.[11] Undoubtedly, a stronger focus on ESG is increasingly demanded by many big institutional investors around the world, so BlackRock embracing sustainability as its new mantra made perfect business sense, irrespective of any moral imperative. Friends of Fink counter that his experiences in Alaska and Botswana in 2019 genuinely rattled him, and sparked BlackRock's new crusade.

Yet this is not without potential pitfalls. No matter how worthy and important the issue, it will inevitably drag index fund providers into politically controversial territory. The biggest challenge in the coming era of passive investing will be to navigate the balance between being passive and active owners, especially at a time of intense political and cultural polarization.

For the index fund companies, the multitude of often conflicting attacks is frustrating. Barbara Novick, BlackRock's steely former public policy supremo, has described their predicament as a Goldilocks dilemma. "Do asset managers do enough? Do they do too much? Or are they doing just the right amount?" she observed at a Harvard roundtable on corporate governance in 2019.[12]

Already, there are signs of a backlash against BlackRock in particular, with some executives and rivals riled by what they see as Fink's sanctimonious pontificating. "I didn't know Larry Fink had been made God," Sam Zell, a prominent real estate billionaire, complained in 2018.[13] Yet this griping paled next to the reaction to Fink's 2020 climate change letter, which some saw as BlackRock piggybacking on the money it manages on behalf of other investors to throw its weight around in areas of public policy.

A group of conservative American business leaders organized under an umbrella group they called the Shareholder Equity Alliance lambasted Fink in a public letter, arguing that he was playing politics with his investors' money. "Whether done to intimidate corporations into toeing the vacuous and amorphous 'sustainability' line, or to force 'unacceptable' corporations out of business, the net effect is the same, namely the creation of an overtly ideological and extra-legal regulatory regime," the letter argued.[14]

Fink came under equally vociferous attacks from the other side of the political spectrum, where activists argue that BlackRock is not doing enough to avert the climate crisis—a potent example of being caught in the crossfire of one of our time's biggest topics. Even Al Gore has weighed in. "I think the large passive managers have a real difficult decision to make. Do they want to continue to finance the destruction of human civilization, or not?" the former vice president once asked.[15] "Their model makes it difficult for them to execute some of the strategies that active managers have available to them, I understand that. They are trying, they are not succeeding yet."

Fink admits that he didn't enjoy the potshots from both the left and right that followed his 2020 letter on climate change. But he insists that it was the right thing to do, quite simply to fulfill BlackRock's role as a steward of people's money. "We have to focus on long-term purpose, and long-term purpose is doing the right thing . . . as a fiduciary of our clients' money," he says. "And our job is to help them understand the impact of climate change." Moreover, he notes that investors on the whole seem to agree, judging by BlackRock's continued growth. "We're doing something right, as I'm getting killed on the right and the left. But investors are awarding us more business, and our voice is more important than ever before," he says.

Yet it is notable that even Warren Buffett, often seen as the investment industry's moral voice, is not a fan of the ESG push, pointing out that many shareholders would in reality prefer companies to focus on making profits rather than "doing good," and arguing that ultimately real change has to come with democratic legitimacy.[16] Indeed, some governments are beginning to take a closer look at the potentially adverse impact of mammoth investment groups on the dynamism of capitalism.

▲

THE ANODYNE GREENBERG LOUNGE IN New York University Law School's Vanderbilt Hall was an unlikely setting for a testy meeting of investors, regulators, and economists on December 8, 2018. But the hearing, arranged by the Federal Trade Commission, tackled one of the most controversial theories dogging the index fund industry: "Common ownership."

The common ownership theory is that companies have fewer incentives to invest in new products or services, or to compete on price, if they know that their biggest shareholders also own big chunks of their rivals. The suggestion is not that they engage in overtly anticompetitive deals thrashed out in secretive smoke-filled rooms, merely that significant cross-shareholding may have an indirect, almost psychological dampening effect on the competitive urge of companies. Although this applies to any pooled, large investment vehicle—such as mutual funds—the de facto oligopoly of the index fund industry makes it a particularly pertinent issue for BlackRock, Vanguard, and State Street, which collectively are the largest shareholders of over four-fifths of all S&P 500 companies.

The basic theory was first proposed by the economist Julio Rotemberg back in 1984, but was brought into the limelight by three young economists in a bombshell 2014 paper titled "Anticompetitive Effects of Common Ownership."[17] José Azar, Isabel Tecu, and Martin Schmalz had found evidence from granular airline industry data that ticket prices were probably higher than they should be, because the overlapping shareholdings of the likes of BlackRock, State Street, Vanguard, and Berkshire Hathaway— which owned big slices of American Airlines, Delta, Southwest, and United at the time—had an effect on routes.

The implications were much wider. Perhaps common ownership was more broadly blunting the competitive drive that is the foundation stone of modern capitalism? An active investor in, say, JPMorgan might actively encourage the bank to take on its rivals, but an index fund that owns shares in all US banks might be less inclined to do so.

Initially the common ownership theory was dismissed as a loony idea from ivory-tower economists. After all, the airline industry is infamously bankruptcy-prone and looked like poor evidence of anticompetitive behavior, overt or otherwise. Richard Branson, the billionaire entrepreneur, once joked that the best way to become an aviation millionaire was to be a billionaire and invest in an airline. However, the theory gradually started to garner attention. "Are Index Funds Evil?" was the provocative title of one piece examining the subject in *The Atlantic* in 2017.[18]

By late 2018, the Federal Trade Commission—the US government agency tasked with tackling antitrust issues—held an open hearing on the subject. In addition to a bevy of lawyers, law professors, curious financial journalists, and several commissioners from the FTC and the Securities and Exchange Commission, Martin Schmalz was there to present the three economists' viewpoint, and— underlining how seriously it took the subject—BlackRock's Novick attended to argue against them. "This debate is not just academic," Noah Phillips, an FTC commissioner, stressed at the conference.[19]

"Antitrust enforcers around the world are watching its development, as we are today, and incorporating common ownership into their analyses."

Other studies commissioned by the likes of BlackRock, Vanguard, and the Investment Company Institute have reached different conclusions on the evidence of any common ownership effect. Anyway, the indexing giants point out that they still remain minority shareholders in almost every company, and given their exposure to the entire economy, they would also be hurt by any anticompetitive behavior.

For example, they might benefit from airlines refraining from price wars, but that would dampen air travel and crimp businesses for the hotels they invest in. Bogle himself thought it "absurd," given the myriad other forces affecting the behavior of companies. For example, executive compensation is often tied to the performance of a company's stock, directly encouraging management to do whatever they can to boost it, irrespective of whether Vanguard or BlackRock also owns shares in their competitors.

Yet there are indications that some antitrust officials are starting to take the theory seriously. When the European Commission examined the proposed merger of DuPont and Dow Chemical in 2017, the high level of common ownership across the industry was a factor in its deliberations, and helped spur a demand for the combined group to offload its pesticide business to receive approval for the merger.[20] Soon afterward, Margrethe Vestager, the Commission's powerful competition supremo, said that it was looking "carefully" at the common ownership issue.[21]

Some legal scholars say that we are already far beyond needing a careful look, and argue that concrete action is needed. "Horizontal shareholding poses the greatest anticompetitive threat of our time, mainly because it is the one anticompetitive problem we are doing nothing about," Einer Elhauge, a professor at Harvard Law School specializing in antitrust issues, concluded in a 2020 paper reviewing all the historiography in the field.[22] "This enforcement passivity is unwarranted."

▲

PERHAPS THE DEBATE SURROUNDING corporate governance and common ownership is merely a by-product of a deeper, more profound, but even trickier issue. Maybe all the academics and analysts scrambling to get a handle on these issues are like the proverbial blind men touching different parts of an elephant and describing what they feel as a snake or a tree trunk? The elephant in this case is the sheer size and growth of the indexing industry's giants. Bigness itself, above all, is the broader inchoate but central, thorny issue.

This is relevant to virtually every industry—especially "Big Tech" is under fire these days. But what is unique about index funds is that size is indisputably an advantage. Traditional active funds typically see their performance atrophy as they grow big, yet index funds are entirely commoditized. The larger they are, the cheaper they are to run. That allows fees to be lower, and investor flows will follow. Bigger ETFs are generally also more actively traded, increasing their attraction. Thus the big becoming bigger is an embedded feature of index funds, raising the prospect of just a handful of vast, multitrillion-dollar investment groups with fingers in every corporate pie in the world.

This was the subject of an eye-catching paper by Harvard Law professor John Coates, entitled "The Problem of Twelve," where he argued that the "mega-trend" of passive investing threatened to hand unsurpassed power to just a dozen or so people working inside the index fund giants, the proxy advisors, and a handful of traditional investment groups that will likely continue to thrive.[23]

"Unless law changes, the effect of indexation will be to turn the concept of 'passive' investing on its head and produce the greatest concentration of economic control in our lifetimes," Professor Coates warned. "The prospect of twelve people even potentially controlling most of the economy poses a legitimacy and accountability issue of the first order—one might even call it a small 'c' constitutional challenge."

This may seem shrill, but in the United States, the birthplace of index investing, the trend is now stark, entrenched, and accelerating. Over the past decade, about 80 cents of every dollar that has gone into the US investment industry has ended up at Vanguard, State Street, and BlackRock. As a result, the combined stake in S&P 500 companies held by the Big Three has quadrupled over the past two decades, from about 5 percent in in 1998 to north of 20 percent today.[24] Because not all investors actually vote at annual meetings, Vanguard, BlackRock, and State Street account for about a quarter of all shareholder votes, according to a study by Harvard Law School's Lucian Bebchuk and Boston University's Scott Hirst.

Assuming that past trends continue, they estimate that the Big Three will account for over a third of all voting shareholders within the next decade, and about 41 percent inside the next twenty years. "In this 'Giant Three' scenario, three investment managers would largely dominate shareholder voting in practically all significant U.S. companies that do not have a controlling shareholder," Bebchuk and Hirst pointed out in a 2019 paper.[25]

Naturally, Fink thinks this focus is preposterous. He points out that despite the size of BlackRock and its biggest rivals, asset management remains less concentrated than many industries. Moreover, if there ever is consensus that their size is having a deleterious effect on corporate governance or pooling too much influence, then he could address it by divvying up holdings into separate, smaller legal entities, each with its own research and stewardship teams. It would be expensive and complicated, but not prohibitively so. "If society believes this is going to be a big issue, it is solvable," Fink says. "And I could still provide transparency, convenience, and [low] pricing."

Nonetheless, this is the crux of the issue that nagged at Bogle in his final days. When does the ephemeral societal cost of success and size outstrip the real and quantifiable benefits brought to investors? Can anything be done to ameliorate the downsides while preserving the boon to millions of people that index funds have brought?

"It's hard to know how big we can get, and the consequences. But it does raise issues that we need to address," Bogle admitted in one of his last interviews before passing away in January 2019.[26] "We cannot ignore them. But to solve this we should not destroy the greatest invention in the history of finance."

EPILOGUE

TWO AND A HALF CENTURIES AGO, Amsterdam was the world's commercial center, but many of its wealthy merchants were reeling from one of the world's first financial crises. The shares of the British East India Company had collapsed, culminating in a series of bank failures, government bailouts, and ultimately nationalization, a debacle that rippled across the continent's nascent markets. For a little-known Dutch merchant and stockbroker, it proved the inspiration for an idea ahead of its time.

In 1774, Abraham von Ketwich set up a novel, pooled investment trust he called Eendragt Maakt Magt—Dutch for "Unity Creates Strength." This would sell two thousand shares for five hundred guilders each to individual investors, and invest the proceeds into a diversified portfolio of fifty bonds. These were divided into ten different categories, from plantation loans, bonds backed by Spanish or Danish toll road payments, to an assortment of European government bonds. At the time, bonds were physical certificates written on paper or even goatskin, and these were stored in a solid iron chest with three locks, which could be opened only by Eendragt Maakt Magt's board and an independent notary. The aim was to pay a 4 percent annual dividend, and disburse the final proceeds only after twenty-five years, hoping that the diversity of the portfolio would protect investors.[1]

As it turns out, a subsequent Anglo-Dutch war in 1780 and Napoleon's occupation of Holland in 1795 wreaked havoc on Eendragt Maakt Magt. The annual payments never materialized, and investors didn't receive their money back until 1824, albeit then receiving 561 guilders a share. Nonetheless, Eendragt Maakt Magt was a brilliant invention that would go on to inspire the birth of investment trusts in Great Britain and eventually the mutual fund we know today. It is also arguably the ultimate intellectual forefather of today's index funds, given its minimal trading, diversified approach, and low fees, charging a mere 0.2 percent a year.

This historical detour to eighteenth-century Amsterdam may seem odd. Yet Eendragt Maakt Magt highlights how the financial industry is in constant evolution, and the importance of many inventions is often missed at first. So it is with the initially inauspicious index fund. The physicist Niels Bohr once quipped that it is hard to make predictions, especially about the future. But we can start to glimpse the contours of what the future landscape looks like for the global investment industry, and guess what it means for markets: Barring a cataclysm, it is possible that within a generation the majority of all the global investment industry's money will be in an index fund or strategy of some kind.

Financial markets may not always be popular, and often seem mysterious, fickle, and even dangerous to outsiders. But they are the bedrock of the modern capitalist system, and such a seismic shift will have a profound effect on many facets of the global economy. You may not think that the era of the index fund matters to you, but it does, in countless ways that we are only starting to fathom. This

is one of the most profound forces to rip through the finance industry in history, and it could ultimately help reshape capitalism itself.

However, despite the litany of problematic potential side effects
examined in the last few chapters, it is important not to lose sight of
Bogle's point: In the annals of Wall Street, the index fund is one of
the few truly, nearly unambiguously beneficial inventions, a disruptive technology that has already saved investors hundreds of billions
of dollars, sums that will undoubtedly reach trillions in years to
come. Just consider the implications for a moment. Pretty much everyone saving for their retirement, to send their kids to university, to
buy a house, or just for a rainy day indirectly or directly reaps the
benefits of the humble index fund.

Yes, index funds are subtly rewiring modern finance. But so did
mutual funds before them, or the investment trusts before that. Despite legitimate concerns about the concentration of power in just a
few hands, the era of less dispersed, more long-term ownership might
actually prove a boon for corporate governance. If not, we have the
tools to minimize the dangers.

The determined, iconoclastic renegades of the 1970s who
birthed the index are some of the most consequential if underappreciated disruptors of the modern era. While it is important to
recognize and attempt to address some of the downsides that might
emerge from the revolution they unleashed, the benefits are real,
and enormous.

ACKNOWLEDGMENTS

THIS BOOK MAY HAVE ONLY one author, but in reality it represents the work of a multitude, whether they know it or not.

First and foremost, I must thank all the people who gave so generously of their time to tell me their stories. A journalist lives and dies by their sources, and I have been exceptionally lucky to have the help of so many in writing this book—some even before there was a book to talk about. Several sources may have asked me to not use their names, but I am immensely grateful to everyone for their help. You know who you are.

Many have not just spent hours with me on the phone, but also patiently answered follow-up emails checking up on details. That in some cases they did so in the middle of a pandemic and the disruptions it caused makes me even more grateful. Notably, a lot of the early pioneers are in their seventies, eighties, or even nineties, but their energy and intellectual sizzle still puts me to shame.

In particular, I want to acknowledge the effervescent Jack Bogle, whom I spoke to several times for an *FT Weekend Magazine* piece that became the kernel of this book. In late December 2018, he graciously called me just to check that I had everything I needed, as he was heading to the hospital and feared he might not be long for this world. A month later, he passed away, aged eighty-nine and indisputably one of history's great men.

A special thank-you to my agent, Julia Eagleton, and my editor, Leah Trouwborst. Julia had followed my work at the *Financial Times* and saw the potential for a great story before even I did. She has been a pillar of support and advice throughout the whole process, even as she was herself in the middle of a mid-pandemic, cross-Atlantic, cross-agency move. Leah luckily agreed with Julia that the story of the index fund could make a decent book, and I'll be forever grateful to her. It proved to be far more fun than I dared hope, and that is largely thanks to her zeal and willingness to humor my incessant emails. Noah Schwartzberg then picked up the tiller and steered this ship to shore with aplomb. Lucy Woods did sterling work fact-checking my opus, and appreciated my sneaky Terry Pratchett reference. Any remaining bloopers are naturally my fault.

I've also had plenty of outside help from friends and contacts, ranging from moral support and writing tips to checking over chunks of my raw verbiage for glaring omissions or mistakes, and passing on their own contacts. I want to single out Charley Ellis, Ewan Kirk, John Woerth, Jim Riepe, Jan Twardowski, Eric Clothier, Larry Tint, Fred Grauer, Felix Salmon, and Cliff Weber, who all helped me check different sections of my book for factual problems or interpretative shortfalls. If there are still some there, blame me. Charley was also an inspiration for me doing this book—and is an inspiration in general. Both Dimensional Fund Advisors and BlackRock sent me their own internal history books, which were vital guides for those chapters. Kip McDaniel kindly opened up *Institutional Investor*'s archives. For a finance history nerd like me, it was like a day in heaven.

I'm lucky enough to work with some wonderful colleagues at the *Financial Times*, who aside from the intellectual fizz they bring to work every day were a particular joy to natter with through the om-nishambles of 2020, when this book was largely written. The likes of Katie Martin, Ian Smith, Ben McLannahan, Tony Tassell, Geoff Dyer, Harriet Arnold, Adam Samson, and the rest of the *FT*'s crack squad of editors had to suffer plenty of my moans, but they did so (mostly) with patience. There are too many awesome colleagues on the broader markets and investing teams to name them all here, but I love you all, and the first round is on me. In truth, the entire *FT* family has been a delight since I joined a dozen years ago, and for that I have to thank Roula Khalaf and Andrew England, who took a chance on me all those years ago, and James Drummond, who broke me in. That was a lucky break that not many journalists get.

All journalists stand on the shoulders of giants, whether they ad-mit it or not. In many cases, my book was vastly enhanced by the su-perlative work of other journalists, writers, and financial historians, who have themselves explored some of the subjects and themes I have tried to knit together in one sweeping narrative. Peter Bernstein is a huge inspiration, and his books were of tremendous help for some of the earlier chapters, as was Colin Read's *The Efficient Market Hypoth-esists*. Lewis Braham's biography of Jack Bogle is essential reading for anyone interested in the tumultuous life of Vanguard's founder. Ralph Lehman's *The Elusive Trade* was exhaustively detailed on the genesis of ETFs, and Anthony Bianco's *The Big Lie* vividly tells the story of WFIA/BGI in the Pattie Dunn era. I have also learned an enormous amount from working with or admiring from afar financial journal-ists like John Authers, Gillian Tett, James Mackintosh, Philip Cog-gan, and Jason Zweig, as well as industry experts such as Deborah Fuhr, Ben Johnson, Eric Balchunas, and David Nadig. They are all titans upon whose shoulders I nervously perch.

But someone closer to home deserves the biggest acknowledg-ment. In the middle of the coronavirus-induced lockdown, my daughter wrote a riddle and proudly presented it to me. Scrawled on the page, it said, "What works and works and is never finished?" To my horror I realized that the answer was me.

I'm one of the lucky people who truly loves their job. Unfortunately, that can come at a cost to those around me. My wife, Gunvor, has over the years been extraordinarily patient, including letting me sequester myself in solitary cabin confinement for several weeks to finish this book. But at least she vaguely knew who she was marrying. I owe everything to my wonderful parents, Willen and Peter, yet they must share the blame for making me a workaholic. My brother, Philip, thinking I am far smarter than I really am, is an enormous encouragement, but he has luckily been shielded from any consequences of my inability to switch off.

So this book is first and foremost dedicated to my children, Matilde and Finn, whose antics make every day brighter.

NOTES

Unless otherwise noted here, the quotes in this book are from interviews I have conducted myself over the course of 2018–2020.

CHAPTER 1: BUFFETT'S BET

1. Carol Loomis, "Buffett's Big Bet," *Fortune*, June 2008.
2. Ted Seides, "Dear Warren," letter to Buffett.
3. Stephen Gandel, "The 1975 Buffett Memo That Saved WaPo's Pension," *Fortune*, August 15, 2013.
4. Chris Welles, "Fred Alger, Portrait of a Star," *Institutional Investor*, January 1968.
5. Warren Buffett, "The Superinvestors of Graham-and-Doddsville," speech, Columbia Business School, May 17, 1984.
6. Loomis, "Buffett's Big Bet."
7. Ahmed Kabil, "How Warren Buffett Won His Multi-Million Dollar Long Bet," *Medium*, February 17, 2018.
8. "Over a ten-year period commencing on January 1, 2008, and ending on December 31, 2017, the S&P 500 will outperform a portfolio of funds of hedge funds, when performance is measured on a basis net of fees, costs and expenses," Long Bets Project, 2008.
9. Berkshire Hathaway annual report, 2017.
10. Loomis, "Buffett's Big Bet."
11. Jack Bogle, "Warren Buffett Gave Me a Surprise Shoutout at Berkshire Meeting," *Omaha World-Herald*, April 10, 2018.
12. Bogle, "Warren Buffett Gave Me a Surprise Shoutout at Berkshire Meeting."
13. Berkshire Hathaway annual report, 2016.
14. Justin Baer, "Fidelity Reports Record Operating Profit, Revenue," *Wall Street Journal*, March 3, 2020.

15. Paul Singer, "Comfortably Numb," Elliott Management letter to investors, 2017.

CHAPTER 2: THE GODFATHER

1. Peter Bernstein, *Capital Ideas: The Improbable Origins of Modern Wall Street* (New York: Wiley, 1992), 23.
2. Bernstein, *Capital Ideas*, 23.
3. Mark Davis, "Louis Bachelier's Theory of Speculation," talk, Imperial College, https://f-origin.hypotheses.org/wp-content/blogs.dir/1596 /files/2014/12/Mark-Davis-Talk.pdf.
4. L. Carraro and P. Crépel, "Louis Bachelier," Encyclopedia of Math, www.encyclopediaofmath.org/images/f/f1/LouisBACHELIER.pdf.
5. Carraro and Crépel, "Louis Bachelier."
6. Colin Read, *The Efficient Market Hypothesists: Bachelier, Samuelson, Fama, Ross, Tobin, and Shiller* (Basingstoke, UK: Palgrave Macmillan, 2013), 48.
7. Bernstein, *Capital Ideas*, 18.
8. John Kenneth Galbraith, *The Great Crash, 1929* (Boston: Mariner Books, 2009; originally published by Houghton Mifflin, 1955), 27.
9. Bernstein, *Capital Ideas*, 29.
10. Alfred Cowles, "Can Stock Market Forecasters Forecast?," paper read at a joint meeting of the Econometric Society and the American Statistical Association, Cincinnati, Ohio, December 31, 1932, https://cowles.yale .edu/sites/default/files/files/pub/misc/cowles-forecasters33.pdf.
11. Bernstein, *Capital Ideas*, 33.
12. Cowles, "Can Stock Market Forecasters Forecast?"
13. Alfred Cowles, "Stock Market Forecasting," *Econometrica* 12, no. 3/4 (July–October 1944): 206–14, http://e-m-h.org/Cowl44.pdf.
14. Bernstein, *Capital Ideas*, 35.
15. Bernstein, *Capital Ideas*, 36.
16. Alfred Cowles, *Cowles Commission for Research in Economics* (Monograph No. 3), 2.
17. Robin Wigglesworth, "Passive Attack: The Story of a Wall Street Revolution," *Financial Times*, December 20, 2018.
18. Louis Engel, "What Everybody Ought to Know . . . About This Stock and Bond Business," *New York Times*, October 19, 1948, https:// swiped.co/file/about-this-stock-bond-louis-engel/.
19. David Bird, "Louis Engel Jr., Ex-Merrill Lynch Partner, Dies," *New York Times*, November 8, 1982, www.nytimes.com/1982/11/08 /obituaries/louis-engel-jr-ex-merrill-lynch-partner-dies.html.
20. James H. Lorie, "Current Controversies on the Stock Market," speech to American Statistical Association, September 1965, www.crsp .uchicago.edu/50/images/lorie.pdf.

21. Tonya Maxwell, "In Memory of James H. Lorie," *Chicago Tribune*, August 11, 2005, www.dailyspeculations.com/vic/JimLorie.html.
22. Maxwell, "In Memory of James H. Lorie."
23. "Lorie Developed Chicago Approach to Management Education," *University of Chicago Chronicle*, October 6, 2005, http://chronicle .uchicago.edu/051006/obit-lorie.shtml.
24. Lorie, "Current Controversies on the Stock Market."
25. Lorie, "Current Controversies on the Stock Market."
26. Lorie, "Current Controversies on the Stock Market."
27. L. Fisher and J. Lorie, "Rates of Return on Investments in Common Stocks," *Journal of Business* 37, no. 1 (January 1964): 1–21, at 2.
28. Center for Research in Security Prices, "Louis Engel: The Man Who Brought Wall Street to Main Street," *50th Anniversary Issue: Rates of Return of Investments in Common Stocks*, www.crsp.org/research /louis-engel-man-who-brought-wall-street-main-street.
29. Center for Research in Security Prices, "James Lorie: Recognized the Importance of CRSP for Future Research," *50th Anniversary Issue: Rates of Return of Investments in Common Stocks*, www.crsp.org /research/james-lorie-recognized-importance-crsp-future-research.
30. Lorie, "Current Controversies on the Stock Market."
31. Michael Jensen, "The Performance of Mutual Funds in the Period 1945–1964," *Journal of Finance*, May 1968.
32. Paul F. Miller Jr., "The Dangers of Retrospective Myopia," in *The Book of Investing Wisdom: Classic Writings by Great Stock-Pickers and Legends of Wall Street*, ed. Peter Krass (New York: Wiley, 1999), 49.
33. Edward Renshaw and Paul Feldstein, "The Case for an Unmanaged Investment Company," *Financial Analysts Journal*, 1960.
34. John B. Armstrong, "The Case for Mutual Fund Management," *Financial Analysts Journal*, 1960.
35. Prasanna Chandra, *Behavioural Finance* (New Delhi: McGraw-Hill Education, 2016), 7.
36. Charles D. Ellis, "The Loser's Game," *Financial Analysts Journal*, 1975.
37. Ian Liew, "SBBI: The Almanac of Returns Data," Index Fund Advisors, July 19, 2019, www.ifa.com/articles/draft_dawn_creation _investing_science_bible_returns_data/.
38. Lorie, "Current Controversies on the Stock Market."
39. Bernstein, *Capital Ideas*, 97.
40. Lorie, "Current Controversies on the Stock Market."

CHAPTER 3: TAMING THE DEMON OF CHANCE

1. Russell R. Wasendorf Sr. and Russell R. Wasendorf Jr., "Feature Interview: Harry M. Markowitz, Nobel Laureate," *SFO Magazine*, July

2008, 2, www.altavra.com/docs/thirdparty/interview-with-nobel
-laureate-harry-markowitz.pdf.

2. UBS, "Harry Markowitz," Nobel Perspectives, www.ubs.com
/microsites/nobel-perspectives/en/laureates/harry-markowitz.html.

3. Wasendorf and Wasendorf, "Feature Interview: Harry M. Markowitz,
Nobel Laureate," 3.

4. Peter Bernstein, *Capital Ideas Evolving* (Hoboken, NJ: Wiley, 2007),
xiii.

5. Robin Wigglesworth, "How a Volatility Virus Infected Wall Street,"
Financial Times, April 12, 2018, https://www.ft.com/content
/be68aac6-3d13-11e8-b9f9-de94fa33a81e.

6. Wasendorf and Wasendorf, "Feature Interview: Harry M. Markowitz,
Nobel Laureate," 3.

7. Wasendorf and Wasendorf, "Feature Interview: Harry M. Markowitz,
Nobel Laureate," 3.

8. Natalie Marine-Street, William F. Sharpe interview, Stanford
Historial Society, 2018.

9. Marine-Street, William Sharpe interview.

10. Ronald N. Kahn, *The Future of Investment Management* (CFA Institute
Research Foundation, 2018), 19, www.cfainstitute.org/-/media
/documents/book/rf-publication/2018/future-of-investment
-management-kahn.ashx.

11. Marine-Street, William Sharpe interview.

12. The Nobel Prize, "Eugene F. Fama" (biography).

13. Colin Read, *The Efficient Market Hypothesists: Bachelier, Samuelson,
Fama, Ross, Tobin, and Shiller* (Basingstoke, UK: Palgrave Macmillan,
2013), 93.

14. The Nobel Prize, "Eugene F. Fama."

15. The Nobel Prize, "Eugene F. Fama."

16. Eugene Fama, "A Brief History of Finance and My Life at Chicago,"
Chicago Booth Review, April 7, 2014, https://review.chicagobooth.edu
/magazine/fall-2013/a-brief-history-of-finance.

17. The Nobel Prize, "Eugene F. Fama."

18. Tyler Vigen, "Spurious Correlations," www.tylervigen.com/spurious
-correlations.

19. Eugene Fama, "The Behavior of Stock-Market Prices," *Journal of
Business* 38, no. 1 (January 1965).

20. Read, *The Efficient Market Hypothesists*, 102.

21. *Institutional Investor*, April 1968.

22. Roger Ibbotson, "Random Talks with Eugene Fama," Ibbotson
Associates, 2000.

23. Burton Malkiel, *A Random Walk Down Wall Street* (New York: Norton,
1973).

CHAPTER 4: THE QUANTIFIERS

1. Peter Bernstein, *Capital Ideas: The Improbable Origins of Modern Wall Street* (New York: Wiley, 1992), 237.
2. Bernstein, *Capital Ideas*, 238, and author interviews with McQuown.
3. Bernstein, *Capital Ideas*, 238.
4. Bernstein, *Capital Ideas*, 238.
5. John McQuown, "A Personal History of Modern Finance," speech, 2011.
6. McQuown, "A Personal History of Modern Finance."
7. McQuown, "A Personal History of Modern Finance."
8. *Institutional Investor*, April 1968.
9. Bernstein, *Capital Ideas*, 241.
10. Robin Wigglesworth, "Passive Attack: The Story of a Wall Street Revolution," *Financial Times*, December 20, 2018.
11. Jeanette Cooperman, "The Return of the King," *St. Louis* magazine, June 23, 2009, www.stlmag.com/The-Return-of-the-King/.
12. Donald MacKenzie, *An Engine, Not a Camera: How Financial Models Shape Markets* (Cambridge, MA: MIT Press, 2006), 100.
13. Deborah Ziff Soriano, "Index Fund Pioneer Rex Sinquefield," *Chicago Booth Magazine*, May 2019, www.chicagobooth.edu/magazine /rex-sinquefield-dimensional.
14. Margaret Towle, "Being First Is Best: An Adventure Capitalist's Approach to Life and Investing, a Conversation with Dean LeBaron," *Journal of Investment Consulting* 14, no. 2 (November 2013).
15. Towle, "Being First Is Best."
16. LeBaron family history, courtesy of Donna Carpenter-LeBaron.
17. LeBaron family history.
18. LeBaron family history.
19. *Pensions & Investments*, November 26, 1973.
20. *Pensions & Investments*, January 1975.
21. *Pensions & Investments*, February 17, 1975.

CHAPTER 5: BASTIONS OF UNORTHODOXY

1. *Institutional Investor*, July 1972.
2. Peter Bernstein, *Capital Ideas: The Improbable Origins of Modern Wall Street* (New York: Wiley, 1992), 242.
3. *Institutional Investor*, July 1972.
4. Email from James Vertin via Charley Ellis.
5. Bernstein, *Capital Ideas*, 240.
6. Myron Scholes, "Derivatives in a Dynamic Environment," Nobel Lecture, December 1997.
7. Perry Mehrling, *Fischer Black and the Revolutionary Idea of Finance* (Hoboken, NJ: Wiley, 2011), 105.
8. Mehrling, *Fischer Black and the Revolutionary Idea of Finance*, 101.

9. James Hagerty, "Bill Fouse Taught Skeptical Investors to Love Index Funds," *Wall Street Journal*, October 31, 2019.
10. "William Lewis Fouse," *San Francisco Chronicle* (obituary), October 17, 2019.
11. Robin Wigglesworth, "William Fouse, Quantitative Analyst, 1928–2019," *Financial Times*, October 24, 2019.
12. Bernstein, *Capital Ideas*, 243.
13. Bernstein, *Capital Ideas*, 244.
14. Bill Fouse, "His Early Bosses Thought Fouse's Indexing Idea Was a Melon," *Pensions & Investments*, October 19, 1998.
15. Bernstein, *Capital Ideas*, 245.
16. Mehrling, *Fischer Black and the Revolutionary Idea of Finance*, 106.
17. Mehrling, *Fischer Black and the Revolutionary Idea of Finance*, 107.
18. Donald MacKenzie, *An Engine, Not a Camera: How Financial Models Shape Markets* (Cambridge, MA: MIT Press, 2006), 85.
19. Frank Fabozzi, *Perspectives on Equity Indexing* (New York: Wiley, 2000), 44.
20. Bernstein, *Capital Ideas*, 248.
21. Deborah Ziff Soriano, "Index Fund Pioneer Rex Sinquefield," *Chicago Booth Magazine*, May 2019, www.chicagobooth.edu/magazine /rex-sinquefield-dimensional."
22. *Pensions & Investments*, June 23, 1975.
23. Dean LeBaron, speech to Atlanta Society of Financial Analysts, January 22, 1975.
24. George Miller, "First to Sell, but Not First to Invent," *Wall Street Journal*, September 18, 2011.
25. *Institutional Investor*, February 1976.
26. *New York Times*, March 26, 1977.
27. *Institutional Investor*, July 1972.
28. *Institutional Investor*, February 1974.
29. *Institutional Investor*, April 1980.
30. Bernstein, *Capital Ideas*, 248.
31. Jonathan Laing, "Bye-Bye, Go-Go?," *Wall Street Journal*, June 7, 1973.
32. Laing, "Bye-Bye, Go-Go?"
33. Eric Balchunas, "Passive Funds' Effect on Stocks," Bloomberg, September 18, 2019.
34. Lawrence Rout, "Firms' Pension Fund Managers Often Are Failing to Manage—Instead, They Are Indexing, Without Admitting It, and Charging High Fees," *Wall Street Journal*, January 31, 1979.
35. Charles D. Ellis, *The Index Revolution: Why Investors Should Join It Now* (Hoboken, NJ: Wiley, 2016), 43.
36. *Institutional Investor*, February 1976.
37. Fabozzi, *Perspectives on Equity Indexing*, 43

38. *Institutional Investor*, June 1977.
39. *Institutional Investor*, February 1976.
40. Fabozzi, *Perspectives on Equity Indexing*, 42.
41. Paul Samuelson, "Index-Fund Investing," *Newsweek*, August 1976.

CHAPTER 6: THE HEDGEHOG

1. Jack Bogle, *Stay the Course: The Story of Vanguard and the Index Revolution* (Hoboken, NJ: Wiley, 2018), 262.
2. Lewis Braham, *The House That Bogle Built: How John Bogle and Vanguard Reinvented the Mutual Fund Industry* (New York: McGraw-Hill, 2011), chapter 1, ePub.
3. Gene Colter, "Change of Heart," *Wall Street Journal*, September 24, 2004.
4. Braham, *The House That Bogle Built*, chap. 1, ePub.
5. Bogle, *Stay the Course*, 258.
6. Bogle, *Stay the Course*, 258.
7. Braham, *The House That Bogle Built*, chap. 1, ePub.
8. Bogle, *Stay the Course*, 9.
9. Braham, *The House That Bogle Built*, chap. 2, ePub.
10. Braham, *The House That Bogle Built*, chap. 1, ePub.
11. "Big Money in Boston," *Forbes*, April 1949.
12. Jack Bogle, "The Economic Role of the Investment Company" (Princeton thesis, 1951).
13. Braham, *The House That Bogle Built*, chap. 2, ePub.
14. Braham, *The House That Bogle Built*, chap. 3, ePub.
15. Braham, *The House That Bogle Built*, chap 3, ePub.
16. Philadelphia Area Archives Research Portal, Jack C. Bogle Papers, Princeton University Library.
17. Braham, *The House That Bogle Built*, chap. 4, ePub.
18. Bogle, *Stay the Course*, 264.
19. Bogle, *Stay the Course*, 20.
20. Braham, *The House That Bogle Built*, chap. 4, ePub.
21. Braham, *The House That Bogle Built*, chap. 4, ePub.
22. Bogle, *Stay the Course*, 21.
23. *Institutional Investor*, January 1968.
24. *Institutional Investor*, January 1968.
25. *Institutional Investor*, July 1972.
26. *Institutional Investor*, July 1972.
27. *Institutional Investor*, July 1972.
28. Bogle, *Stay the Course*, 24.
29. Braham, *The House That Bogle Built*, chap. 5, ePub.
30. Braham, *The House That Bogle Built*, chap. 5, ePub.
31. Braham, *The House That Bogle Built*, chap. 5, ePub.

32. Bogle, *Stay the Course*, 23, and *Institutional Investor*, July 1972.
33. Braham, *The House That Bogle Built*, chap. 5, ePub.
34. Robin Wigglesworth, "Passive Attack: The Story of a Wall Street Revolution," *Financial Times*, December 20, 2018."
35. Braham, *The House That Bogle Built*, chap. 5, ePub.
36. Bogle, *Stay the Course*, 25.

CHAPTER 7: BOGLE'S FOLLY

1. Lewis Braham, *The House That Bogle Built: How John Bogle and Vanguard Reinvented the Mutual Fund Industry* (New York: McGraw-Hill, 2011), chap. 6, ePub.
2. Jack Bogle, *Character Counts: The Creation and Building of the Vanguard Group* (New York: McGraw-Hill, 2002), 7.
3. Jack Bogle, *Stay the Course: The Story of Vanguard and the Index Revolution* (Hoboken, NJ: Wiley, 2018), 32.
4. Braham, *The House That Bogle Built*, chap. 6, ePub.
5. Braham, *The House That Bogle Built*, chap. 7, ePub.
6. Braham, *The House That Bogle Built*, chap. 6, ePub.
7. Jack Bogle, "Born in Strife," *Philadelphia Inquirer*, September 24, 2014.
8. Bogle, *Character Counts*, 7.
9. Paul Samuelson, "Challenge to Judgment," *Journal of Portfolio Management*, Fall 1974.
10. Bogle, *Stay the Course*, 39.
11. Bogle, *Stay the Course*, 189.
12. Charles Ellis, "The Loser's Game," *Financial Analysts Journal*, July/August 1975.
13. Bogle, *Stay the Course*, 44.
14. Bogle, *Stay the Course*, 41.
15. Bogle, *Stay the Course*, 45.
16. Paul Samuelson, "Index-Fund Investing," *Fortune*, June 1976, 66.
17. Bogle, *Stay the Course*, 47.
18. Richard Phalon, "Beating the Market or 'Indexing' It?," *New York Times*, March 26, 1977.
19. *Boston Globe*, August 24, 1976, via Bogle, *Stay the Course*, 47.
20. Bogle, *Stay the Course*, 47.
21. Bogle, *Stay the Course*, 58.
22. Braham, *The House That Bogle Built*, chap. 12, ePub.
23. Braham, *The House That Bogle Built*, chap. 7, ePub.
24. Bogle, *Stay the Course*, 55.
25. Braham, *The House That Bogle Built*, chap. 7, ePub.
26. Braham, *The House That Bogle Built*, chap. 7, ePub.
27. Bogle, *Stay the Course*, 63.

CHAPTER 8: VANGUARD RISING

1. Lewis Braham, *The House That Bogle Built: How John Bogle and Vanguard Reinvented the Mutual Fund Industry* (New York: McGraw-Hill, 2011), chap. 11, ePub.
2. Jack Bogle, *Stay the Course: The Story of Vanguard and the Index Revolution* (Hoboken, NJ: Wiley, 2018), 146.
3. Braham, *The House That Bogle Built*, chap. 10, ePub.
4. Braham, *The House That Bogle Built*, chap. 9, ePub.
5. Ben Yagoda, "Mutually Exclusive," *Philadelphia* magazine, August 1993.
6. Bogle, *Stay the Course*, 147.
7. Bogle, *Stay the Course*, 48.
8. Braham, *The House That Bogle Built*, chap. 12, ePub.
9. John Hechinger and Pui-Wing Tam, "Vanguard 500 Surpasses Fidelity Magellan in Size," *Wall Street Journal*, April 6, 2000.
10. Pui-Wing Tam and John Hechinger, "Vanguard 500 Is Set to Pass Magellan as Biggest Fund," *Wall Street Journal*, January 12, 2000.
11. Bogle, *Stay the Course*, 51.
12. Bogle, *Stay the Course*, 146.
13. Bogle, *Stay the Course*, 146.
14. Bogle, *Stay the Course*, 147.
15. Bogle, *Stay the Course*, 91.
16. J. M. Lawrence, "Frank Brennan, 93; Banker Had an Honest, Caring Way," *Boston Globe*, April 6, 2010.
17. Bill Lane, "Frank Brennan: An Elder Statesman Keeps on Going," *Boston Business Journal*, June 22, 1998.
18. Bogle, *Stay the Course*, 148.
19. Braham, *The House That Bogle Built*, chap. 12, ePub.
20. Braham, *The House That Bogle Built*, chap. 1, ePub.
21. Bogle, *Stay the Course*, 143.
22. Erin Arvedlund, "Vanguard Founder Bogle and Surgeons Gather for a Heart-Transplant Reunion," *Philadelphia Inquirer*, February 21, 2017.
23. Braham, *The House That Bogle Built*, chap. 12, ePub.
24. Robert McGough and Pui-Wing Tam, "Vanguard May Ask Bogle to Retire from Its Board," *Wall Street Journal*, August 12, 1999.
25. Braham, *The House That Bogle Built*, chap. 12, ePub.
26. Bogle, *Stay the Course*, 263.
27. Robin Wigglesworth, "Passive Attack: The Story of a Wall Street Revolution," *Financial Times*, December 20, 2018.

CHAPTER 9: NEW DIMENSIONS

1. Lydialyle Gibson, "Return on Principles," *University of Chicago Magazine*, January–February 2009, http://magazine.uchicago.edu/0902/features/booth.shtml.
2. Lydialyle Gibson, "Return on Principles."

3. Shawn Tully, "How the Really Smart Money Invests," *Fortune*, July 6, 1998.
4. Lydialyle Gibson, "Return on Principles."
5. David Booth and Eduardo Repetto, "Dimensional Fund Advisors at Thirty," Dimensional Fund Advisors, 2011, 24.
6. Booth and Repetto, "Dimensional Fund Advisors at Thirty," 25.
7. Booth and Repetto, "Dimensional Fund Advisors at Thirty," 27.
8. Investment Company Institute retirement factbook.
9. Booth and Repetto, "Dimensional Fund Advisors at Thirty," 25.
10. Thom Hogan, "IBM Announces New Microcomputer System," *InfoWorld*, September 14, 1981.
11. Booth and Repetto, "Dimensional Fund Advisors at Thirty," 25.
12. Booth and Repetto, "Dimensional Fund Advisors at Thirty," 28.
13. Booth and Repetto, "Dimensional Fund Advisors at Thirty," 43.
14. Crain News Service, "Chicago Money Managers Betting on 'Scrap Heap' Fund," *Crain's Chicago Business*, March 1982.

CHAPTER 10: BIONIC BETAS

1. Anise Wallace, "Perils and Profits of Pension Advisers," *New York Times*, September 11, 1983.
2. David Booth and Eduardo Repetto, "Dimensional Fund Advisors at Thirty," Dimensional Fund Advisors, 2011, 31.
3. Wallace, "Perils and Profits of Pension Advisers."
4. A. F. Ehrbar, "Giant Payoffs from Midget Stocks," *Fortune*, June 30, 1980.
5. Rolf Banz, "The Relationship Between Return and Market Value of Common Stocks," *Journal of Financial Economics*, March 1981.
6. Booth and Repetto, "Dimensional Fund Advisors at Thirty," 29.
7. Fischer Black and Myron Scholes, "From Theory to a New Financial Product," *Journal of Finance*, May 1974.
8. Chris Welles, "Who Is Barr Rosenberg? And What the Hell Is He Talking About?," *Institutional Investor*, May 1978.
9. Narasimhan Jegadeesh and Sheridan Titman, "Returns to Buying Winners and Selling Losers: Implications for Stock Market Efficiency," *Journal of Finance*, March 1993.
10. Robert Huebscher, "Sharpe Ratio Inventor: 'When I Hear Smart Beta It Makes Me Sick,'" *Business Insider*, May 22, 2014.
11. Eugene Fama and Kenneth French, "The Cross-Section of Expected Stock Returns," *Journal of Finance*, June 1992.
12. Robin Wigglesworth, "Can Factor Investing Kill Off the Hedge Fund?," *Financial Times*, July 22, 2018.
13. Booth and Repetto, "Dimensional Fund Advisors at Thirty," 31.
14. Booth and Repetto, "Dimensional Fund Advisors at Thirty," 32.
15. Booth and Repetto, "Dimensional Fund Advisors at Thirty," 41.

16. Jason Zweig, "Making Billions with One Belief: The Markets Can't Be Beat," *Wall Street Journal*, October 20, 2016.

17. Booth and Repetto, "Dimensional Fund Advisors at Thirty," 56.

18. Michael Lewis, "The Evolution of an Investor," *Condé Nast Portfolio*, December 2007.

CHAPTER 11: THE SPIDER'S BIRTH

1. Robin Wigglesworth, "Passive Attack: The Story of a Wall Street Revolution," *Financial Times*, December 20, 2018."

2. Jack Bogle, *Stay the Course: The Story of Vanguard and the Index Revolution* (Hoboken, NJ: Wiley, 2018), 108.

3. Wigglesworth, "Passive Attack."

4. Bogle, *Stay the Course*, 110.

5. Jennifer Bayot, "Nathan Most Is Dead at 90; Investment Fund Innovator," *New York Times*, December 10, 2004.

6. Ralph Lehman, *The Elusive Trade: How Exchange-Traded Funds Conquered Wall Street* (Dallas: Brown Books, 2009), 50.

7. Lehman, *The Elusive Trade*, 51.

8. Lehman, *The Elusive Trade*, 51.

9. Bayot, "Nathan Most Is Dead at 90; Investment Fund Innovator."

10. Lehman, *The Elusive Trade*, 52.

11. Lehman, *The Elusive Trade*, 53.

12. Edwin Hill, "The Strangest Stock Market in the World," *Munsey's Magazine*, February 1920.

13. Eric Balchunas, "The ETF Files: How the US Government Inadvertently Launched a $3 Trillion Industry," *Bloomberg Markets*, March 7, 2016.

14. Lawrence Carrel, *ETFs for the Long Run: What They Are, How They Work, and Simple Strategies for Successful Long-Term Investing* (New York: Wiley, 2008), 13.

15. Donald Katz, "Wall Street Rocket Scientists," *Worth*, February 1992.

16. Laurence Arnold, "Ivers Riley, Who Helped Introduce Spider ETFs, Dies at 82," Bloomberg, February 19, 2015.

17. Lehman, *The Elusive Trade*, 67.

18. Gary Gastineau, *The Exchange-Traded Funds Manual* (New York: Wiley, 2010), 33.

19. Jim Wiandt, "Nate Most, Exchange-Traded Fund Inventor, Dies at Age 90," ETF.com, December 8, 2004.

20. State Street Global Advisors, "SPY: The Idea That Spawned an Industry," January 25, 2013, www.sec.gov/Archives/edgar/data /1222333/000119312513023294/d473476dfwp.htm.

21. Carrel, *ETFs for the Long Run*, 22.

22. State Street Global Advisors, "SPY: The Idea That Spawned an Industry."

23. Balchunas, "The ETF Files."

24. Mark Rubinstein, "The SuperTrust," unpublished paper, December 20, 1990.

25. Lehman, *The Elusive Trade*, 103.

26. Divya Balji, "The $6 Trillion ETF Revolution Began 30 Years Ago in Toronto," Bloomberg, March 9, 2020.

27. Lehman, *The Elusive Trade*, 121.

28. Lehman, *The Elusive Trade*, 127.

29. Lehman, *The Elusive Trade*, 125.

30. Lehman, *The Elusive Trade*, 128.

31. Carrel, *ETFs for the Long Run*, 28.

32. Lehman, *The Elusive Trade*, 129.

33. Eric Balchunas, *The Institutional ETF Toolbox: How Institutions Can Understand and Utilize the Fast-Growing World of ETFs* (Hoboken, NJ: Wiley, 2016), 72.

34. Lehman, *The Elusive Trade*, 129.

35. Rachel Evans, Vildana Hajric, and Tracy Alloway, "The Fate of the World's Largest ETF Is Tied to 11 Random Millennials," Bloomberg, August 9, 2019.

CHAPTER 12: WFIA 2.0

1. Anthony Bianco, *The Big Lie: Spying, Scandal, and Ethical Collapse at Hewlett Packard* (New York: PublicAffairs, 2010), 105.

2. Bianco, *The Big Lie*, 107.

3. Andrew Pollack, "Wells Fargo and Nikko Set Advisory Venture," *New York Times*, June 28, 1989.

4. Bianco, *The Big Lie*, 108

5. Peter Truell, "Barclays to Acquire a Unit of Wells Fargo and Nikko," *New York Times*, June 22, 1995.

6. Truell, "Barclays to Acquire a Unit of Wells Fargo and Nikko."

7. Joel Chernoff, "It's Dunn Deal Now at BGI," *Pensions & Investments*, July 13, 1998.

8. Bianco, *The Big Lie*, 113.

9. Chernoff, "It's Dunn Deal Now at BGI."

10. Bianco, *The Big Lie*, 99.

11. James Stewart, "The Kona Files," *New Yorker*, February 2007.

12. Bianco, *The Big Lie*, 106.

13. Barclays annual report, 1998.

14. Tom Lauricella, "How Barclays Became a Force in ETFs," *Wall Street Journal*, November 1, 2004.

15. Investment Company Institute data.

16. Barclays annual report, 2007.

17. Bianco, *The Big Lie*, 119.

18. Bianco, *The Big Lie*, 119.

CHAPTER 13: LARRY'S GAMBIT

1. Suzanna Andrews, "Larry Fink's $12 Trillion Shadow," *Vanity Fair*, April 2010.
2. "Larry Fink," Crain's New York Business Hall of Fame, www .crainsnewyork.com/awards/larry-fink.
3. Larry Fink, "Built on the 'Ashes of Failure,'" UCLA commencement speech, June 10, 2016.
4. Richard Henderson and Owen Walker, "BlackRock's Black Box," *Financial Times*, February 24, 2020.
5. BlackRock Official History, shared with author.
6. David Carey and John Morris, *King of Capital: The Remarkable Rise, Fall, and Rise Again of Steve Schwarzman and Blackstone* (New York: Crown Business, 2010), 179.
7. Carey and Morris, *King of Capital*, 180.
8. BlackRock Official History.
9. BlackRock Official History.
10. Carey and Morris, *King of Capital*, 263.
11. BlackRock Official History.
12. Carey and Morris, *King of Capital*, 358.
13. Blackstone statement to author.
14. Devin Banerjee, "Schwarzman Says Selling BlackRock Was 'Heroic' Mistake," Bloomberg, September 30, 2013.
15. BlackRock Official History.
16. Blackstone statement.
17. Chrystia Freeland, "View from the Top: Larry Fink," *Financial Times*, April 24, 2007.
18. Ranjay Gulati, Jan Rivkin, and Aldo Sesia, "BlackRock: Integrating BGI," Harvard Business School, November 13, 2017.
19. Charlie Gasparino, "Merrill Taps Thain After Fink Demanded Full Tally," CNBC, November 14, 2007.
20. Andrews, "Larry Fink's $12 Trillion Shadow."
21. Henderson and Walker, "BlackRock's Black Box."

CHAPTER 14: DEAL OF THE CENTURY

1. David Ricketts and Mark Cobley, "Inside BlackRock's 'Once in a Lifetime' Deal with Barclays, 10 Years Later," *Financial News*, June 11, 2019.
2. BlackRock Official History.
3. Ricketts and Cobley, "Inside BlackRock's 'Once in a Lifetime' Deal with Barclays."
4. Elena Holodny, "The Founder of $5tn Investing Behemoth BlackRock Helped Launch Maroon 5," *Business Insider*, April 18, 2017.
5. Larry Fink, UCLA commencement speech.
6. Investment Company Institute data.

CHAPTER 15: PURDEY SHOTGUNS

1. Robert Netzly, "The Inspire Story," Inspire Investing, www
   .inspireinvesting.com/story.
2. Netzly, "The Inspire Story."
3. Netzly, "The Inspire Story."
4. Lewis Braham, *The House That Bogle Built: How John Bogle and
   Vanguard Reinvented the Mutual Fund Industry* (New York:
   McGraw-Hill, 2011), chap. 12, ePub.
5. Ben Johnson, "Ready, Fire, Aim: The ETF Industry Blasts Its
   Spaghetti Cannon," Morningstar, June 17, 2016.
6. Janet Levaux, "Vanguard CEO Pleads for Slowdown on ETF
   Rollouts," *ThinkAdvisor*, January 25, 2016.
7. Index Industry Association, "Index Industry Association's Third
   Annual Survey Finds 2.96 Million Indexes Globally," Business Wire,
   October 25, 2019.
8. OECD, "Who Are the Owners of the World's Listed Companies and
   Why Should We Care?," October, 17, 2019.
9. Inigo Fraser-Jenkins, "The Man Who Created the Last Index,"
   Bernstein, November 23, 2018.
10. Jeff Cox, "BlackRock Distances Itself from the Products That Have
    Freaked Out the Market," CNBC, February 6, 2018.
11. J. P. Morgan Global ETF Study, 2020, https://am.jpmorgan.com/lu
    /en/asset-management/adv/insights/portfolio-insights/etf-perspectives
    /global-etf-survey.

CHAPTER 16: THE NEW CAPTAINS OF CAPITAL

1. Peter Santilli, "Tesla Stock Joins the S&P 500: A Game Changer,"
   Wall Street Journal, December 21, 2020.
2. Hudson Lockett and Daniel Shane, "Investors Lose Billions as Bubble
   in Two HK Companies Bursts," *Financial Times*, November 21, 2019.
3. Patricia Hurtado, "S&P Index Manager Charged with $900,000
   Insider-Trading Scheme," Bloomberg, September 22, 2020.
4. Benjamin Bennett, René Stulz, and Zexi Wang, "Does Joining the
   S&P 500 Index Hurt Firms?," National Bureau of Economic Research,
   July 2020.
5. Noel Randewich, "Tesla to Join S&P 500, Spark Epic Index Fund
   Trade," Reuters, November 16, 2020.
6. Gabriel Rauterberg and Andrew Verstein, "Index Theory: The Law,
   Promise and Failure of Financial Indices," *Yale Journal on Regulation*,
   2013.
7. Nicole Bullock, "Investors Hail S&P 500 Move over Multiple Class
   Shares," *Financial Times*, August 1, 2017.
8. "Unilever Ditches Plan to Move to Rotterdam After Shareholder
   Pressure," DutchNews.nl, October 5, 2018.

9. Johannes Petry, Jan Fichtner, and Eelke Heemskerk, "Steering Capital: The Growing Private Authority of Index Providers in the Age of Passive Asset Management," *Review of International Political Economy*, December 10, 2019.

10. Steve Johnson, "MSCI Peru Ruling Threatens to Unbalance Frontier Index," *Financial Times*, April 29, 2016.

11. Andres Schipani, "Peru Stocks Remain in MSCI EM Indices," *Financial Times*, June 15, 2016.

12. Tracy Alloway, Dani Burger, and Rachel Evans, "Index Providers Rule the World—For Now, at Least," *Bloomberg Markets*, November 27, 2017.

13. Mike Bird, "How China Pressured MSCI to Add Its Market to Major Benchmark," *Wall Street Journal*, February 3, 2019.

14. Shelly Banjo and Jenny Leonard, "Rubio Duels with MSCI over Investors' Money in Chinese Stocks," Bloomberg, October 21, 2019.

15. Michelle Price, "US Senator Queries MSCI over Inclusion of Chinese Shares in Major Benchmark," Reuters, June 13, 2019.

16. Vladyslav Sushko and Grant Turner, "The Implications of Passive Investing for Securities Markets," *BIS Quarterly Review*, March 2018.

17. Joe Rennison, Robert Armstrong, and Robin Wigglesworth, "The New Kings of the Bond Market," *Financial Times*, January 22, 2020.

18. Tomas Williams, Nathan Converse, and Eduardo Levy-Yayati, "How ETFs Amplify the Global Financial Cycle in Emerging Markets," Institute for International Economic Policy Working Paper Series, September 2018.

19. Henry Hu and John Morley, "A Regulatory Framework for Exchange-Traded Funds," *Southern California Law Review*, March 13, 2018.

20. John Coumarianos, "How a Dividend ETF Was Bitten by the Index It Mimics," *Barron's*, January 24, 2020.

21. Jason Zweig, "The Stock Got Crushed. Then the ETFs Had to Sell," *Wall Street Journal*, January 21, 2020.

CHAPTER 17: THIS IS WATER

1. Sam Levine, "David Foster Wallace's Famous Commencement Speech Almost Didn't Happen," *Huffington Post*, May 24, 2016.

2. Miles Weiss, "Peter Thiel Had $244 Million Bet on Volatility Jump at Year-End," Bloomberg, February 16, 2018.

3. Michael Green, "Policy in a World of Pandemics, Social Media and Passive Investing," Logica Capital Advisers, March 26, 2020.

4. Brian Scheid, "Top 5 Tech Stocks' S&P 500 Dominance Raises Fears of Bursting Bubble," S&P Global Market Intelligence, July 27, 2020.

5. Hao Jiang, Dimitri Vayanos, and Lu Zheng, "Tracking Biased Weights: Asset Pricing Implications of Value-Weighted Indexing," CEPR Discussion Paper, December 23, 2020.

6. Marco Pagano, Antonio Sanchez Serrano, and Josef Zechner, "Can ETFs Contribute to Systemic Risk?," European Systemic Risk Board, June 2019.

7. Itzhak Ben-David, Francesco Franzoni, and Rabih Moussawi, "Do ETFs Increase Volatility?," *Journal of Finance*, September 22, 2018.

8. Kenechukwu Anadu, Mathias Kruttli, Patrick McCabe, Emilio Osambela, and Chae Hee Shin, "The Shift from Active to Passive Investing: Potential Risks to Financial Stability?," Federal Reserve Bank of Boston, 2018.

9. Matthew Goldstein and Alexandra Stevenson, "Carl Icahn Calls BlackRock a 'Very Dangerous Company,'" *New York Times*, July 15, 2015.

10. Joe Rennison, "How the Fed Helped Bond ETFs Meet Their Biggest Challenge," *Financial Times*, March 26, 2020.

11. Robin Wigglesworth, "All That Drama About Fixed-Income ETFs Was Overplayed," *Financial Times*, April 22, 2020.

12. Rohan Arora, Sebastien Betermier, Guillaume Ouellet Leblanc, Adriano Palumbo, and Ryan Shotlander, "Concentration in the Market of Authorized Participants of US Fixed-Income Exchange-Traded Funds," Bank of Canada, November 2020.

13. Anadu, Kruttli, McCabe, Osambela, and Shin, "The Shift from Active to Passive Investing."

14. Robin Wigglesworth, Owen Walker, and Josephine Cumbo, "UK Universities Pension Fund Closes Stockpicking Team," *Financial Times*, February 13, 2020.

15. Wigglesworth, Walker, and Cumbo, "UK Universities Pension Fund Closes Stockpicking Team."

16. William Sharpe, "The Arithmetic of Active Management," *Financial Analysts Journal*, 1991.

17. Lasse Heje Pedersen, "Sharpening the Arithmetic of Active Management," *Financial Analysts Journal*, 2018.

18. Berlinda Liu and Phillip Brzenk, "Does Past Performance Matter? The Persistence Scorecard," S&P Dow Jones Indices, December 2019.

19. Robin Wigglesworth, "Active Fund Managers Pray for Turnround as Exodus Continues," *Financial Times*, January 3, 2020.

20. Myles Udland, "Jack Bogle Envisions 'Chaos, Catastrophe' in Markets If Everyone Were to Index," Yahoo Finance, May 6, 2017.

21. Luke Kawa, "Bernstein: Passive Investing Is Worse for Society Than Marxism," Bloomberg, August 23, 2016.

22. Sanford Grossman and Joseph Stiglitz, "On the Impossibility of Informationally Efficient Markets," *American Economic Review*, June 1980.

23. Ben Johnson, "The Cost Matters Hypothesis," Morningstar, February 10, 2016.

24. Michael Mauboussin, Dan Callahan, and Darius Majd, "Looking for Easy Games. How Passive Investing Shapes Active Management," Credit Suisse, January 4, 2017.

25. Robin Wigglesworth, "Why the Index Fund 'Bubble' Should Be Applauded," *Financial Times*, September 23, 2019.

26. Mary Childs, "Gary Shteyngart's View from Hedge Fund Land," *Barron's*, September 7, 2018.

CHAPTER 18: OUR NEW CORPORATE OVERLORDS

1. Mike Murphy, "David Hogg Calls for Investors to Boycott BlackRock, Vanguard over Gun Holdings," MarketWatch, April 18, 2018.

2. BlackRock, "BlackRock's Approach to Companies That Manufacture and Distribute Civilian Firearms," press release, March 2, 2018.

3. Jack Bogle, "Bogle Sounds a Warning on Index Funds," *Wall Street Journal*, November 29, 2018.

4. Simone Foxman, "Paul Singer Says Passive Investing Is 'Devouring Capitalism,'" Bloomberg, August 3, 2017.

5. Bill McNabb, "Getting to Know You: The Case for Significant Shareholder Engagement," speech at Lazard's 2015 Director Event.

6. Larry Fink, "A Sense of Purpose," annual letter to CEOs, 2018.

7. Ian Appel, Todd Gormley, and Donald Keim, "Passive Investors, Not Passive Owners," *Journal of Financial Economics*, 2016.

8. Paul Singer, "Comfortably Numb," Elliott Management letter to investors, 2017.

9. Elizabeth Harball, "'There Is No Silver Lining': Why Alaska Fires Are a Glimpse of Our Climate Future," *Guardian*, August 23, 2019.

10. Larry Fink, "A Fundamental Reshaping of Finance," BlackRock 2020 letter to CEOs.

11. Billy Nauman and Leo Lewis, "Moral Money Special Edition: Hiro Mizuno, Japan's $1.6tn Man," *Financial Times*, December 12, 2019.

12. David McLaughlin and Annie Massa, "The Hidden Dangers of the Great Index Fund Takeover," *Bloomberg BusinessWeek*, January 9, 2020.

13. Andrew Ross Sorkin, "World's Biggest Investor Tells CEOs Purpose Is the 'Animating Force' for Profits," *New York Times*, January 17, 2019.

14. Shareholder Equity Alliance, Letter to Lawrence Fink, press release, April 15, 2020.

15. Gillian Tett, Billy Nauman, Patrick Temple-West, Leslie Hook, Mehreen Khan, Anna Gross, Tamami Shimizuishi, and Andrew Edgecliffe-Johnson, "Al Gore Blasts BlackRock," *Financial Times*, December 11, 2019.

16. Robert Armstrong, "Warren Buffett on Why Companies Cannot Be Moral Arbiters," *Financial Times*, December 29, 2019.

17. José Azar, Martin Schmalz, and Isabel Tecu, "Anti-competitive Effects of Common Ownership," *Journal of Finance*, May 2018.

18. Frank Partnoy, "Are Index Funds Evil?," *Atlantic*, September 2017.
19. Brooke Fox and Robin Wigglesworth, "Common Ownership of Shares Faces Regulatory Scrutiny," *Financial Times*, January 22, 2019.
20. McLaughlin and Massa, "The Hidden Dangers of the Great Index Fund Takeover."
21. Marc Israel, "Renewed Focus on Common Ownership," White & Case LLP, May 18, 2018.
22. Einer Elhauge, "How Horizontal Shareholding Harms Our Economy—And Why Antitrust Law Can Fix It," *Harvard Business Law Review*, 2020.
23. John Coates, "The Future of Corporate Governance Part 1: The Problem of Twelve," Harvard Public Law Working Paper, October 2018.
24. Lucian Bebchuk and Scott Hirst, "The Specter of the Giant Three," National Bureau of Economic Research, June 2019.
25. Bebchuk and Hirst, "The Specter of the Giant Three."
26. Robin Wigglesworth, "Passive Attack: The Story of a Wall Street Revolution," *Financial Times*, December 20, 2018.

EPILOGUE

1. Jan Sytze Mosselaar, *A Concise Financial History of Europe* (Rotterdam: Robeco, 2018).

INDEX